McGraw-Hill Ryerson

BIOLOGY 11
Study Guide

Authors

Briar Ballou
Science Writer

Glen Hutton
Educational Writer

Contributing Author

Julie Kretchman
Science Writer

Reviewer

Clyde Ramlochan
Toronto District School Board

Study Tips Reviewer

Donna Zuccato
Peel District School Board

McGraw-Hill Ryerson

Toronto Montréal Boston Burr Ridge, IL Dubuque, IA Madison, WI New York San Francisco
St. Louis Bangkok Bogotá Caracas Kuala Lumpur Lisbon London Madrid Mexico City
Milan New Delhi Santiago Seoul Singapore Sydney Taipei

Biology 11 Study Guide

ISBN-13: 978-0-07-105100-2
ISBN-10: 0-07-105100-7

http://www.mcgrawhill.ca

2 3 4 5 6 7 8 9 MP 1 9 8 7 6 5 4 3 2 1 0

Printed and bound in Canada

Care has been taken to trace ownership of copyright material contained in this text. The publishers will gladly accept any information that will enable them to rectify any reference or credit in subsequent printings.

PUBLISHER: Diane Wyman
PROJECT MANAGEMENT: Julie Kretchman
DEVELOPMENT: First Folio Resource Group Inc. (Loretta Johnson, Julie Kretchman)
MANAGER, EDITORIAL SERVICES: Crystal Shortt
SUPERVISING EDITOR: Alexandra Savage-Ferr
EDITORIAL ASSISTANTS: Erin Hartley, Michelle Malda
MANAGER, PRODUCTION SERVICES: Yolanda Pigden
PRODUCTION COORDINATOR: Sheryl MacAdam
COVER DESIGN: Liz Harasymczuk
ART DIRECTION: Pronk & Associates
ELECTRONIC PAGE MAKE-UP: Pronk & Associates

COPIES OF THIS BOOK MAY BE OBTAINED BY CONTACTING:

McGraw-Hill Ryerson Ltd.

WEB SITE:

http://www.mcgrawhill.ca

E-MAIL:

orders@mcgrawhill.ca

TOLL-FREE FAX:

1-800-463-5885

TOLL-FREE CALL:

1-800-565-5758

OR BY MAILING YOUR ORDER TO:

McGraw-Hill Ryerson
Order Department
300 Water Street
Whitby, ON L1N 9B6

Please quote the ISBN and title when placing your order.

Student Text ISBN:
978-0-07-091580-0
0-07-091580-6

Biology 11 Study Guide

Table of Contents

Using this Study Guide

This Study Guide has been designed to help you understand important ideas about biology. Use it with your textbook and in addition to the work you do in class for the most successful learning experience.

Here are some of the Study Guide's key features, and suggestions for how to use them.

Study Guide feature	Where you can find it	How it can help you
Self assessment	at the beginning of each chapter	After you've read a chapter in the textbook, the self assessment in the Study Guide can help you identify any areas you still need help with, and tell you what pages of the study guide will help you.
Summary	for each topic	Information is often presented in point form, in tables, or as diagrams to help you understand the key points.
Learning Check questions	for each topic	Use these questions to help you decide if you have understood each summary. Check your answers against those in the back of the Study Guide.
Study Tips	in the margin of every topic summary	Everyone learns differently. Try the questionnaire on page VIII to help you identify your preferred learning styles, read the suggestions on page IX, then use the Study Tips in the margins of this guide to help you learn effectively. These Study Tips also help you create your own organized notes that will help you study for tests and exams.
Bringing It All Together/ Unit Review	at the end of every chapter and every unit	These pages provide opportunities for you to demonstrate what you have learned by organizing and connecting ideas in a table or another graphic organizer. Some ideas are provided to get you started.
Practice Tests	at the end of every chapter and every unit	When you think you are ready, these Practice Tests will help you see how much you have learned. They also tell you where to look for anything you need a bit more help with.

Learning Preferences Self Assessment

People learn in many different ways. If you know what learning styles suit you, you can choose activities to help you learn more effectively.

Take a few minutes to complete this questionnaire. Choose one way to complete each sentence. Use the table to record the number of times you choose A, B, and C.

1. I remember ideas best if I
- ☐ **A.** write them down.
- ☐ **B.** explain them to someone.
- ☐ **C.** practise or demonstrate the concept.

2. I spend a lot of my free time
- ☐ **A.** watching TV or reading.
- ☐ **B.** talking to friends.
- ☐ **C.** doing or making things.

3. When I'm figuring out how to spell a word, I
- ☐ **A.** visualize the word in my head.
- ☐ **B.** sound out the word.
- ☐ **C.** write the word on paper or in the air.

4. To teach someone how to do something, I prefer to
- ☐ **A.** write down instructions.
- ☐ **B.** tell them.
- ☐ **C.** show them.

5. I am most easily distracted by
- ☐ **A.** movements.
- ☐ **B.** sounds.
- ☐ **C.** people doing things around me.

6. When working in a group, I prefer to
- ☐ **A.** document the activity
- ☐ **B.** lead the discussion
- ☐ **C.** conduct the activity

7. When listening to music, I
- ☐ **A.** follow along with the printed lyrics.
- ☐ **B.** just listen.
- ☐ **C.** dance.

8. I find it easiest to remember
- ☐ **A.** faces.
- ☐ **B.** names.
- ☐ **C.** things I have done.

9. When making a presentation, I prefer to create
- ☐ **A.** a written report.
- ☐ **B.** an oral report.
- ☐ **C.** a model, a poster, or a demonstration.

10. I prefer it when the teacher uses
- ☐ **A.** written notes, tables, or diagrams.
- ☐ **B.** discussions, debates, or guest speakers.
- ☐ **C.** 3-D models and hands-on activities.

A visual learning (looking)	B auditory learning (listening)	C kinesthetic learning (doing)

If you chose more As, you usually prefer to learn things by looking at them. This can include reading notes, looking at maps and diagrams, and associating shapes.

If you chose more Bs, you usually prefer to learn things by hearing them. This can include listening to someone talk, and getting involved in discussions yourself.

If you chose more Cs, you usually prefer to learn things by doing them. This can include doing experiments and building models.

Most people choose a combination of As, Bs, and Cs.

On the next page, you will find some strategies to help you learn Biology in ways that suit your style.

Using Study Tips

There are many ways to study. It's a good idea to use a variety of strategies. You'll find several Study Tips suggested in the margins of this Study Guide. Try those as well as your own ideas.

If you know how you prefer to learn, you can choose tools that will help you with any topic in Biology. You can also customize Study Tips to suit your own preferred learning styles.

Here are some ideas:

A. If you prefer to learn by **reading, writing, and viewing:**
- draw labeled diagrams.
- keep organized notes. Focus on the main ideas, and organize them on the page so they are easy to find when you study.
- Use highlighters to add visual cues to your notes.
- make graphic organizers. See pages 654 of your textbook for some ideas.
- make vocabulary cards. (Write the new term on the front. Divide the back into four sections, and:
  1. write the definition in your own words
  2. sketch a diagram
  3. use the term in a sentence
  4. describe how the term fits into the big picture

B. If you prefer to learn by **listening and talking:**
- use your vocabulary cards or your textbook to quiz a classmate.
- read out loud to yourself, to a classmate, or to a family member.
- work with a classmate to summarize paragraphs out loud.
- ask questions and suggest ideas in class.
- have an argument. Record pros and cons, or advantages and disadvantages, then discuss the issue with a classmate.

C. If you prefer to learn by **moving and doing:**
- build a model. You can also do this when the book suggests drawing a diagram. Use simple materials, and focus on representing important features.
- see for yourself. For example, to learn about vein patterns in leaves, go for a walk and look at some leaves.
- create a graphic organizer on the computer, or with physical materials. For example, you can create a Venn diagram with hoops or string, then place items in the circles. You can build a flowchart by writing down ideas, then cutting them out and arranging them in order.
- act out a process—on your own or with a classmate.

To ensure that you learn the most, study in ways that match the ways you learn.

Unit 1 Diversity of Living Things

Chapter 1 Classifying Life's Diversity

Genetic diversity, species diversity, and ecosystem diversity play crucial roles in maintaining healthy ecosystems.

Biologists use appearance, breeding patterns, evolutionary relationships, and DNA evidence to classify the wide variety of species on Earth. All organisms are members of one of three domains:

- Bacteria,

- Archaea, or

- Eukarya. Within each domain are smaller groups, forming a hierarchical system of classification.

From the most general to the most specific, the categories of taxonomy are:

Domain → Kingdom → Phylum → Class → Order → Family → Genus → Species

This classification system helps scientists to describe organisms, understand relationships, and to predict and track the spread of diseases, or develop strategies to maintain biodiversity.

Most organisms are named using a two name system. The organism's scientific name is made up of its *Genus* and its *species*.

Chapter 2 Diversity: From Simple to Complex

The Kingdoms of Bacteria, Archaea, and Protista are all comprised of unicellular organisms.

- Viruses are not capable of living independently outside of a living cell. Like cells, viruses contain genetic material but must rely on the machinery of the host's cells in order to reproduce.

- Organisms in the Bacteria and Archaea domains are prokaryotic cells. Bacteria and Archaea differ in the ways they obtain nutrition, the habitats in which they live, and how they reproduce.

- Protists are eukaryotes that are not plants, fungi, or animals. The organisms in this kingdom are roughly divided into three groups: plant-like, animal-like, and fungus-like protists.

- Endosymbiosis is a theory of evolution in which two or more prokaryotic cells permanently merged to form a eukaryotic cell. In this theory, one cell engulfed a different type of cell. The engulfed cell survived and became an organelle in the engulfing cell.

- Sexual life cycles are unique to eukaryotes. These cycles alternate between meiosis, which produces eggs and sperm, and fertilization, which merges eggs and sperm.

Chapter 3 Multicellular Diversity

Considerable diversity exists among multicellular organisms, as well.

• Algae, especially green algae, are the evolutionary link between the plant-like protists and the plant kingdom. The transition from a primarily aquatic existence of protists to living on dry land required the evolution of a number of adaptations.

• Plants can be divided into two main groups: the non-vascular plants (Bryophytes) and the vascular plants, which include seedless ferns, gymnosperms, and angiosperms.

• Fungi are heterotrophs made of a vegetative mycelium and a variety of sporeproducing and gamete-producing structures. Lichens are composite organisms made of a fungus and a photosynthetic partner.

• Animals are heterotrophic, food ingesting organisms whose cells do not have a cell wall.

• Animals are grouped into two main categories: animals without backbones (invertebrates) or animals with backbones (vertebrates).

• Modern threats to biodiversity constitute the biodiversity crisis. Climate change is predicted to have particularly significant impacts on species and their ecosystems.

CHAPTER 1

Classifying Life's Diversity

Self Assessment

1. What criteria can be used to classify an organism as a particular species?
   - **A.** geographic location
   - **B.** name
   - **C.** rate of reproduction
   - **D.** production of fertile offspring
   - **E.** average life span

2. Morphology is the branch of biology that deals with
   - **A.** change in organisms
   - **B.** reproductive success of a species.
   - **C.** genetic inheritance of an organism.
   - **D.** evolutionary history of a species.
   - **E.** appearance or form of organisms.

3. What is the correct format for the species name for humans?
   - **A.** homo sapiens
   - **B.** *homo sapiens*
   - **C.** *Homo sapiens*
   - **D.** *Homo* sapiens
   - **E.** *homo Sapiens*

4. What is the broadest category in the hierarchical classification system?
   - **A.** Domain
   - **B.** Family
   - **C.** Kingdom
   - **D.** Phylum
   - **E.** Species

5. Which term describes the study of the structure of organisms?
   - **A.** morphology
   - **B.** anatomy
   - **C.** physiology
   - **D.** genetics
   - **E.** biology

6. DNA evidence has shown that animals and fungi are
   - **A.** more closely related to each other than protists and plants.
   - **B.** more closely related to each other than plants and fungi.
   - **C.** less closely related to each other than protists and fungi.
   - **D.** less closely related to each other than plants and animals.
   - **E.** both descended from plants

7. How many kingdoms are used in the current system for classifying organisms?
   - **A.** two
   - **B.** three
   - **C.** four
   - **D.** five
   - **E.** six

8. Eukaryotic cells
   - **A.** have a membrane-bound nucleus.
   - **B.** lack a membrane-bound nucleus.
   - **C.** lack genetic material.
   - **D.** have very few organelles.
   - **E.** have no organelles

9. Which kingdoms are classified in the domain Eukarya?

   A. Archea, Fungi, Protista

   B. Bacteria, Animalia, Plantea

   C. Bacteria, Fungi, Animalia

   D. Archea, Bacteria, Animalia

   E. Animalia, Fungi, Protista

10. What is a dichotomous key used for?

   A. distinguishing between two organisms

   B. identifying and classifying organisms

   C. sequencing an organism's genome

   D. predicting population growth

   E. analyzing environmental conditions

11. Which statement is true?

   A. Plant and animal cells both have cell walls.

   B. Animal cells lack cell walls.

   C. Plant cells lack cell walls.

   D. Fungi cells lack cell walls.

   E. All Archaea have cell walls.

12. Which kingdom includes only heterotrophs?

   A. Archaea   **B.** Bacteria   **C.** Fungi

   D. Plantae   **E.** Protista

13. The sum total of the variety of organisms on Earth is often referred to as

   A. biodiversity.   **B.** ecosystem.   **C.** community.

   D. species   **E.** gene pool.

14. Ecosystems are diverse due to variations in

   A. temperature.   **B.** precipitation

   C. biotic factors only.   **D.** both abiotic and biotic factors.

   E. changes due to humans.

Self Study Guide

Question	If you answered this question incorrectly, see this Study Guide page for further review.	After completing your review, be sure to answer these questions in the Chapter 1 Practice Test.	Question	If you answered this question incorrectly, see this Study Guide page for further review.	After completing your review, be sure to answer these questions in the Chapter 1 Practice Test.
1	SG-6	10	8	SG-10	9
2	SG-7	3	9	SG-10	4, 6
3	SG-8	11	10	SG-11	12
4	SG-10	1, 2	11	SG-10	12
5	SG-8	3, 10	12	SG-10	12
6	SG-8	10	13	SG-12	7
7	SG-10	2, 4, 8	14	SG-11, SG-12, SG-13	7

Key Terms

species

morphology

phylogeny

taxonomy

binomial nomenclature

genus

classification

hierarchical classification

rank

taxon

ancestor

anatomy

physiology

phylogenetic tree

structural diversity

prokaryotic

eukaryotic

dichotomous key

autotroph

heterotroph

species diversity

genetic diversity

ecosystem diversity

gene pool

resilience

Study Tip

Many ideas in science are alike in some ways and different in others. You can use a **Venn diagram** to help you recognize the **similarities** and the **differences** between the ideas, as in question 1.

Defining a Species (1.1)

A **species** is a group of related organisms. Biologists use several different concepts to help define species.

Species concept	Concept is based on	Advantages and disadvantages
Morphological	appearance	simple, but there is often significant variation in appearance within a species
Biological	behaviour and ability to mate and produce fertile offspring	widely used, but cannot be used with many extinct species or separated species
Phylogenetic	evolutionary relationships	can be used with extinct species and makes use of DNA evidence, but evolutionary relationships are not always known

Learning Check

1. **C** **K/U** Make a Venn diagram with three circles. Use it to show the similarities and differences among the three concepts used to define species.

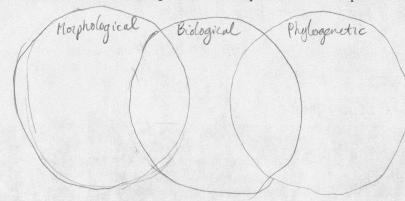

Morphological   Biological   Phylogenetic

2. **A** **C** Which species concept would you use to identify each of the following? Explain why you chose each concept.

a. A chicken and a duck.

   Morphological

b. A mule combines the traits of it horse dam (female) and donkey sire (male) to create a new animal with its own distinctive characteristics. The mule is a sterile hybrid.

   biological

c. Two distinct species of lizards had a common ancestor.

   Phylogenetic

Using Hierarchical Categories to Identify and Name Organisms (1.1)

Organisms are formally known by scientific names, made up of two parts: the **genus** and the species. This **binomial nomenclature** helps identify organisms accurately, and helps scientists around the world communicate with one another.

All species are classified by being placed in eight nested, or hierarchical, ranks. The process of identifying, naming, and classifying species is known as **taxonomy**. For example, this table shows the **classification** of human beings, *Homo sapiens*:

Rank	Domain	Kingdom	Phylum	Class	Order	Family	Genus	Species
Taxon	Eukarya	Animalia	Chordata	Mammalia	Primate	Hominidae	*Homo*	*sapiens*

There are millions of species in the domain Eukarya, including plants, animals, and fungi. There are fewer species in the kingdom Animalia but mammals, fish, and insects are all members of this kingdom. As you move from left to right in the table above, each rank includes fewer species. Species that share the same **genus** are more closely related than those that share only the same domain and kingdom.

Learning Check

1. **K/U** Which scientific name of the black bear is written correctly?

   A. *Americanus ursus*

   B. *Ursus americanus* ⟵ (circled)

   C. *ursus Americanus*

   D. *Ursus Americanus*

   E. *ursus americanus*

2. **K/U** Place these ranks in order from the rank that includes the most species to the rank that includes the fewest species:

   Class, Domain, Family, Genus
       2   1   3   4

3. **C** Draw a diagram, create a T-chart, or write sentences to show how the hierarchical classification of organisms is similar to the address of your home.

   Planet   Continent   Country   Province   City   Street
   Earth   North America   Canada   Ontario   Toronto   Council cres
                                                         Number 26

Study Tip

An analogy is a connection between two ideas that are similar in some way. For example, the Sun is similar to a light bulb because both produce heat and light. Developing an **analogy** as in **question 3**, can help you strengthen your understanding of ideas in biology.

4. **A** **T/I** This table shows the classification of the Canada goose.

Rank	Domain	Kingdom	Phylum	Class	Order	Family	Genus	Species
Taxon	Eukarya	Animalia	Chordata	Aves	Anseriformes	Anatidae	*Branta*	*canadensis*

   a. What is the scientific name for the Canada goose?

   Branta canadensis

   b. What ranks do human beings share with the Canada goose?

   Domain, Kingdom, Phylum,

   c. Which organism is more closely related to the Canada goose: *Branta sandvicensis* (Hawaiian goose) or *Chen caerulescens* (snow goose)? How do you know?

   Branta sandvicensis because they share the same Genus; *Branta*

Determining Relationships Among Species (1.2)

Scientists try to classify organisms in a way that reflects their morphological (physical) similarities as well as evolutionary history. If two organisms share much of the same evolutionary history, it means they have a fairly recent common ancestor, and are closely related.

Three types of evidence are used to how closely species are related:

1. Anatomical evidence refers to physical characteristics such as size, shape, and other physical features. Although birds and dinosaurs seem quite different, anatomical evidence such as the makeup and shape of bones show that they are related.

2. Physiological evidence refers to the functioning of organisms, including the proteins they make. The proteins any species makes are determined by the species' genes. Even though two species may look similar, if their bodies create very different proteins, they are probably not closely related.

3. DNA evidence refers to similarities in the long strands of material that makes up the genes. Genes are complex molecules that are passed from one generation to the next. Closely related species will have similar DNA sequences. Fungi and plants are similar in many ways, but DNA evidence shows that fungi are in fact more closely related to animals than to plants.

Analyzing the relationships among species allows scientists to construct **phylogenetic trees**, such as this one. It shows that some species of plant-eating, hoofed mammals are more closely related than others. They have a more recent common **ancestor**.

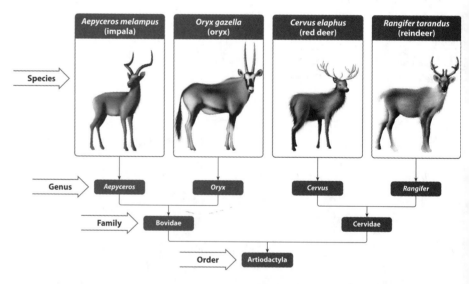

Understanding the evolutionary relationships among species and groups of organisms can help scientists

• discover sources of new pharmaceutical drugs

• trace the transmission of disease

• plan conservation projects

1. (K/U) Which shows physiological evidence of a relationship?

   A. Two species of corn produce similar proteins.

   B. Insects have six jointed legs and exoskeletons.

   C. Two organisms are in the same kingdom.

   D. Lynxes and housecats share many of the same genes.

   E. Birds and dinosaurs share common bone characteristics.

2. (K/U) Refer to the phylogenetic tree on the previous page.

   a. To what order do all four animals belong? _Artiodactyla_

   b. Which two animals belong to the Bovidae family? _impala & oryx_

   c. To which other animal shown is *Oryx gazella* most closely related? How do you know? _The impala_

3. (A) Dogs, wolves, seals, cats, and hyenas are all members of the order carnivora and share a common ancestor. Dogs, wolves, and seals are more closely related to one another than they are to cats or hyenas. Cats and hyenas are more closely related to each other than they are to dogs, wolves, or seals. Draw a phylogenetic tree to show these relationships.

4. (A) (T/I) Describe the relationships among the gooseberry, tomato, and potato.

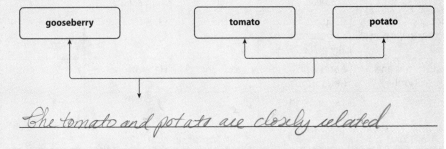

The tomato and potato are closely related

5. (K/U) 93% of human DNA is the same as chimpanzee DNA.

   a. What does this suggest about our relationship with chimpanzees?

   We are very closely related to chimps

   b. What type of evidence is this? _DNA evidence_

6. (T/I) Why might someone who works to control the spread of new diseases be interested in knowing how closely humans and chimpanzees are related?

   To use chimps for testing

7. (T/I) (A) By examining hundreds of fossils, scientists have developed a phylogenetic tree for the modern horse and its relatives (both living and extinct).

   a. Describe in detail the types of evidence scientists may have used to decide how closely two fossils were related. _Anatomical evidence_ _DNA evidence_

   b. How can knowing the evolutionary relationships among horses and their relatives help people who work with horses? _Knowing which bred is suitable for their environment etc._

Study Tip

Drawing a **diagram** (**question 3**) can help you:

- understand relationships
- understand key terms
- remember what things look like
- remember how things work

You can review scientific diagrams on page 653 of your textbook.

What are Kingdoms and Domains? (1.3)

There is far too much structural diversity among organisms to compare them all at the species level. For this reason, biologists look for similarities and differences at much higher taxonomic levels, such as kingdom and even domain.

There are two main cell types that help biologists classify organisms into the three domains. **Prokaryotic** cells, such as bacteria, do not have a membrane-bound nucleus. Most species are unicellular. However, some species live in colonies while others are filamentous. No species of prokaryotes are multicellular. **Eukaryotic** cells do have a membrane-bound nucleus. They also have a more complex internal structure, and are usually larger than prokaryotic cells. Some organisms with eukaryotic cells are unicellular, and others, such as humans, are multicellular.

The three domains in our current classification system are Bacteria, Archaea, and Eukarya. Bacteria and Archaea are both prokaryotic, and include only one Kingdom each. However, the number of Archaea and Bacteria Kingdoms could increase as new species are discovered. Eukarya includes four kingdoms, all of which are eukaryotic.

As well as cell types, nutrition (autotrophs capture energy from sunlight), and means of reproduction are used to distinguish among domains and kingdoms.

Domain	Bacteria	Archaea	Eukarya			
Kingdom	Bacteria	Archaea	Protista	Plantae	Fungi	Animalia
Example	Staphylococcus	Sulfolobus archaea	Amoeba	Maple tree	Mushroom	Rabbit
Cell type	Prokaryote	Prokaryote	Eukaryote	Eukaryote	Eukaryote	Eukaryote
Number of cells	Unicellular	Unicellular	Unicellular & multicellular	Multicellular	Mostly multicellular	Multicellular
Cell wall material	Peptidoglycan	Not peptidoglycan; occasionally no cell wall	Cellulose in some; occasionally no cell wall	Cellulose	Chitin	No cell wall
Nutrition	**Autotrophs** and **heterotrophs**	Autotrophs and heterotrophs	Autotrophs and heterotrophs	Autotrophs	Heterotrophs	Heterotrophs
Primary means of reproduction	Asexual	Asexual	Asexual and sexual	Sexual	Sexual	Sexual

Study Tip

These parts of a word can help you understand the word's meaning:

- **root**
- **prefix**
- **suffix**

For example, "karyotype" means a diagram of all the chromosomes in a nucleus. "Prokaryotic" means before the nucleus. "Eukaryotic" means true nucleus.

Learning Check

1. **K/U** Which kingdom exhibits a prokaryotic cell plan?
   A. Animalia   **B.** Archaea (circled)   **C.** Fungi
   D. Protista   **E.** Plantae

2. **K/U** Why does our classification system divide organisms into large, general groups such as domains and kingdoms, as well as specific groups like species?

   _____

   _____

3. **K/U** Three new species are discovered. State which domain each species is in and how you know.
   a. Species A is multicellular. _____Eukarya_____
   b. Species B is unicellular, has no membrane around its nucleus, and has a cell wall composed of petidoglycan. _____Bacteria_____
   c. Species C is unicellular and has no membrane around its nucleus. Although Species C doesn't have a cell wall, most representatives of its domain have a cell wall that is not composed of petidoglycan. _____Archaea_____

Using a Dichotomous Key (1.3)

It is easier to choose between two options than it is to consider many options at the same time. A **dichotomous key** allows us to make simple choices, one at a time, to help identify organisms. Dichotomous keys are usually used to help identify a species but can also be used to identify an order, a family, or another rank.

To use a dichotomous key, make the first choice, and follow instructions to other choices.

This dichotomous key will help identify which kingdom an organism is in.

1a. prokaryotic	go to 2	**1b.** eukaryotic	go to 3
2a. peptidoglycan in cell wall	Bacteria	**2b.** no peptiglycan in cell wall	Archaea
3a. chitin in cell wall	Fungi	**3b.** no chitin in cell wall	go to 4
4a. unicellular	Protist	**4b.** multicellular	go to 5
5a. autotroph	Plantae	**5b.** heterotroph	Animalia

Learning Check

Use the dichotomous key above for questions 1–3.

1. **(K/U)** Which traits tell you that an organism is in the Kingdom Plantae?

  A. prokaryotic, peptidoglycan in cell wall

  B. eukaryotic, peptidoglycan in cell wall

  C. eukaryotic, cell wall made of cellulose

  D. eukaryotic, no chitin in cell wall, multicellular, heterotroph

  E. eukaryotic, cell wall made of cellulose, multicellular, autotroph

2. **(T/I)** Choice 4 tells you that if the organism is unicellular it is a Protist. Bacteria are also unicellular. Why are Bacteria not listed as a possibility in choice 4?

  Because Bacteria is unique in that it has peptidoglycan in the cell wall.

3. **(C)** Why is the choice between autotroph and heterotroph not made first?

  Because too many fall into that category

4. **(A)** This is part of a dichotomous key for species of birch trees.

1a. twigs are fragrant	go to 2	**1b.** twigs are not fragrant	go to 3
2a. leaves widest near the middle *Betula alleghaniensis*		**2b.** leaves are widest near the base *Betula lenta*	
3a. mature bark is dark brown or gray	go to 4	**3b.** mature bark is white	go to 5
4a. Leaves yellowish green and shiny *Betula occidentalis*		**4b.** leaves dark green and hairy *Betula kenaica*	

You have found a birch tree and want to identify it.

  a. What is the first thing you need to do. _____

  b. The twigs of the birch tree are not fragrant, and the bark is dark brown. What is the next decision you need to make, and what will that tell you about the tree? _____

  _____

Study Tip

You can **draw arrows** from one step of the dichotomous key to the next to help you answer **question 4b**.

What Types of Biodiversity Are There? (1.4)

Biological diversity is important for the health of the environment. There are three main types of diversity.

Genetic diversity describes the variety of inherited characteristics within a group. These characteristics are controled by genes in the organism's cells. Genetically diverse groups have many visible and invisible characteristics that differ between individuals. Individuals in groups with no genetic diversity are identical to one another.

Species diversity describes the variety and abundance of species in a given area. These species can include representatives from all six Kingdoms.

Ecosystem diversity describes the variety of ecosystems found on Earth. These can differ in biotic and abiotic factors, in relationships, and in size. Some ecosystems are as large as a tropical rainforest. Others are as small as a single plant and the organisms that grow on it.

Learning Check

1. **K/U** Decide if each example shows species, genetic, or ecosystem diversity.
   a. In one day, you count 40 types of bird in a park. _____species_____
   b. On one side of a hill is grassland, at the top is a forest, and on the other side is a lake. _____ecosystem_____
   c. Two cats in a litter are black, two are grey, and one is striped. _____genetic_____

2. **A** Describe the types of diversity this illustration shows.

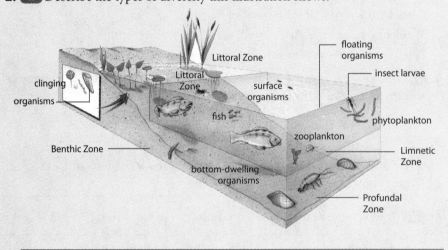

_____

_____

_____

3. **C** Complete this diagram to show the relationships among the three types of biodiversity.

(Genetic diversity)

4. **A C** a. Describe an example of species diversity near your home.

_____

b. Describe an area with limited species diversity.

_____

Why Is Biodiversity Important? (1.4)

Genetic diversity is important in any kind of environmental change, such as the introduction of a new disease. If none of the individuals in a population have the ability to survive a disease, they will all die. However, if some, have different genetic characteristics that allow them to survive, the population will carry on. Similarly, if the environment becomes drier and some individuals have the ability to survive with less water, the population will survive.

Species diversity is important for healthy ecosystems. Ecosystem services are the benefits provided by ecosystems to their members. These include regulation of carbon dioxide and oxygen, pollination, providing food, removing waste, and preventing erosion. A diverse ecosystem is more able to provide these various services to its members.

Ecosystem diversity ensures that a wide variety of species can survive and thrive on Earth.

Learning Check

1. **K/U** How can genetic diversity in a stand of Jack Pine (*Pinus banksiana*) help a population survive when a winter is much colder than normal?

_____

_____

2. **K/U** How can species diversity help a marine ecosystem provide food and other ecosystem services for whales?

_____

_____

3. **A** Many of the crops that are grown for food have very little species diversity. What are some advantages and disadvantages of this lack of diversity? Use this T-chart to record your answer.

Advantages	Disadvantages

4. **A** Living frozen zoos preserve reproductive cells (sperm and embryos) and genetic material in a frozen state, at $-196°C$ in liquid nitrogen. How could this practice help endangered species?

_____

_____

5. **T/I** **C** How do you think these types of diversity will help individual species survive global warming?

_____

_____

_____

Study Tip

Real life issues often do not have one clear answer. A **T-chart** (**question 3**) can help you consider **advantages** and **disadvantages**.

Human Impact on Biodiversity (1.4)

Humans often cause changes to ecosystems in order to increase the ecosystem services that are avaiable to us. Many of these changes reduce biodiversity, but some of the changes increase biodiversity. Sometimes it is difficult to tell what the overall effect of a change is.

Herbicides are used in agriculture to control the growth of weeds. The use of herbicides causes more food to be produced for human consumption. However, it also causes weeds to die, reducing biodiversity. When rainwater carries herbicides into rivers and lakes, it can reduce biodiversity in those ecosystems, as well.

Restoring habitats such as wetlands, and planting wildflowers in city gardens can increase biodiversity.

Stocking lakes with fish may seem like it increases biodiversity. In fact, introducing non-native fish into a lake ecosystem can result in native organisms being eaten, or having their normal food source taken by the new fish. New diseases may also be introduced in this way, reducing biodiversity.

Learning Check

1. **K/U** List three ways humans have changed the ecosytems around your local community. For each one, explain whether the change has resulted in increased or decreased biodiversity.

   _____

   _____

   _____

   _____

   _____

2. **A** In what ways can each activity affect biodiversity?

   a. Introducing new plant species to a forest.

   _____

   b. Building a hydroelectric dam on a river.

   _____

   c. Building new roads through a natural area.

   _____

   d. Allowing plants on the sides of highways to grow naturally.

   _____

3. **C** **T/I** Create a flowchart to show the long term effects of one of the changes in question 2.

Study Tip

You can understand many events by thinking about **causes** and **effects**. You can use a **flowchart** (**question 3**) to illustrate relationships between events.

Bringing It All Together

Complete this hierarchical classification system. Add examples, and other information that you have learned.

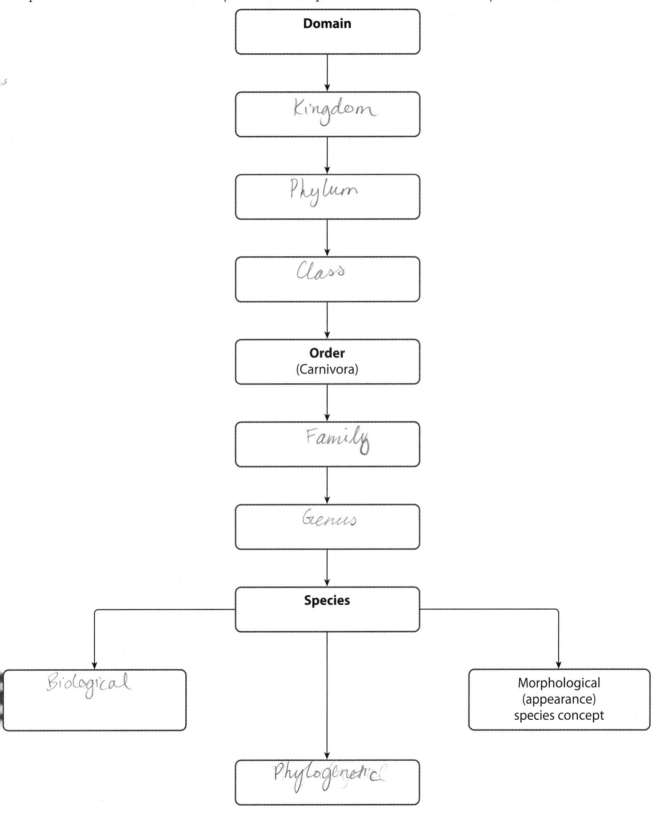

649 705 8939

1. **K/U** The hierarchical classification system arranges species in categories
   A. according to number of organisms involved.
   B. according to relative size of the organism.
   C. from simplest to most complex.
   D. from fewest organelles to most organelles
   E. from most general to most specific.

2. **K/U** Which term represents the narrowest category for classifying organisms?
   A. Class   B. Domain
   C. Kingdom   D. Species
   E. Genus

3. **A** What does this diagram show?

Whale	Bat	Horse
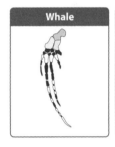		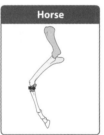

   A. These animals evolved from different ancestors.
   B. These animals have a shared evolutionary history.
   C. These animals adapted to environmental changes.
   D. These animals share common genes.
   E. These animals are related to modern birds and dinosaurs.

4. **K/U** What domain includes Protista?
   A. Archaea
   B. Plantae
   C. Prokarya
   D. Eukarya
   E. Bacteria

5. **K/U** Which term decribes organisms that must consume other organisms to obtain energy-yielding food?
   A. omnivore   B. autotrophic
   C. eukaryotic   D. heterotrophic
   E. prokaryotic

6. **K/U** Organisms in which kingdom have cell walls that contain peptidoglycan?
   A. Bacteria
   B. Archaea
   C. Plantae
   D. Protista
   E. Fungi

7. **T/I** Which of the following is a result of genetic diversity?
   A. decreased reproduction rates
   B. increased reproduction rates
   C. decreased resistance to disease
   D. increased resistance to disease
   E. sexual reproduction

8. **T/I** What led scientists to add a rank higher than kingdom to the classification system?
   The study of cell types and genes

9. a. **A** Add labels to this diagram.

cell membrane
nucleus
chromo
riboso
rough beceu lined with ribosomes

   b. What type of cell is this?
   Eukaryotic

   c. What evidence did you use to reach this conclusion?
   Because the cell has a membrane bound nucleus

10. C T/I Compare the advantages and disadvantages of using morphology and phylogeny to classify a species.

The advantages of using morphology is that its simple but there are so many individuals that its hard to find the difference in variation. Phylogeny is good for fossil specimens but sometimes we don't know the evolutionary history of every species

11. C List five things to remember when naming a species using the binomial nomenclature system.

   i. *When typing: in italics*
   ii. *Genus is capitalized.*
   iii. *Species is not capitalized*
   iv. *Underline when handwriting*
   v. *2 parts, the 1st is the Genus, then Species*

12. K/U Complete the following table.

Domain	Eukarya	*Eukarya*		Archaea
Kingdom	*Bacteria*	Protista		
Cell type				
Nutrition				autotrophs
Cell wall material	No cell wall		Not peptidoglycan; occasionally no cell wall	

Self Study Guide

Question	If you answered this question incorrectly, see this Study Guide page for further review.	Question	If you answered this question incorrectly, see this Study Guide page for further review.
1	SG-7	7	SG-12, SG-13
2	SG-7	8	SG-10
3	SG-8	9	SG-10
4	SG-10	10	SG-6
5	SG-10	11	SG-7
6	SG-10	12	SG-10

978-0-07-105100-2   Chapter 1 Classifying Life's Diversity • MHR   SG-17

Diversity: From Simple to Complex

Self Assessment

1. Which organisms are prokaryotes?
   - **A.** archaea, protists
   - **B.** archaea, bacteria
   - **C.** bacteria, plants
   - **D.** fungi, animals
   - **E.** protists, plants

2. Which statement about viruses is true?
   - **A.** They contain only RNA.
   - **B.** They exist only in eukaryotic cells.
   - **C.** They cannot live independently outside of cells.
   - **D.** They cause disease only in animals.
   - **E.** They contain membrane-bound organelles.

3. In the lytic cycle, where does the replication process occur?
   - **A.** In the capsid of the virus.
   - **B.** In the genetic material of the virus.
   - **C.** In the DNA of the host cell.
   - **D.** In the cytoplasm of the host cell.
   - **E.** In the proteins of the host cell.

4. Prions are composed of which substance?
   - **A.** carbohydrates
   - **B.** lipids
   - **C.** proteins
   - **D.** nucleic acids
   - **E.** triglycerides

5. What are the most common forms of bacteria and archaea?
   - **A.** spirals and cones
   - **B.** spirals and rods
   - **C.** cones and spheres
   - **D.** rods and cones
   - **E.** spheres and rods

6. By which process do cyanobacteria obtain energy?
   - **A.** decomposition
   - **B.** methanogenesis
   - **C.** parasitism
   - **D.** photosynthesis
   - **E.** chemosynthesis

7. In which environment have only halophilic Archaea been found?
   - **A.** sea water with high salt concentrations
   - **B.** deep sea vents with hot temperatures
   - **C.** craters of volcanoes
   - **D.** sediments of landfills
   - **E.** internal organs of animals

8. Which process involves the exchange of genetic material?
   - **A.** regeneration
   - **B.** meiosis
   - **C.** mitosis
   - **D.** binary fission
   - **E.** conjugation

9. What is a plasmid?

   A. a small loop of DNA

   B. a small loop of RNA

   C. a combination of RNA and DNA

   D. the identical copy of the genome

   E. the viral copy of the genome

10. What characteristic do modern biologists use to classify prokaryotes?

   A. size   **B.** shape   **C.** movement

   D. DNA   **E.** nutrition

11. Which organelle provides the strongest evidence of endosymbiosis in early eukaryotes?

   A. cell wall   **B.** chloroplast   **C.** nucleus

   D. ribosomes   **E.** vacuole

12. Mitochondria divide by which method?

   A. binary fission   **B.** conjugation   **C.** meiosis

   D. regeneration   **E.** cloning

13. Which statement accurately describes haploid cells?

   A. They contain one set of chromosomes.

   B. They contain two sets of chromosomes.

   C. They are produced when egg and sperm fuse.

   D. They are produced only during asexual reproduction.

   E. They occur only in prokaryotic cells.

14. Which is the best description of a protist?

   A. unicellular prokaryote   **B.** multicellular eukaryote

   C. unicellular eukaryote   **D.** multicellular plant

   E. unicellular fungi

Self Study Guide

Question	If you answered this question incorrectly, see this Study Guide page for further review.	After completing your review, be sure to answer these questions in the Chapter 1 Practice Test.	Question	If you answered this question incorrectly, see this Study Guide page for further review.	After completing your review, be sure to answer these questions in the Chapter 1 Practice Test.
1	SG-24	9	8	SG-21	3
2	SG-20	2	9	SG-21	3
3	SG-20	12	10	SG-21	1, 8
4	SG-20	2	11	SG-24	5, 9, 14
5	SG-21	3	12	SG-24	9, 14
6	SG-22	4	13	SG-25	10
7	SG-21	4	14	SG-27, SG-28	6, 7, 11

Key Terms

virus

structural diversity

capsid

replication

lytic cycle

lysogenic cycle

prion

bacterium

archaeon

coccus

bacillus

methanogenesis

extremophile

mesophile

binary fission

conjugation

endospore

Gram stain

endosymbiosis

gamete

zygote

protist

parasite

pseudopod

cilium

flagellum

plasmodium

pseduoplasmodium

red tide

Study Tip

Before you read a passage from the textbook, look at the **illustrations** to get an idea of the topic. As you read the chapter, review the graphics to help you remember key concepts.

Viruses and Prions Cause Diseases in Plants and Animals (2.1)

Viurses are not classified in any kingdom of living things. Like living organisms, viruses contain genetic material (DNA or RNA) but they are unable to reproduce on their own. Instead, they use a host cell to produce multiple copies of themselves. Viruses are classified by the shape of the protein coat (**capsid**) that protects their genetic material or by the diseases they cause.

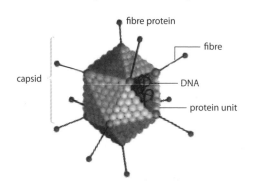

Despite their diversity, all viruses have an outer capsid composed of protein subunits and a nucleic acid core that is composed of either DNA or RNA.

Viruses are best known for causing diseases in plants and animals. Once viruses enter a host cell, some follow a **lytic** replication cycle resulting in the host cell breaking open (lysis) releasing new viral particles to infect other cells. Others follow a **lysogenic** cycle in which the virus's genetic information enters the host cell's chromosomes forming a provirus. The genetic material of the provirus is copied and spread as the host cell reproduces. The provirus can separate from the host chromosomes and spread as in the lytic cycle.

Prions are pathogenic variants of proteins that are naturally produced in nerve cells and certain other cells. They cause several degenerative brain diseases.

Learning Check

1. a. (K/U) What characteristic supports the idea that viruses are living organisms?

_____

b. (K/U) Why are viruses not classified in any kingdom of living organisms?

_____

2. (A) Does a prion have a prokaryotic cell plan, a eukaryotic cell plan, or no cell plan? Explain your reasoning.

_____

_____

3. (C) On a separate sheet of paper, draw a diagram comparing the lytic cycle and lysogenic cycle in the replication of viruses. Refer to your textbook for details.

Comparing Two Domains: Archaea and Bacteria (2.2)

Morphology

Prokaryotes are represented by two domains: Archaea and Bacteria. Generally, species in these two domains are of similar size and shape. They are the smallest, simplest organisms on Earth and are abundant in the air, water, soil, and on most objects. All species in Archaea and Bacteria are unicellular, but some form colonies or link up to form filaments. Species in both domains can occupy aerobic and anaerobic environments. Some species in both groups occupy extreme environments, such as those with high temperatures or high salt levels. These species are known as **extremophiles**.

Archaea and Bacteria are classified as **bacillus**, **coccus**, or spirillium, based on their shape.

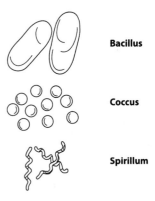

Bacillus

Coccus

Spirillum

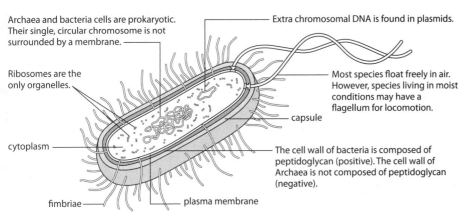

Archaea and bacteria cells are prokaryotic. Their single, circular chromosome is not surrounded by a membrane.

Extra chromosomal DNA is found in plasmids.

Ribosomes are the only organelles.

Most species float freely in air. However, species living in moist conditions may have a flagellum for locomotion.

capsule

cytoplasm

The cell wall of bacteria is composed of peptidoglycan (positive). The cell wall of Archaea is not composed of peptidoglycan (negative).

fimbriae

plasma membrane

Reproduction

All species of both domains reproduce asexually by binary fission. The steps in this process are summarized below.

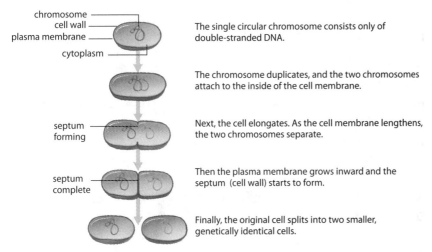

chromosome
cell wall
plasma membrane
cytoplasm

The single circular chromosome consists only of double-stranded DNA.

The chromosome duplicates, and the two chromosomes attach to the inside of the cell membrane.

septum forming

Next, the cell elongates. As the cell membrane lengthens, the two chromosomes separate.

septum complete

Then the plasma membrane grows inward and the septum (cell wall) starts to form.

Finally, the original cell splits into two smaller, genetically identical cells.

Sexual reproduction does not occur in Archaea or Bacteria. However, genetic recombination does occur. This process, called **conjugation**, involves one bacterium making a copy of a portion of DNA, called a plasmid, and transferring that copy to another bacterium by way of a long, tube-like pilus.

Importance of Bacteria and Archaea

Characteristic	Arachaea	Bacteria
Disease-causing	• no known disease-causing species	• many cause diseases in plants and animals • for example, strep throat, ear infections, and cavities in humans
Symbiotic relationships	• many are mutualists or commensals	• some are mutualists or commensals
Role in ecosystems	• some fix atmospheric carbon dioxide • some are methanogenic; they live in intestines of ruminants (cows) and release methane gas which may contribute to global warming	• some fix nitrogen • decomposers break down organic matter • cyanobacteria perform photosynthesis
Human use	• biotechnology: enzymes can function in extreme environments • antibiotics: new class of potentially useful antibiotics recently discovered • bioremediation: some metabolize metal ions in polluted areas	• biotechnology: genetic engineering • antibiotics: some are important sources of antibiotics • food production: some are used in the production of yogurt, cheese, wine, and beer

Learning Check

1. **K/U** What are the most common shapes of Bacteria and Archaea?
   A. polyhedral, spherical, cylindrical
   B. gametic, zygotic, sporic
   C. spherical, rod, spiral
   D. animal-like, fungus-like, plant-like
   E. ciliated, flagellated, amoebic

2. **K/U** What is the key difference between Archaea and Bacteria?
   A. Archaea have a prokaryotic cell plan while Bacteria have a eukaryotic cell plan.
   B. Archaea can live in anaerobic conditions while Bacteria can only live in aerobic conditions.
   C. Archaea can only live in less extreme conditions (mesophiles) while Bacteria can live in more extreme conditions (extremophiles).
   D. Archaea do not use photosynthesis as a source of metabolic energy while some Bacteria can use photosynthesis as a source of metabolic energy.
   E. Archaea have membrane-bound organelles while Bacteria do not have membrane-bound organelles.

3. a. (K/U) Identify the primary reproductive strategy used by species of Archaea and Bacteria.

_____

b. (C) Use a flow chart or another graphic organizer to summarize the steps in this process.

4. (C) Draw and label a generic prokaryotic cell. Identify the features that are unique to prokayrotic cells.

5. (A) Individual bacterial cells may have plasmids with the genes that protect the bacterial cells from antibiotics. Explain how this trait may be passed on to other bacterial cells in the colony.

_____

_____

_____

6. (C) Use a graphic organizer to compare the importance of Archaea and Bacteria to life on Earth.

Evolution of the Eukaryotic Cell (2.3)

In evolutionary history, scientists believe that two prokaryotic cells formed a symbiotic team that, over millions of years, evolved into a single organism. The result of this union was the first eukaryotic cell. This hypothesis of the evolution of a eukaryotic cell is known as the endosymbiotic hypothesis.

In **endosymbiosis**, as illustrated below, heterotrophic bacteria became mitochondria, and cyanobacteria became chloroplasts after being taken up by host cells. The flagella associated with animal cells may have arisen when spiral-shaped bacteria were incorporated into evolving eukaryotic cells.

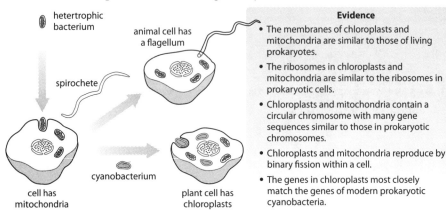

Evidence
- The membranes of chloroplasts and mitochondria are similar to those of living prokaryotes.
- The ribosomes in chloroplasts and mitochondria are similar to the ribosomes in prokaryotic cells.
- Chloroplasts and mitochondria contain a circular chromosome with many gene sequences similar to those in prokaryotic chromosomes.
- Chloroplasts and mitochondria reproduce by binary fission within a cell.
- The genes in chloroplasts most closely match the genes of modern prokaryotic cyanobacteria.

Learning Check

1. **(K/U)** Which statement is *not* evidence supporting the theory of endosymbiosis?
   A. Membranes of the chloroplasts and mitochondria are similar to living prokaryotes.
   B. Ribosomes in these organelles are similar to ribosomes in prokaryotes.
   C. The mitochondria and chloroplasts reproduce by binary fission.
   D. The chloroplasts and mitochondria have a circular chromosome.
   E. The genes in the chloroplast closely match the genes found in the chloroplasts of modern plants.

2. **(C)** On a separate sheet of paper, draw a spider map to summarize the evidence supporting the endosymbiotic hypothesis.

3. **(C)** Read the study tip on this page. Explain how the meanings of the prefix *endo* and the root word *symbiosis* relate to the endosymbiotic hypothesis.

   _____

   _____

4. **(A)** As you learned in Chapter 1, a phylogenetic tree is a branching diagram showing assumed evolutionary relationships among organisms. Draw a phlogenetic tree to show the evolutionary relationships among prokaryotic cells (Bacteria and Archaea) and eukaryotic cells (animals, fungi, and plants only). Include where you think the first mitochondria and then the first chloroplasts must have arisen. Explain your reasoning.

Study Tip

You can use parts of a word to help you understand the word's meaning.

For example, *endosymbiosis*.
- The prefix *endo* means "within."
- *Symbiosis* is a term used to describe two or more different species living in close association.

Eukaryotes: Life Cycles and Reproduction (2.3)

Asexual Reproduction

Some eukaryotic, multicellular organisms reproduce by budding or fragmentation. This form of reproduction involves mitosis, cell division in which daughter cells receive the exact chromosome and genetic makeup as the parent cell. The cells produced are genetically identical (clones).

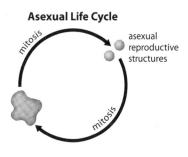

Sexual Reproduction

Gametic Life Cycle

Animals and some brown algae have a gametic life cycle. In meiosis, a diploid cell (with two copies of each chromosome) produces haploid gametes (each with only one copy of each chromosome). In fertilization, the **gametes** fuse, resulting in a diploid zygote. The zygote undergoes mitosis resulting in a diploid organism. The only haploid cells in the life cycle of these organisms are the gametes (egg or sperm).

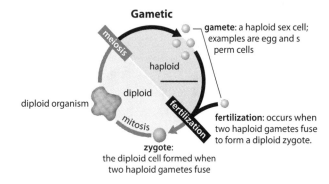

Zygotic Life Cycle

All fungi, some green algae, and many protozoans have a zygotic life cycle. In a zygotic life cycle, the zygote undergoes meiosis. The only diploid cell is the zygote. All the other cells in the organism are haploid.

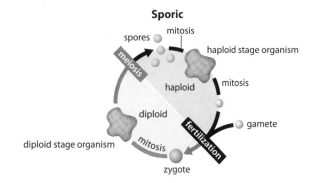

Sporic Life Cycle

Plants and many algae have a sporic life cycle. In these organisms, mitosis occurs in both the diploid and haploid phases. Organisms with this life cycle display an alternation of generations, which features a spore-producing *sporophyte generation* and gamete-producing *gametophyte generation*.

1. **K/U** Compare and contrast each pair of terms.

a. haploid and diploid

_____

_____

b. gamete and zygote

_____

_____

c. meiosis and mitosis

_____

_____

2. a. **T/I** This diagram shows the life cycle of a corn plant. Add labels to complete the diagram.

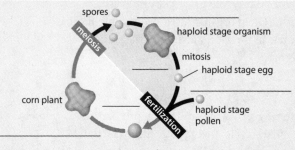

Sporic

spores _____

haploid stage organism

mitosis

haploid stage egg

corn plant

haploid stage pollen

_____

_____

b. **A** Briefly describe three important features of this life cycle.

_____

_____

3. **C** Draw a diagram illustrating the gametic life cycle of a mammal. Use these terms to label your diagram: haploid phase, diploid phase, meiosis, mitosis, fertilization, and zygote. You may need to use some terms more than once.

4. **A** Compare the life cycle of a bacterium to the life cycle of a fish. How are they similar? How are they different?

_____

_____

_____

Kingdom Protista (2.4)

The kingdom Protista inlcudes all eukaryotic organisms except animals, plants, and fungi. There are three groups of unicellular protists. *Protozoans* are aquatic animal-like heterotrophs that ingest or absorb their food. Slime moulds (terrestrial) and *water moulds* (aquatic) are fungus-like, heterotrophic protists. *Diatoms, dinoflagellates* and *euglenoids* are plant-like, autotrophic protists.

Protozoans

Protozoans are one-celled, heterotrophic protists. They live in water, soil, and living and dead organisms. Protozoans contain special vacuoles for digesting food and getting rid of excess water. They are classified according to how they move.

For more information about types of protists, see pages 73 to 77 in your textbook.

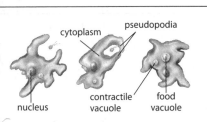

Carcazoans move and engulf their prey by producing limb-like extensions of their cytoplasm called peusdopodia (phagocytosis). Digestion occurs in a food vacuole.

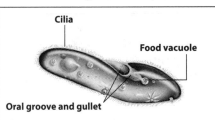

Ciliates move using short, hair-like **cilia**. These rapidly swimming protists sweep bacteria into the oral groove. A food vacuole forms and the food is digested.

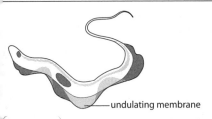

Flagellates use one or more long **flagella** to move through aquatic environments. Some species are free-living, some are parasites, and some live in symbiotic relationships.

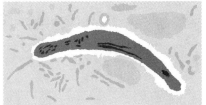

Sporozoans have no way of moving on their own. All are parasites that live in and feed on the blood of humans and other animals. They have a complex life cycle, adapted to transferring their offspring from one host to another.

Fungus-like Protists

Like fungi, fungus-like protists produce spores. Like protozoa, they glide from place to place and ingest food. Like plants, they have cellulose cell walls.

Plasmodial slime moulds share some characteristics with protozoans. During part of their life cycle, cells move by means of psuedopods and behave like amoebas. Plasmodial slime moulds reproduce with spores the way fungi do.

Cellular slime moulds spend part of their life cycle as an independent amoeboids that feed, grow, and divide by cell division. When food grows scarce, these cells join with hundreds or thousands of others to reproduce.

Water moulds live in water or moist places and appear as fuzzy, white growths on decaying matter. They grow as a mass of threads over a plant or animal, digest it, and then absorb the organism's nutrients. Unlike fungi, however, they produce reproductive cells with flagella.

Plant-like Protists

Plant-like protists are unicellular, aquatic, chlorophyll-containing organisms. Although once classified as plants, they do not have leaves, stems, roots, or water-conducting tissues.

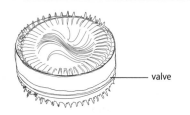

Diatoms have a body made of two halves. They have yellow-brown chloroplasts enabling them to photosynthesize. Their cell wall contains silica.

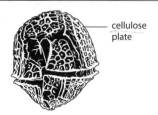

Dinoflagellates live in oceans. They have protective coats made of cellulose plates. Most have two flagella; one is free, but the other lies in a groove. *Gonyaulax* sp. shown here contains a red pigment and is responsible for "**red tides**."

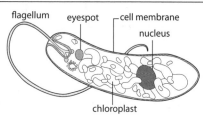

Euglenoids have both plant and animal characteristics. They have chloroplasts but lack a cell wall and swim by means of a flagella. An eyespot allows these protists to find light, after which photosynthesis can occur in the numerous chloroplasts. They can also absorb nutrients across their cell membrane.

Learning Check

Use the dichotomous key above for questions 1–3.

1. **K/U** **a.** Explain why the kingdom Protista can be called an artificial group.

_____

b. How is this different from the other kingdoms?

_____

2. **K/U** What is the function of the two vacuoles exhibited by many protozoans?

_____

3. **A** For each description identify the phylum or group. List key characteristics and give an example.

There may be more than one phylum or group presented in Chapter 2 that fits each description. The first one has been done for you.

a. Description: Heterotrophic, unicellular, with no permanent locomotory apparatus

Phylum: Cercozoa; Characteristics: move by pseudopodia; Example: amoeba

b. Description: Autotrophic, unicellular

_____

_____

c. Description: Hetertrophic, unicellular, with permanent locomotory apparatus

_____

_____

d. Description: Non-motile, spore-formers

_____

_____

Study Tip

Question 3 asks you to apply the information in the textbook using a different set of **criteria**. Reorganizing the information you learn into different **patterns** will help you make **connections**.

Ann Duo

Bringing It All Together

Complete the chart to compare Archaea, Bacteria, and Protista.

Kingdom	Arachaea	Bacteria	Protista
Cell type	_prokaryotic_	• prokaryotic	
Number of cells		• most are unicellular • some live in colonies or filamentous chains	
Locomotion	• most cannot move • some have flagella		• some have pseudopods, cilia, or flagella
Classification based on characteristics	• cocci (round) • bacilli (rod-shape) • spirilli (spiral shape)		• animal-like • plant-like • fungus-like
Classification based on Gram staining	• Gram positive: thick cell wall, purple stain • Gram negative: thinner cell wall, pink stain	• does not apply	• does not apply
Petidoglycan cell wall	• yes		
Membrane-bound organelles	• no chloroplast, mitochondria, or other membrane-bound organelles		
DNA and chromosomes	• single, circular chromosome • extra-chromosomal DNA in plasmids		
Ribosomes in cytoplasm	• yes	• yes	• yes
Reproduction			• asexual and sexual (mitosis and meiosis)
Extremophiles or mesophiles		• both	• only mesophiles
Other characteristics			

Practice Test

1. (K/U) Which statement is true for prokaryotic cells?
   A. DNA is in a nucleus bound by a membrane.
   B. Mitochondria are present.
   C. Most forms are multicellular.
   D. Cell division occurs by mitosis and meiosis.
   E. The genome is made up of a single chromosome.

2. (K/U) Which characteristic can be used to identify the HIV virus?
   A. crystalline appearance of protein coat
   B. multiple sides originating from a protein structure
   C. presence of a head-like structure attached to a protein tail
   D. spherical capsid
   E. cylindrical capsid

3. (K/U) Which name describes rod shaped bacteria?
   A. bacilli
   B. cocci
   C. spiral
   D. cubodial
   E. pyramidal

4. (K/U) Methanogenesis occurs in environments lacking which substance?
   A. carbon dioxide
   B. carbon monoxide
   C. methane
   D. nitrogen
   E. oxygen

5. (K/U) How many years ago do scientists believe that large complex eukaryotes first developed?
   A. 230 million
   B. 550 million
   C. 1.2 billion
   D. 2 billion
   E. 3.5 billion

6. (K/U) Amoebas are best known for the presence of which feature?
   A. cilia
   B. flagella
   C. plasmodium
   D. pseudopods
   E. sporozoites

7. (K/U) Which organism is known to cause an algal bloom resulting in a red tide?
   A. diatom
   B. dinoflagellate
   C. slime mould
   D. paramecia
   E. phytoplankton

8. (A) How would you describe the cell wall of a bacterium that stains purple when exposed to Gram staining techniques?

   _____

9. (K/U) Name two organelles in eukaryotic cells that scientists believe originated as independent cells.

   _____

10. (C) Compare and contrast a haploid cell with a diploid cell.

    _____

    _____

11. (T/I) Name the group each protist belongs to and explain how you know.
    a. Diatom_____

    _____

    _____

    b. Water mould_____

    _____

    _____

    c. Ciliate_____

    _____

    _____

12. (A) Describe how genetic engineers can use viruses to redirect cell activity.

_____

_____

_____

13. (C) Draw a diagram to illustrate your answer to question 12.

14. (K/U) (T/I) **In the 1960's, biologist Lynn Margulis first presented the concept of endosymbiosis.**

a. Describe the evidence that scientists use to explain the evolution of the eukarytoic cell.

_____

_____

_____

_____

b. Which endosymbiotic event occurred first: the evolution of chloroplasts or the evolution of mitochondria? Explain your answer.

_____

_____

_____

Self Study Guide

Question	If you answered this question incorrectly, see this Study Guide page for further review.	Question	If you answered this question incorrectly, see this Study Guide page for further review.
1	SG-21	8	SG-21
2	SG-20	9	SG-24
3	SG-21	10	SG-25
4	SG-22	11	SG-27, SG-28
5	SG-24	12	SG-20
6	SG-27, SG-28	13	SG-20
7	SG-28	14	SG-24

Self Assessment

1. Algae belong to which kingdom?
   A. Plantae   **B.** Animalia   **C.** Fungi
   D. Protista   **E.** Archaea

2. In vascular plants, xylem allows for which process?
   A. transport of large molecules like sugar from root systems
   B. transport of water and minerals from root systems
   C. gas exchange that occurs in the leaves
   D. absorption of sunlight to help with photosynthesis
   E. storage of food in the form of glycogen

3. Sporic reproduction involves which reproductive cells?
   A. haploid gametophytes and haploid spores
   B. haploid sporophytes and haploid spores
   C. diploid gametophytes and diploid spores
   D. haploid sporophytes and diploid spores
   E. diploid gametophytes and haploid spores

4. Which groups are bryophytes?
   A. algae, ferns, mosses
   B. hornworts, liverworts, mosses
   C. ferns, liverworts, gymnosperms
   D. hornworts, mosses, gymnosperms
   E. angiosperms, ferns, gymnosperms

5. The sporophyte generation is the most dominant stage in the life cycle of which organism?
   A. ferns   **B.** mosses   **C.** green algae
   D. brown algae   **E.** liverworts

6. What is the meaning of the term *gymnosperm*?
   A. vascular plant   **B.** flowering plant   **C.** naked seed
   D. fruit bearing   **E.** single seed

7. What basic structural units make up the body of a fungus?
   A. sori   **B.** mycellium   **C.** fruiting body
   D. hyphae   **E.** rhizoid

8. The mould Pencillum belongs to which group?
   A. Chytrids   **B.** Club Fungi   **C.** Sac Fungi
   D. Zygospore Fungi   **E.** Fungi Imperfecti

9. Which of the following is a composite organism made of a fungus and a photosynthetic organism?
   A. bread mould   **B.** truffles   **C.** lichen
   D. mushroom   **E.** Roquefort cheese

10. In which phylum have the largest number of animal species been identified?

    A. Annelida   **B.** Arthropoda   **C.** Chordata

    D. Platyhelminthes   **E.** Porifera

11. Which animals have a body plan with bilateral symmetry?

    A. corals, jellyfish, clams   **B.** sea anemones, worms, turtles.

    C. jellyfish, starfish, birds   **D.** insects, worms, mammals

    E. insects, starfish, mammals

12. What evidence can be used to link birds to reptiles?

    A. Reptiles are ectothermic.

    B. Birds are endothermic.

    C. Reptiles have a three-chambered heart.

    D. Birds have a four-chambered heart.

    E. Birds have scales on their legs.

13. Modern threats to species and their ecosystems are creating

    A. a biodiversity crisis.   **B.** climate change.

    C. evolutionary change.   **D.** stable environments for all organisms.

    E. predictable precipitation patterns.

14. What effect is global warming is having on mountainous regions?

    A. stabilizing of temperatures

    B. increase in number of alpine species

    C. habitat loss

    D. genetic diversity

    E. reduction in lowland species

15. Which event has been linked to the effects of climate change?

    A. increase of caribou populations in West Greenland

    B. increase in vegetation zones in mountainous regions

    C. increase in genetic diversity of plant populations

    D. decrease in pollination of plants

    E. decrease in consumption of oxygen by fish

Self Study Guide

Question	If you answered this question incorrectly, see this Study Guide page for further review.	After completing your review, be sure to answer these questions in the Chapter 3 Practice Test.	Question	If you answered this question incorrectly, see this Study Guide page for further review.	After completing your review, be sure to answer these questions in the Chapter 3 Practice Test.
1	SG-34	1, 2	9	SG-40	7, 10
2	SG-36, SG-37	4	10	SG-41, SG-42	7, 10
3	SG-36, SG-37	3, 11	11	SG-41	7, 10
4	SG-36	13	12	SG-41, SG-42	7, 10
5	SG-36	5	13	SG-44	12
6	SG-39	9, 13	14	SG-44	12
7	SG-41, SG-42	6, 13	15	SG-44	12
8	SG-40	11			

Key Terms

alga

plant

embryo

lignin

sporic reproduction

gametophyte

sporophyte

bryophyte

gymnosperm

angiosperm

cone

flower

fruit

dicot, monocot

fungus

hypha

mycelium

fruiting body

zygospore

ascus

basidium

lichen

invertebrate, vertebrate

radial symmetry

bilateral symmetry

coelom

segmentation

polyp

medusa

mantle

exoskeleton

notochord

cartilage

tetrapod

ecotothermy, endothermy

mammary gland

placenta

mass extinction

biodiversity

modelling

temperature sex determination

pollination

Algae – The Evolutionary Link Between Protists and the Plant Kingdom (3.1)

Algae (singular: **alga**) are classified in the kingdom Protista. Like plants, algae are autotrophic by photosynthesis, store food energy in the form of starch, and have common DNA sequences. However, because their zygote and embryo are not protected algae can only live in aquatic or moist environments. Algae also lack true roots, stems, and leaves. All algae contain chlorophyll, but may also contain other pigments that mask the green colour of the chlorophyll. They are commonly named for the type of pigment they contain; brown, red, and green algae.

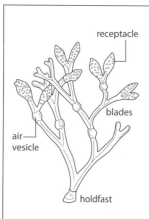

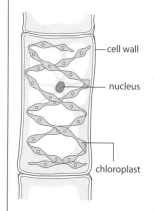

- **Brown algae** are structurally diverse, ranging from simple filaments to large blade forms up to 100 m in length.
- Large brown algae are called sea weeds or kelp and are found in marine ecosystems along rocky shorelines.
- Brown algae are anchored by holdfasts. When the tide is in, their broad, flattened blades are buoyed by air vescicles keeping them close to the surface of the water and in the sunlight.

- **Red algae** are smaller and more delicate than brown algae. Many have filamentous branches or are multicellular.
- Some species can live at depths of 175 m in the ocean. Their red pigment (phycoerythrin) allows them to absorb the limited amount of light that penetrates to those depths for photosynthesis
- Like coral, coralline red algae build up a layer of carbonate around themselves forming reefs.

- **Green algae** range from one-celled organisms such as *Chlamydomonas* to multicellular *Ulva* (sea lettuce).
- Most green algae live in water. Some species can live in other environments, including trunks of trees or on other organisms.
- Green algae are believed to be closely related to green plants. Both groups (1) have a cell wall that contains cellulose, (2) possess chlorophylls *a* and *b*, and (3) store food as starch.

Transition to Living on Dry Land

Unlike algae, **plants** are adapted to living on land where light is more available and carbon dioxide diffuses freely in the air. The land environment, however, requires adaptations to deal with the constant threat of drying out and to support the plant against the force of gravity.

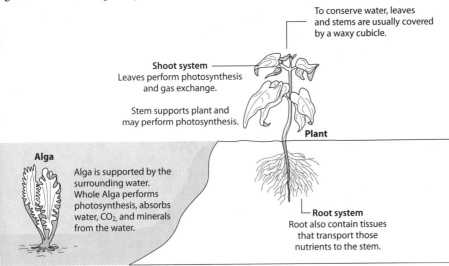

To conserve water, leaves and stems are usually covered by a waxy cubicle.

Shoot system
Leaves perform photosynthesis and gas exchange.

Stem supports plant and may perform photosynthesis.

Plant

Alga
Alga is supported by the surrounding water. Whole Alga performs photosynthesis, absorbs water, CO_2, and minerals from the water.

Root system
Root also contain tissues that transport those nutrients to the stem.

These additional adaptations allowed plants to move onto dry land.

- A cellulose cell wall prevents plant cells from drying out and provides support.
- Plants have a sporic life cycle (with alternation of generations).
- Most plants enclose the **embryo** to protect it and keep it from drying out, and use wind to disperse spores or seeds.
- Vascular plants have tube-like, elongated xylem tissues that carry water and nutrients from the roots and living phloem tissue that transports the carbohydrates manufactured during photosynthesis throughout the plant. Xylem tissue contains a tough support material called **lignin**, which allows trees to grow to great heights.

Learning Check

1. **C** Construct a Venn diagram or other graphic organizer that compares algae to plants.

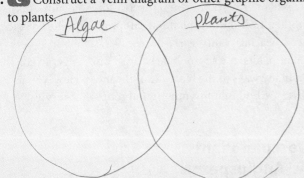

Algae   Plants

2. **K/U** Choose three adaptations that green plants have which allow them to survive in dry, terrestrial environments. Explain why each adaptation is helpful.

_____

_____

_____

Study Tip

Descriptions and examples of **graphic organizers** appear on pages 654–656 of your textbook. Use those pages to help you choose an organizer that suits the content and your preferred learning style.

Kingdom Plantae (3.2)

Plants are categorized as nonvascular plants, seedless vascular plants, and seed-producing vascular plants on the basis or the presence or absence of vascular tissue and the type of structure (seed or spore) that disperses the species.

- A seed is a plant organ that contains an embryo, along with a food supply, and is covered by a protective coat. In seed plants, the act of fertilization (union of the male and female cells) takes place before the seed leaves the parent plant.

- A spore is a reproductive cell that forms without fertilization and produces a new organism. Spores have very little stored food but are surrounded by a protective coat. In spore-producing plants, fertilization takes place after the spore leaves the parent.

Non-vascular Plants: The Bryophytes

The non-vascular plants, including liverworts and the mosses, do not have vascular tissue and therefore lack true roots, stems, and leaves.

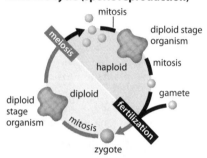

Moss life cycle (sporic reproduction)

The life cycle of a moss, like all plants, is characterized by an alternation of generations. The adult generation (**sporophyte**) produces spores, while the spore generation (**gametophyte**) produces sex cells (gametes). The evolution of windblown spores to disperse the species allowed these plants to reproduce on land.

Seedless Vascular Plants

Vascular plants have vascular tissue. Xylem transports water and minerals and also supports plants against the pull of gravity. Phloem transports organic nutrients from one part of the plant to another. Like the bryophytes, ferns produce spores, yet they have vascular tissue like seed-bearing plants. Ferns have leaves, stems, and roots.

In the life cycle of vascular plants, the sporophyte is larger and longer lived. The fern's life cycle is similar in many ways to the life cycle of the moss. However, the sporophyte and gametophyte are both photosynthetic and capable of survival and growth without the other.

Seed-Producing Vascular Plants: Gymnosperms and Angiosperms

A seed contains a plant embryo and stored food. Within the seed are all the parts needed to produce a new plant. Seeds contain the next sporophyte generation.

Seed plants have a life cycle that is fully adapted to a terrestrial environment. Two types of spores develop inside the body of the sporophyte: the pollen grain (reduced gametophyte) produces non-flagellated sperm, and the female gametophyte (located in the ovule) produces the egg.

Gymnosperms

The conifers are the largest group of gymnosperms. They have well developed vascular tissue that extends from the roots, through the stem to the needle-like leaves. Gymnosperms produce seeds that are uncovered (naked).

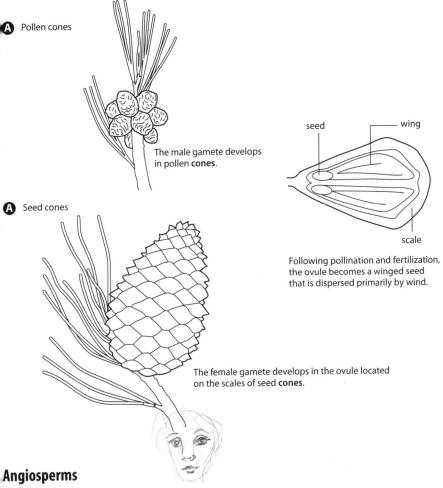

A Pollen cones

The male gamete develops in pollen **cones**.

A Seed cones

seed | wing

scale

Following pollination and fertilization, the ovule becomes a winged seed that is dispersed primarily by wind.

The female gamete develops in the ovule located on the scales of seed **cones**.

Angiosperms

Angiosperms, which include the flowering plants, produce seeds that are covered by **fruits**. The petals of **flowers** attract pollinators, and the ovary develops into a fruit that aids seed dispersal. Angiosperms provide much of the food that sustains terrestrial animals, and are the source of many products used by humans. Sexual reproduction in flowering plants takes place in a flower. Angiosperms are classified as **monocots** (one cotyledon) or **dicots** (two cotyledons). A cotyledon is a seed leaf inside the seed.

Learning Check

1. a. **K/U** Name the three general categories of plants.

_____

_____

_____

Study Tip

If you are having trouble with the vocabulary in biology, you could write out each term as it is pronounced. For example, *gymnosperm* could be written as *gym – no – sperm*. It does not have to be dictionary-correct, just meaningful to you.

b. **C** Use a table or another graphic organizer to compare these characteristics for each group of plants identified in part a.

- vascular tissue

- dominant generation

- species dispersal

2. **K/U** How do seeds and spores differ?

_____

_____

_____

3. **C** The diagram below illustrates the life cycle of plants. It outlines the alternation of generations of diploid sporophytes with haploid gametophytes. Use your knowledge of life cycles to complete the diagram.

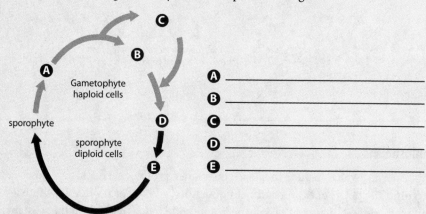

A _____

B _____

C _____

D _____

E _____

4. **T/I** Explain why vascular plants are more likely to survive in a dry environment than non-vascular plants.

_____

_____

_____

5. **C** Construct a list or T-chart comparing the characteristics that distinguish moncots from dicots.

Kingdom Fungi (3.3)

With the exception of yeast, fungi are multicellular eukaryotes that are heterotrophic by absorption. They send out digestive enzymes into the immediate environment, and absorb nutrient molecules through their cell membrane.

The basic structural units of multicellular fungi are threadlike filaments called **hypahae** that develop from fungal spores. Hyphae elongate at their tips and branch extensively to form a network of filaments called a **mycelium**.

At one point, fungi were classified as plants. However, fungal cells are quite different from plant cells. Fungal cells lack chloroplasts. The cell wall of a fungus is composed of chitin while plant cell walls are composed of cellulose.

Fungi produce windblown spores during both sexual and asexual reproduction. The major phyla of fungi are distinguished through their reproductive strategies and the structure of their **fruiting body**.

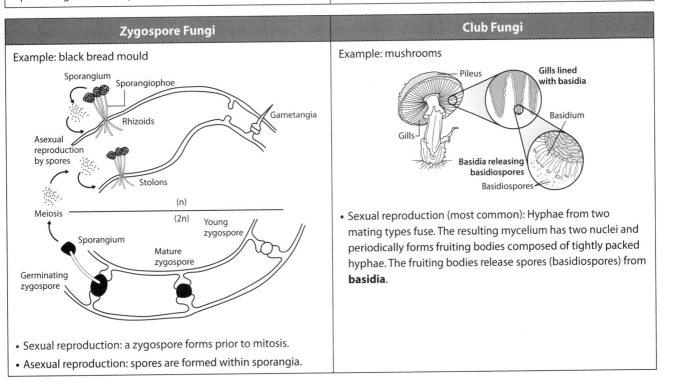

Chytrids	Sac Fungi
The chytrids are single-celled and considered the most primitive of the fungi.	Examples: red bread mould, cup fungi, morels, and truffles.

Chytrids

- Sexual reproduction: male and female motile gametes fuse to create a resting spore.
- Asexual reproduction: cytoplasm cleaves in a sporangium, producing motile zoospores.

Sac Fungi

- Sexual reproduction: sac fungi produce ascospores within asci, usually within a fruiting body.
- Asexual reproduction (most common): spores are produced.
- Yeasts are unicellular sac fungi that reproduce asexually by mitosis or budding.

Zygospore Fungi

Example: black bread mould

- Sexual reproduction: a zygospore forms prior to mitosis.
- Asexual reproduction: spores are formed within sporangia.

Club Fungi

Example: mushrooms

- Sexual reproduction (most common): Hyphae from two mating types fuse. The resulting mycelium has two nuclei and periodically forms fruiting bodies composed of tightly packed hyphae. The fruiting bodies release spores (basidiospores) from **basidia**.

Fungi Imperfecti

Fungi imperfecti cannot be classified into one of the other phyla because their mode of sexual reproduction is unknown. They always reproduce asexually by producing spores at the ends of certain hyphae.

Lichens

Lichens are a symbiotic relationship between a fungus and a cyanobacterium or a green alga. Although most references describe the symbiotic relationship as mutualism (both benefit), some studies indicate that this relationship is actually a form of parasitism of the algal cells by the fungus.

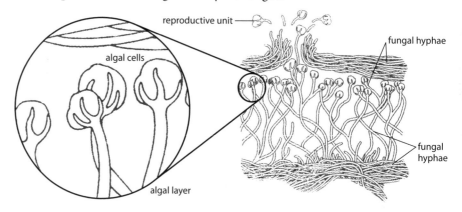

A section of lichen shows the placement of the algal cells and the fungal hyphae, which encircle and penetrate the algal cells.

Study Tip

When reading textbooks, be sure to "read":

- pictures
- tables
- diagrams
- photographs.

Sometimes these are easier to read than words. For example, what are three facts you can learn from Figure 3.22 on page 109 in your textbook?

Learning Check

1. **K/U** Identify the main characteristics of the kingdom Fungi.

_____

_____

2. **K/U** What role do most fungi play in food chains and food webs?

_____

3. **A** Why are lichens examples of composite organisms?

_____

_____

4. **C** Create a table or another graphic organizer comparing and contrasting the reproductive strategies of the chytrids, sac fungi, zygospore fungi, and club fungi.

Kingdom Animalia (3.4)

Animals are members of the domain Eukarya and the kingdom Animalia. The more than 30 animal phyla are believed to have evolved from protists.

Homo sapiens are members of the Phylum Chordata, animals with a **notochord**. Most members of Chordata are **vertebrates**—they have an internal skeleton of bone or **cartilage**. A few members of Chordata are **invertebrates**.

In general, animals

- are hetrotrophic and acquire food by ingestion followed by digestion.
- have the power of motion or locomotion by means of muscle fibres.
- are multicellular, and have specialized cells that form tissues and organs.
- have a life cycle in which the adult is diploid.
- reproduce sexually and produce an embryo that undergoes developmental stages.

The classification of animals is based on the anatomical features shown below.

Anatomical Features	Variation Between Groups
Level of Organization	• Cells not organized into tissues. • Cells organized into tissues. • Tissues organized into organs. • Organs organized into system.
Number of Body Layers	• Two cell layers: ectoderm (outside) and endoderm (inner). • Three cell layers: ectoderm, endoderm, and mesoderm.
Symmetry	• Asymmetrical: Body shape is irregular. • Radial: Any longitudinal cut through the midpoint yields equal halves. • Bilateral: Only one longitudinal cut through the midpoint yields equal halves.
Body Plan	• Sac plan: Mouth used for intake of nutrient molecules and exit of waste molecules. • Tube-within-a-tube plan: Separate openings (mouth and anus) for food intake and waste exit.
Body Cavities	• Acoelomate: Have no **coelom** • Pseudocoelomate: Have false coelom; coelom incompletely lined with mesoderm. • Coelomate: Have true coelom: a fluid-filled body cavity completely lined with mesoderm.
Embryonic openings	• In protostomes the first (*protos*) embryonic opening becomes the mouth (*stoma*) • In deuterostomes the first opening becomes related to the anus, and the second (*deutero*) opening becomes the mouth
Segmentation	• No segmentation (no repeating parts). • A repeating series of parts from anterior to posterior.
Movement	• Sessile: Adults are not able to move around but animal is motile at some point in the life cycle. • Motile: Able to move spontaneously and actively.
Reproduction	• Asexual • Sexual

For more details about each feature and the implications it has for an animal, see pages 112 to 114 of your textbook.

Evolutionary Tree of the Kingdom Animalia

The diagram illustrates the evolutionary relationships among the major phyla in the kingdom Animalia.

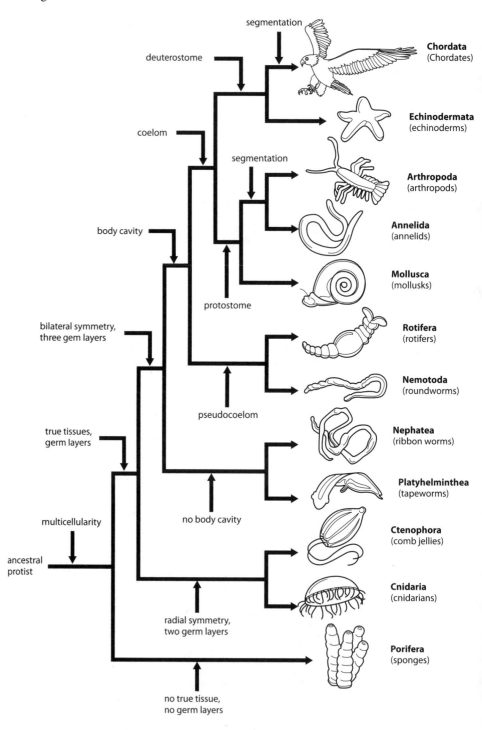

All animals are believed to have descended from protists. The poriferans (sponges), do not have tissues, so they may have evolved separately from the rest of the animals.

1. **K/U** Use the table and evolutionary tree on the previous page, and your textbook, to complete this table.

Characteristic	Sponges	Cnidarians	Flatworms	Roundworms
Level of Organization	cell			
Number of Body Layers	two			
Type of Body Plan	none		Sac plan: incomplete digestive system; only one opening	Tube-within-a-tube plan: complete digestive system; two openings
Type of Symmetry	asymmetrical			
Type of Coelom	none			

Study Tip

Understanding the **origin of some terms** can help you figure out what they mean. For example, ectothermic, from the Greek *ectos,* "outside" and *therme,* "heat," refers to organisms that control their body temperature through external means.

2. **A** Based on the evolutionary tree on the previous page, develop a dichtomous key distinguishing an echinoderm from an arthropod.

3. **T/I** **a.** Identify the one characteristic that separates invertebrates from other groups of animals.

_____

b. Summarize the major characteristics of the invertebrate phyla identified in your textbook. Some information about invertebrate chordates has been included below as an example. Record your answer on a separate sheet of paper or index cards.

Invertebrate Chordates have a dorsal hollow nerve cord, pharyngeal pouches, and postanal tail at some stage of development. They have bilateral symmetry, a well-developed coelom, and segmentation. Examples include tunicates (sea squirts) and the fish-like lancets.

4. **T/I** **a.** Identify the characteristics that separate vertebrates from all other groups of animals.

_____

b. Summarize the major characteristics of the classes of vertebrates identified in your textbook. Record your answer on a separate sheet of paper or index cards.

The Biodiversity Crisis (3.5)

In Chapter 1, you read about genetic diversity, species diversity, and ecosystem diversity. You also read that ecosystems perform services that depend on a high degree of **biodiversity**.

A **mass extinction** is a rapid, world-wide event during which a significant percent of all life on Earth, across many phyla and habitats, becomes extinct.

Extinction is a fact of life, as normal and necessary as species formation is to a stable world ecosystem. Most species, if not all, go extinct. However, the current rate of extinction is abnormally high. Humans have had a devastating effect on genetic, species, and ecosystem biodiversity almost everywhere in the world. This biodiversity crisis may represent the next mass extinction.

Climate Change

Accelerated global warming is predicted as carbon dioxide and other green house gases trap infrared radiation on the surface of the Earth. Climate change, characterized by changing patterns of precipitation and temperature, is a major threat to the survival of species.

Climate change could impact food sources for humans and other animals. It could result in changing habitats and the shifting of the worlds' major terrestrial and aquatic biomes. It could disrupt the reproductive cycles of many organisms including the role of **pollination** in flowering plants.

Learning Check

1. **K/U** Define or describe each term.
   a. species diversity

   _____

   b. genetic diversity

   _____

   c. biodiversity crisis

   _____

   _____

2. **K/U** What criteria are used to identify a mass extinction?

   _____

   _____

   _____

3. **C** Use the information on pages 125 to 127 of your textbook to create a spider map showing the effects of climate change on species diversity. Include information about these factors: food sources, habitat, reproduction, pollination, aquatic and land ecosystems

---

Study Tip

You can use a **spider map** (sometimes called a semantic map) to investigate and organize various aspects of a single theme or topic, which can help you to organize your thoughts (**question 3**). You can see an example on page 654 of your textbook.

Bringing It All Together

Complete the table to compare examples of Plant-like Algae, Plants, Fungi, and Animals.

	Plant-like Algae [Sea lettuce (*Ulva*)]	Plants [Angiosperm]	Fungi [Zygospore Fungi]	Animals [Mammal]
Kingdom				
Cell Type		eukaryotic		
Number of Cells		multicellular		
Locomotion				
Life Cycle (see Chapter 2)	sporoic (alternation of generations)		zygotic	
Nutrition				
Reproduction				sexual only
Other Characteristics				

Practice Test

1. (K/U) Which is a species of multicellular algae?
   A. Chlamydomonas
   B. Volvox
   C. Ulva
   D. Diatom
   E. Euglenoid

2. (K/U) On a phylogenetic tree diagram, green algae would be appear most closely related to which organisms?
   A. animals
   B. plants
   C. fungi
   D. red algae
   E. dinoflagellates

3. (K/U) A sporophyte produces
   A. spores by mitosis.
   B. spores by meiosis.
   C. gametes by mitosis.
   D. gametes by meiosis.
   E. gametes by fertilization.

4. (K/U) The development of vascular tissue lead to the evolution of which structure?
   A. rhizoids
   B. spores
   C. phloem
   D. roots
   E. leaves

5. (K/U) Which organisms formed the first forests?
   A. seedless vascular plants
   B. seed producing vascular plants
   C. gymnosperms
   D. angiosperms
   E. bryophytes

6. (K/U) Which organisms are hetertrophs?
   A. red algae
   B. green algae
   C. mosses
   D. ferns
   E. fungi

7. (K/U) What is a coelom?
   A. The middle layer of a set of tissues.
   B. A tube-shaped sessile body form.
   C. A fluid filled body cavity.
   D. An umbrella-shaped body form.
   E. An internal skeleton that protects organs.

8. (K/U) List two examples of evolutionary changes that lead to the development of land plants.

   _____

   _____

9. (T/I) Describe the main difference between gymnosperms and angiosperms.

   _____

   _____

   _____

10. (T/I) List three characteristics that make animals different from other kingdoms.

    _____

    _____

    _____

11. (C) Draw a diagram that illustrates sporic reproduction (alternation of generations).

12. (T/I) List two examples of climate change affecting species diversity.

    _____

    _____

    _____

13. a. (T/I) Complete the table

Specialized Characteristic	Kingdom	Example
Seedless, vascular		Ferns, club mosses, horsetails, whisk ferns
Link between protists and plants		
	Animalia	
		Bryophytes (mosses, liverworts, hornworts)
Heterotrophic		
		Gymnosperms (conifers)
		Fish, amphibians, reptiles, birds, mammals
Flower producing		

b. (C) (A) Draw a phylogenetic tree to illustrate the evolution of organisms found in the kingdom Plantae.

Self Study Guide

Question	If you answered this question incorrectly, see this Study Guide page for further review.	Question	If you answered this question incorrectly, see this Study Guide page for further review.
1	SG-34	8	SG-35
2	SG-34	9	SG-37
3	SG-36	10	SG-41, SG-42
4	SG-35	11	SG-36, SG-37, SG-41, SG-42
5	SG-35	12	SG-44
6	SG-39, SG-40	13	SG-35
7	SG-40, SG-42		

Add groups of organisms and information about them to this tree diagram to summarize key ideas about the diversity of life. You may need to write sideways in some places.

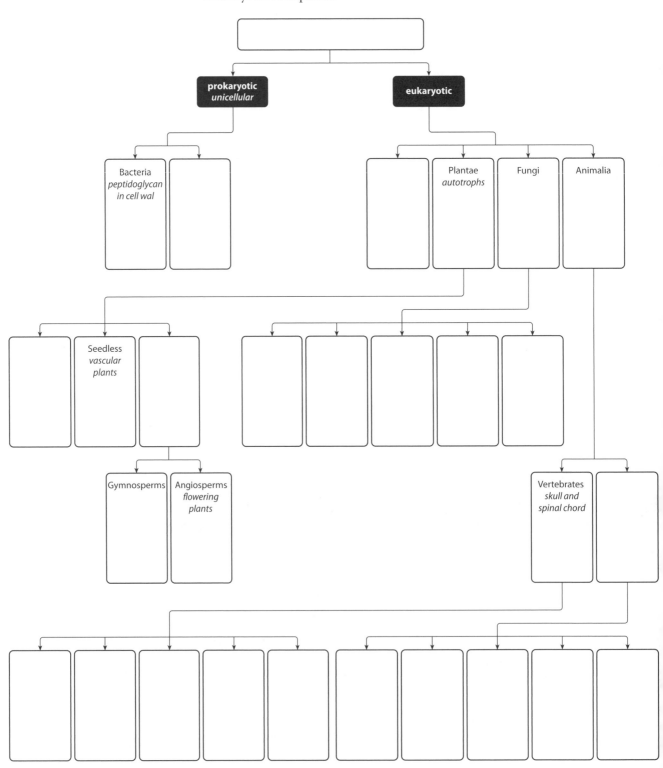

Unit 1 Practice Test

1. **K/U** The phylogenetic species concept is based on what evidence?
   A. body shape and size of organisms
   B. evolutionary history of organisms
   C. ability of organisms to interbreed
   D. structural features of organisms
   E. existing population of a species

2. **K/U** Which category for classifying organisms contains the other four categories?
   A. Family
   B. Species
   C. Phylum
   D. Order
   E. Class

3. **K/U** Which statement best describes organisms found in the kingdom Archaea?
   A. autotrophic and heterotrophic, eukaryote
   B. autotrophic and heterotrophic, prokaryote
   C. heterotrophic, prokaryote
   D. heterotrophic, eukaryote
   E. autotrophic, eukaryote

4. **K/U** Which term describes the ability to maintain balance in ecosystems?
   A. resilience
   B. biodiversity
   C. ecosystem diversity
   D. structural diversity
   E. environmental resistance

5. **K/U** What does a virus do during the lytic cycle after it enters the cell?
   A. forms a provirus
   B. dies
   C. becomes inactive
   D. attaches to the cell wall
   E. replicates

6. **K/U** Which are the three most common shapes of prokaryotes?
   A. bacilli, cocci, spiral
   B. bacilli, cube, rods
   C. cubes, pyramids, rods
   D. cocci, rods, pyramids
   E. cubes, spiral, spherical

7. **K/U** Archaea and bacteria reproduce through which process?
   A. mitosis
   B. meiosis
   C. binary fission
   D. regeneration
   E. mitosis and meiosis

8. **K/U** Which organelles are linked to the theory of endosymbiosis?
   A. endoplasmic reticulum and mitochondria
   B. ribosomes and endoplasmic reticulum
   C. chloroplasts and mitochondria
   D. chloroplasts and golgi bodies
   E. nuclei and nucleolus

9. **K/U** **T/I** What characteristic distinguishes the phylum Zoomastigina from other protists?
   A. parasitic life cycle
   B. extensions of cytoplasm called pseudopods
   C. hair-like projections called cilia
   D. production of spores
   E. presence of one or more flagella

10. **K/U** Which organism is thought to be the first land plant?
    A. ferns
    B. liverworts
    C. club mosses
    D. algae
    E. gymnosperms

11. **K/U** Which statement is true for seedless vascular plants?
    A. The sporophyte is the dominant stage in their life cycle.
    B. The gameophyte is the dominant stage in their life cycle.
    C. Their life cycle is divided equally between sporophytes and gametophytes.
    D. The lack of root systems lead to the development of rhizoids.
    E. Pollen grains are used to form free-living plants.

12. **K/U** Cnidarians have which structure?
    A. bilateral body symmetry
    B. radial body symmetry
    C. a coelomate body plan
    D. three layers of cells
    E. a highly developed nervous system

13. (K/U) What is the main structural difference between prokaryotic and eukaryotic cells?

_____

14. (K/U) What is the process that many organisms in the domain Archaea use to obtain nutrition?

_____

15. (K/U) Scientists hypothesize that eukaryotic cells developed through which process?

_____

16. (K/U) (T/I) What phylum of Algae are the most plant-like?

_____

17. (K/U) (T/I) What classes of animals are known as tetrapods?

_____

18. (K/U) List the categories used to classify species from the broadest category to the narrowest category.

_____

19. (T/I) Describe the research methods a taxonomist would use to classify a species.

_____

_____

20. (T/I) Explain why some scientists do not consider viruses to be living species. Support your answer.

_____

_____

_____

21. (C) Use the table to show the methods of reproduction for bacteria and viruses.

Bacteria	Virus

22. (C) (T/I) Draw a diagram to illustrate the life cycle of a bryophyte.

23. (T/I) Explain why classficiation systems continue to be updated. Give two examples of recent changes.

_____

_____

_____

24. (C) (T/I) Select one organism to represent each of the four kingdoms in the domain Eukarya. Describe the characteristics that place each organism in its respective kingdom.

_____

_____

_____

_____

25. (T/I) (A) **a.** Describe three factors that are contributing to the biodiversity crisis.

_____

_____

_____

b. Explain how one of these factors could be affecting your local community.

_____

_____

Self Study Guide

Question	If you answered this question incorrectly, see this Study Guide page for further review.	Question	If you answered this question incorrectly, see this Study Guide page for further review.
1	SG-6, SG-8	14	SG-22, SG-23
2	SG-7	15	SG-24
3	SG-7, SG-10	16	SG-34
4	SG-12 to SG-14	17	SG-34 (Key Terms)
5	SG-20	18	SG-7
6	SG-21	19	SG-7
7	SG-21	20	SG-20
8	SG-24	21	SG-20, SG-21
9	SG-27, SG-28	22	SG-36
10	SG-35	23	SG-8
11	SG-36	24	SG-27, SG-28, SG-36, SG-37, SG-39 to SG-42
12	SG-41, SG-42	25	SG-44
13	SG-10, SG-21, SG-24		

Unit 2 — Genetic Processes

Chapter 4 Cell Division and Reproduction

- Most diploid (2*n*) somatic (body) cells undergo a continuous sequence of growth and division, referred to as the cell cycle. Through the process of cell division, multicellular organisms grow by:
  - adding new cells,
  - repairing damaged tissues, and
  - replacing dead or dying cells.
- A molecule of DNA is made up of two long strands of nucleotides wound around each other in the shape of a double helix.
- A human karyotype is a photograph of an individual's chromosomes. The chromosome pairs are arranged in order of their length, from longest to shortest, and numbered. The sex chromosomes appear last.
- Meiosis takes place in the reproductive structures of sexually reproducing organisms. Meiosis involves two nuclear divisions to create haploid (*n*) gametes from diploid (2*n*) parent cells. Potential errors during meiosis include changes in chromosome structure and chromosome number that result from mistakes during crossing over and non-disjunction of chromosomes.
- Genetic and reproductive technologies have many useful applications but can also create challenging social and ethical questions.

Chapter 5 Patterns of Inheritance

Gregor Mendel used pea plant crosses to follow the transmission of one or two traits at a time. Given what we know about chromosomes now, we know the genes for the traits he studied were carried on different chromosomes, and each gene had two alleles.

- Mendel's law of segregation states that inherited factors (genes) separate in meiosis. Each individual receives one copy of each gene from each parent.
- The probability of an outcome for a particular event is a number indicating how likely a particular outcome is to occur. This number is calculated by dividing the number of ways the outcome may occur by the number of total possible outcomes for the event.
- Monohybrid crosses are crosses involving only one trait. A test cross breeds an individual with an unknown genotype to a homozygous recessive individual. Punnett squares are based on the principles of probability and can be used to predict the outcomes of genetic crosses.
- Mendel derived his law of independent assortment by observing the transmission of two or more independent traits (where the genes are on different chromosomes.) The chromosome theory of inheritance states that genes are located on chromosomes, and chromosomes provide the basis for the segregation and independent assortment of genes.

- A pedigree is a key tool for geneticists who study the inheritance of human traits. It can provide information about the genotypes and phenotypes of previous generations, and can be used to predict the genotypes and phenotypes of future offspring.

- Analysis of a pedigree indicates whether a trait is autosomal dominant or autosomal recessive.

- Other methods of genetic screening and diagnosis can provide information about human genotypes.

Chapter 6 Complex Patterns of Inheritance

While some genes influence phenotypes according to Mendel's straightforward laws of dominance, many genes influence phenotype in more complex ways.

- Some genes have incompletely dominant alleles. For traits determined by incomplete dominance, heterozygote offspring have phenotypes in between those of the two homozygote parents.

- Some genes have co-dominant alleles. Both alleles are expressed in the phenotype of a heterozygote.

- Some traits are influenced by more than one gene or by environmental conditions, and some traits can be determined by several alleles.

- Linked genes—genes on the same chromosome—do not segregate independently. Instead the probability of recombination is determined by how close the genes are to one another on the chromosome. The frequency of recombination can be used to construct a gene map.

- Sex-linked traits—those controlled by genes on the X or Y chromosome—are expressed in different ratios by male and female offspring.

- Genomic and proteomic studies have built on Mendel's original research and promise to bring unprecedented scientific rewards in the discovery of disease-influencing genes, design of new drugs, understanding developmental processes, and determining the origin and evolution of the human race. However, these studies have also raised many ethical issues.

Self Assessment

1. Which would be classified as somatic cells?
   - **A.** kidney, heart, sperm
   - **B.** egg, skin, blood
   - **C.** spore, seed, zygote
   - **D.** skin, heart, liver
   - **E.** egg, sperm, ovary

2. Which is the longest phase of the cell cycle?
   - **A.** anaphase
   - **B.** interphase
   - **C.** telophase
   - **D.** Growth 2
   - **E.** cytokinesis

3. During which phase of mitosis does the centromere split?
   - **A.** anaphase
   - **B.** interphase
   - **C.** metaphase
   - **D.** prophase
   - **E.** telophase

4. Which process produces exact copies of DNA?
   - **A.** complementarity
   - **B.** replication
   - **C.** translocation
   - **D.** synthesis
   - **E.** fertilization

5. A human female has
   - **A.** 11 autosomal chromosomes and one X chromosome.
   - **B.** 11 autosomal chromosomes and two X chromosomes.
   - **C.** 22 autosomal pairs and one X or Y chromosome.
   - **D.** 22 autosomal pairs and two X chromosomes.
   - **E.** 44 autosomal pairs and two Y chromosomes.

6. What does the fusion of two gametes form?
   - **A.** an egg
   - **B.** a sperm
   - **C.** a zygote
   - **D.** an autosomal cell
   - **E.** a germinal cell

7. What does meiosis produce?
   - **A.** two identical cells
   - **B.** two diploid cells
   - **C.** two haploid cells
   - **D.** four diploid cells
   - **E.** four haploid cells

8. Why is meiosis important for organisms?
   - **A.** It produces diploid cells.
   - **B.** It slows the rate of growth of cells.
   - **C.** It reduces genetic diversity.
   - **D.** It increases genetic variation.
   - **E.** It increases the number of homologous cells.

9. In most female animals, in what organ does oogenesis take place?
   - **A.** oviducts
   - **B.** ovaries
   - **C.** vagina
   - **D.** uterus
   - **E.** cervix

10. The exchange of chromosomal segments between a pair of homologous chromosomes is known as

   A. crossing over.   **B.** independent assortment.

   C. trisomy.   **D.** meiosis.

   E. non-disjunction.

11. Which pre-natal procedure is considered to be non-invasive?

   A. amniocentesis   **B.** chorionic villus sampling

   C. fetoscopy   **D.** maternal blood tests

   E. embryoscopy

12. In humans, what reproductive technique can be used to fertilize egg cells outside a female's body?

   A. artificial insemination   **B.** embryo transfer   **C.** gene cloning

   D. in vitro fertilization   **E.** selective breeding

13. What are stem cells?

   A. unspecialized cells   **B.** specialized cells   **C.** plasmids

   D. somatic (body) cells   **E.** fertilized egg cells

14. Which process can be used to produce human insulin?

   A. embryo transfer   **B.** gene cloning

   C. in vitro fertilization   **D.** amniocentesis

   E. replication of DNA

15. Transgenic organisms are

   A. produced by cloning.

   B. genetically modified.

   C. less resistance to herbicides.

   D. a byproduct of stem cells.

   E. formed by spermatogenesis.

Self Study Guide

Question	If you answered this question incorrectly, see this Study Guide page for further review.	After completing your review, be sure to answer these questions in the Chapter 4 Practice Test.	Question	If you answered this question incorrectly, see this Study Guide page for further review.	After completing your review, be sure to answer these questions in the Chapter 4 Practice Test.
1	SG-59	10	9	SG-62	12
2	SG-59	1, 2, 3	10	SG-61	5, 7, 9
3	SG-60	1, 2, 3, 10	11	SG-62	14
4	SG-56	1, 2	12	SG-63	13
5	SG-58	4	13	SG-63	14
6	SG-61, SG-63	4, 6, 13	14	SG-63	14
7	SG-61	5. 6. 10	15	SG-64	14
8	SG-61	8			

Key Terms

genetics

somatic cell

chromosome

sister chromatid

centromere

spindle fibre

centrosome

genome

sex chromosome

autosome

homologous chromosome

gene

allele

karyotype

asexual reproduction

sexual reproduction

gamete

zygote

fertilization

haploid

diploid

meiosis

germ cell

synapsis

spermatogenesis

oogenesis

crossing over

non-disjunction

monosomy

trisomy

selective breeding

artificial insemination

embryo transfer

in vitro fertilization

cloning

gene cloning

recombinant DNA

therapeutic cloning

reproductive cloning

stem cell

DNA, Genes, and Chromosomes (4.1)

The basic structure of DNA is the nucleotide. Chemical bonds between sugar and phosphate molecules make up the backbone of each DNA strand. **Genes** are segments of DNA on a **chromosome** that contain specific genetic information.

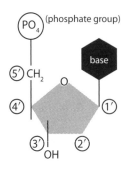

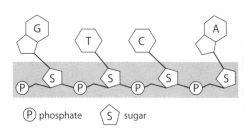

Each DNA nucleotide is composed of a 5-carbon sugar (deoxyribose), a phosphate group, and one of four nitrogen-containing bases: adenine (A), guanine (G), cytosine (C), or thymine (T).

The nitrogenous bases project out from the sugar phosphate backbone of DNA. Double-ringed nitrogenous bases (adenine and guanine) are called purines. Single-ringed nitrogenous bases (thymine and cytosine) are called pyrimidines.

A DNA molecule is made up of two strands of nucleotides, bound together to form a double helix. The two strands are held together by hydrogen bonds between complementary base pairs. Adenine (A) and thymine (T) are base pairs held together by two hydrogen bonds. Guanine (G) and cytosine (C) are held together by three hydrogen bonds.

Homologous chromosomes carry the same genes. They have several characteristics in common such as their length, **centromere** location, and banding pattern.

Although homologous chromosomes appear identical, they carry different forms, or **alleles**, of the same genes at the same location, or locus (plural loci). In these chromosomes, the upper-case and lower-case letters denote different alleles of the same gene.

During DNA replication, two molecules of DNA are made from one. The original double helix unwinds. Two new strands of DNA are assembled using the original strands as templates. The resulting new molecules are identical to the original molecule. Each new molecule contains one original strand of DNA and one new strand.

1. **K/U** **a.** Draw a single DNA nucleotide. Label the parts.

b. One strand in a segment of DNA has the base sequence CCTGA. Draw this segment of DNA. Label the sugar-phosphate backbone and the individual nucleotides.

2. **K/U** What would be the complementary sequence of nucleotides found on the other strand of the DNA molecule you drew in question 1b?

_____

3. **K/U** Label the diagram.

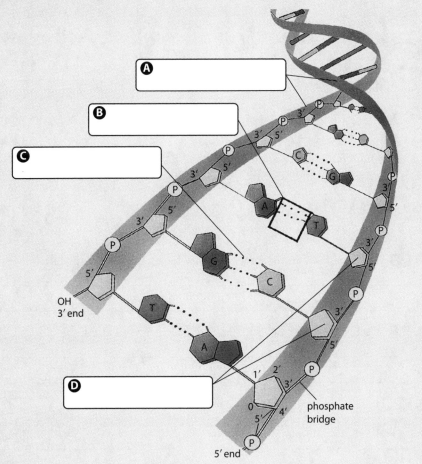

Ⓐ

Ⓑ

Ⓒ

Ⓓ

OH
3′ end

5′ end

phosphate
bridge

4. **A** What characteristics do homologous chromosomes share?

_____

5. **C** Create a flowchart summarizing the events that occur during DNA replication.

Study Tip

A **flowchart** (**question 5**) can help you organize and remember steps in a procedure. As you create a flowchart, check that the steps follow a logical sequence.

Human Karyotypes (4.1, 4.2)

A **karyotype** is a photograph of an individual's chromosomes. To prepare a karyotype, scientists collect a cell sample and use chemicals to stop the cell cycle when the condensed chromosomes are most clearly visible under a light microscope. Then they stain the cells to help them identify the individual chromosomes. Usually, they photograph the stained chromosomes and transfer the images onto a new background. They complete the karyotype by organizing the images into a series of numbered homologous chromosome pairs from longest to shortest. The **sex chromosomes** appear last.

Karyotypes are helpful in diagnosing conditions such as Turner syndrome, where one X chromosome is partly or totally missing (**monosomy** X), and Down syndrome, where there is an extra chromosome 21 (**trisomy** 21).

Learning Check

Use this karyotype to answer the questions below.

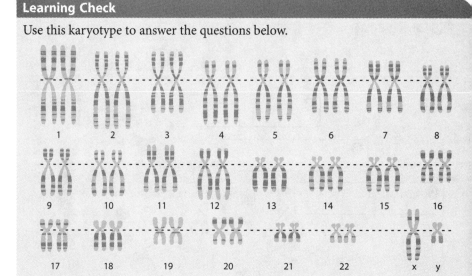

1. **K/U** Which pair of chromosomes does not have a number? Explain why.

_____

_____

2. **A** What is the sex of the individual? Explain how you know.

_____

_____

3. **A** How would the karyotype differ if
a. this individual had Down syndrome?

_____

b. the karyotype were a gamete? What would the chromosome number be?

_____

_____

The Cell Cycle (4.1)

Most **diploid** (2n) **somatic cells** use a continuous sequence of growth and division referred to as the cell cycle. The cell cycle gives rise to all cells and ensures that the diploid parent cell provides an identical set of chromosomes to each of its daughter cells.

The cell cycle is made up of two main stages: interphase and cell division. These stages can be organized into five general phases or processes.

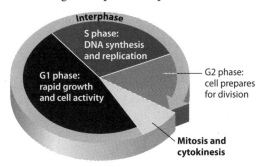

Mitosis is the division of the genetic material and the contents of the nucleus into two complete and separate sets. Cytokinesis is the division of the cytoplasm and the organelles into two separate cells. Together, mitosis and cytokinesis form two new daughter cells with the same genetic information as the parent cell.

Learning Check

1. **K/U** Refer to the diagram above. Summarize the events occurring at each stage in the cell cycle.

a. interphase _____

_____

b. G1 phase _____

_____

c. S phase _____

_____

d. G2 phase _____

_____

e. mitosis _____

_____

f. cytokinesis _____

_____

2. **A** **a.** What is the main purpose of the cell cycle in human skin cells?

_____

b. How would the cell cycle in actively dividing cells differ from the cell cycle in cells that no longer divide?

_____

_____

_____

Mitosis and Cytokinesis (4.1)

Mitosis is the process of nuclear division. The linked processes of mitosis and cytokinesis have three important functions:

- growth of multicellular organisms
- replacing worn out or dead cells
- regenerating damaged tissues

To accomplish these tasks, each new daughter cell must have the correct genetic information. This means that:

- The genetic material of the parent cell must be replicated. This process takes place during the S phase of the cell cycle.
- The replicated chromatin must be condensed and organized as chromosomes in the nucleus. The resulting genetically identical sister chromatids are held together at the centromere.
- The sister chromatids separate during mitosis.

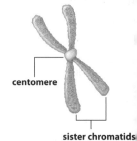

centomere

sister chromatids

Mitosis involves a precise sequence of events. These events are grouped into four phases: prophase, metaphase, anaphase, and telophase. Each phase is defined by a particular arrangement of chromosomes in the dividing cell.

There are two major differences between mitosis of animal cells and mitosis of plant cells:

1. In animal cells, spindle apparatus forms from the centrioles. Plant cells do not have centrioles. They do, however, form a spindle apparatus.
2. During cytokinesis in animal cells, the cell membrane indents to form two daughter cells. In plants, a cell plate develops to form two daughter cells.

See pages 162 to 163 of your textbook for more details on mitosis.

Learning Check

1. **K/U** Name three important functions of mitosis and cytokinesis.

_____

_____

2. **A** Explain why each new daughter cell must have the correct genetic information.

_____

_____

3. **C** On a separate sheet of paper, make a table to describe the major events of each phase of mitosis for a cell with two pairs of chromosomes. Start with interphase. Use diagrams if you wish.

Study Tip

The combination of a verbal description and a clear, **labelled diagram** can help you understand and remember many processes in biology, including the stages of mitosis (**question 3**).

Meiosis (4.2)

In **meiosis**, two nuclear divisions create **haploid** (*n*) gametes from diploid (*2n*) parent cells. Each **gamete** contains only one copy of each type of chromosome that the diploid parent cell contains. Meiosis has two key outcomes: genetic reduction (diploid to haploid) and genetic recombination.

Like mitosis, meiosis involves four distinct phases: prophase, metaphase, anaphase, and telophase. A cell undergoing meiosis will divide twice. In meiosis I, the chromosome number is reduced from diploid to haploid. In meiosis II, the sister chromatids separate.

Two key features of meiosis contribute to genetic variations.

1. Pairing of homologous chromosomes allows for **crossing over**, resulting in the exchange of chromosome sections between non-sister chromatids.

2. Independent assortment of homologous maternal and paternal chromosomes during metaphase I results in gametes that have different combinations of parental chromosomes.

See pages 170 to 171 of your textbook for more details about meiosis.

Gamete Formation in Animals

Different meiotic processes result in the production of human sperm and eggs.

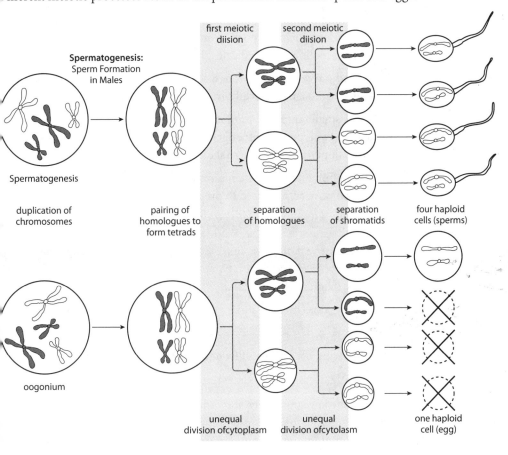

Spermatogenesis: Sperm Formation in Males

first meiotic diision   second meiotic diision

Spermatogenesis

duplication of chromosomes | pairing of homologues to form tetrads | separation of homologues | separation of shromatids | four haploid cells (sperms)

oogonium

unequal division ofcytoplasm | unequal division ofcytolasm | one haploid cell (egg)

Spermatogenesis

Spermatogenesis from spermatogonium cells in the testes starts at puberty.

Meiotic divisions are equal, leading to four spermatozoa from the original spermatogonium cell.

Meiosis II is completed before the sperm are released from testes.

Oogenesis

- All potential gametes are produced before birth in ovaries as an oogonium completes prophase I.
- Meiotic divisions of the primary oocyte are unequal, resulting the formation of one large secondary oocyte and smaller polar bodies (eventually destroyed).
- Puberty releases the "arrested state" of secondary oocytes, leading to ovulation.
- Meiosis II is not completed until fertilization of the secondary oocyte by sperm.

Chromosome Abnormalities

Some chromosomal abnormalities are caused by deletions (chromosomal material is missing), insertions (additional chromosomal material is present), inversions (a portion of the chromosome is 'backwards'), and translocations (chromosomal material has moved from one chromosome to another). Structural abnormalities can occur spontaneously, or they may be caused by agents such as chemicals, radiation, or viral infections.

    Monosomy and **trisomy** are caused by non-disjunction. **Non-disjunction** occurs when chromosomes fail to separate correctly during anaphase I or anaphase II.

Prenatal Testing

- Maternal blood testing provides information about potential physical and chromosomal abnormalities, and indicates the risk for Down syndrome.
- Ultrasound: Sound waves are sent through the amniotic fluid and bounce off the developing fetus. The image produced can reveal physical abnormalities.
- Amniocentesis: A small sample of amniotic fluid is withdrawn from the uterus and used to prepare a karyotype or another genetic analysis. The karyotype can be used to identify non-disjunction chromosomal disorders such as Down syndrome.
- Chorionic villi sampling: Cells can be removed from the chorion, a tissue that surrounds the amniotic sac, and used to prepare a karyotype of the fetus.

Learning Check

1. **C** On a separate sheet of paper, make a table to describe the major events of each phase of meiosis for a cell with two pairs of chromosomes. Start with interphase. Use diagrams if you wish.

2. **T/I** In what ways does meiosis serve a different function than mitosis?

   _____

3. **K/U** How is crossing over different from independent assortment?

   _____

4. **T/I** Compare the key similarities and differences between spermatogenesis and oogenesis.

   _____

   _____

5. **T/I** Explain the significance of meiosis to sexually reproducing organisms.

   _____

   _____

Study Tip

When you learn a new concept or process, compare it to a similar concept or process you already understand. This will help you put the new knowledge in a meaningful **context** and remember it.

Reproduction, Technology, and Society (4.3)

Reproductive technologies have been developed to obtain a large number of offspring from genetically superior animals and to obtain offspring from infertile animals, including humans.

• For thousands of years, human have recognized that offspring resemble parents. People have used this observation to their advantage by using **selective breeding**—choosing and breeding specific plants and animals for particular physical features or behaviours.

• **Artificial insemination** (AI) has been used for decades as a way to promote breeding success among domestic animals. It has also been used by human couples when the male is sterile or infertile. In AI, sperm are collected and concentrated before being placed in the woman's reproductive tract.

• **Embryo transplant** is normally used to increase the number of high quality animals. In farm mammals, early embryos can be removed from the uterus of a donor and transferred to the uterus of other females for development to term. This process usually involves the production of multiple eggs as a result of hormone treatment (superovulation). The donor cow is inseminated several times and then, several days later, the fertilized embryos are removed and examined, and then transferred or frozen for later use.

• **In vitro fertilization** (IVF) offers a solution for women with blocked oviducts. Ultrasound machines are used to identify specific follicles in a woman's ovaries that are close to ovulation. Immature eggs can be retrieved directly from these follicles. The eggs are combined with sperm in laboratory glassware. After fertilization, the developing embryo is placed in the uterus.

In humans, preimplantation genetic diagnosis can be used to identify genetic defects in embryos created through in vitro fertilization (IVF) before pregnancy. Similar screening techniques are applied to embryo transfer programs in animals.

Cloning

Organisms that are genetically identical are said to be clones of one another.

• **Gene cloning** can lead to multiple copies of a gene or to a quantity of the gene product. The gene can be studied in the laboratory or inserted into a bacterium, plant, or animal. The gene product, a protein, can become a commercial product for use as a medicine.

• **Therapeutic cloning** is performed for the purpose of medical treatment. This type of cloning is called somatic cell nuclear transfer and involves extracting the nucleus of a cell, and putting the nucleus into an egg which has had its nucleus removed. The egg is then allowed to divide and grow. The growing egg is used as a source of **stem cells**. The stem cells may be used to treat disorders such as diabetes, Alzheimer's disease, and Parkinson's disease.

• **Reproductive cloning** is used to generate an animal that has the same nuclear DNA as another currently or previously existing animal. Scientists use somatic cell nuclear transfer to insert genetic material from the nucleus of a donor adult cell to an egg whose nucleus has been removed. Once the cloned embryo reaches a suitable stage, it is transferred to the uterus of a female host where it continues to develop until birth. In reproductive cloning, the egg is allowed to grow into a new organism.

Biotechnology Products – Transgenic Organisms

Transgenic organisms have had a foreign gene inserted into them. Recombinant DNA technology has been used to produce transgenic bacteria. These bacteria, containing genetic material from other species, have been used to promote the health of plants, perform bioremediation, extract minerals, and produce chemicals. Transgenic crops, engineered to resist herbicides and pests, are commercially available. Transgenic animals have had foreign DNA inserted into their genome. This foreign DNA must be transmitted through sex cells gametes so that every cell of the animal contains the same modified genetic material. Transgenics has been used with animals for many purposes including:

- increasing milk yield or meat production with genetically engineered hormones
- modifying animal physiology and/or anatomy
- reproducing specific blood lines through cloning
- serving as a source of organs for human transplant patients

Learning Check

1. **K/U a.** Explain how in vitro fertilization might help a couple achieve pregnancy if the woman has a blocked oviduct (fallopian tube). Note: The oviduct carries the ovum (egg) from the ovary to the uterus.

_____

_____

_____

   b. Explain how artificial insemination might help a couple achieve pregnancy if the man has a low sperm count. NOTE: A male with a low sperm count is likely infertile.

_____

_____

_____

2. **K/U a.** Under what circumstances is preimplantation genetic diagnosis (PGD) normally used?

_____

   b. Identify two potential societal issues associated with preimplantation genetic diagnosis.

_____

_____

3. **C** On a separate sheet of paper, draw labelled diagrams to illustrate the steps involved in creating a bacterial cell that can produce human insulin.

4. **T/I** Identical twins form when a single zygote develops into two fetuses. Are identical twins considered to be clones?

_____

5. **T/I** On a separate sheet of paper, make a table to compare gene cloning, therapeutic cloning, and reproductive cloning.

Study Tip

Graphic organizers including **tables (question 5)** and **Venn diagrams** can help you organize comparisons. Choose one that suits your preferred learning styles and the ideas you are comparing.

Bringing It All Together

Examine the diagram and note the similarities and differences between meiosis and mitosis.

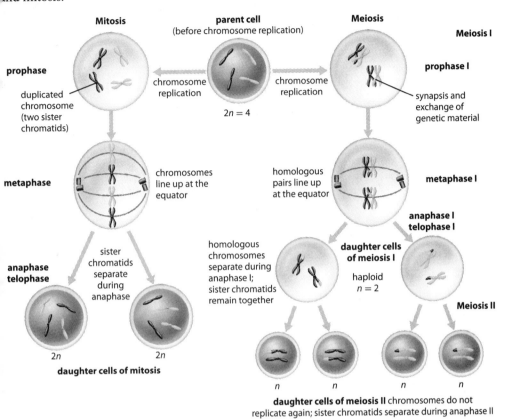

1. Complete the table to compare the differences between mitosis, meiosis I, and meiosis II.

Phase	Mitosis	Meiosis I	Meiosis II
Prophase	• no pairing (synapsis) of chromosomes	pairing of chromosomes (synapsis)	
Metaphase	• duplicated chromosomes at metaphase plate		
Anaphase	• sister chromatids separate, become daughter chromosomes that move to the poles		
Telophase	• chromosomes have one chromatid • two diploid daughter cells form, identical to the parental cell		

2. A diploid cell undergoes _____ nuclear division(s) in mitosis. Mitosis produces _____ diploid daughter cells. A diploid cell undergoes _____ nuclear division(s) in meiosis. Meiosis produces _____ haploid daughter cells.

1. **K/U** Which event occurs during mitosis?
   A. Cells carry out their normal functions.
   B. Microfilaments constrict or pinch the cytoplasm.
   C. The cell's copied genetic material separates.
   D. DNA is copied in the nucleus.
   E. Chromosomes condense into chromatin.

2. **K/U** Which is the correct order for the stages of mitosis?
   A. interphase, metaphase, telophase, anaphase
   B. telophase, anaphase, prophase, interphase
   C. prophase, metaphase, anaphase, interkinesis
   D. interphase, anaphase, metaphase, interkinesis
   E. prophase, metaphase, anaphase, telophase

3. **K/U** During which stage do spindle fibres form in mitosis?
   A. metaphase
   B. anaphase
   C. prophase
   D. telophase
   E. interphase

4. **K/U** Which describes the zygote cell after fertilization?
   A. diploid with 23 pairs of homologous chromosomes
   B. diploid with 23 non-homologous chromosomes
   C. haploid with 23 pairs of homologous chromosomes
   D. haploid with 23 autosomal chromosomes
   E. diplohaplontic with 23 pairs of autosomal chromosomes

5. **K/U** During which phase do the centromeres separate in meiosis?
   A. prophase II
   B. anaphase II
   C. telophase I
   D. anaphase I
   E. prophase I

6. **K/U** Which describes the process and products of meiosis?
   A. one division, produces two haploid daughter cells
   B. one division, produces two diploid daughter cells
   C. two divisions, produces two haploid daughter cells
   D. two divisions, produces four haploid daughter cells
   E. two divisions. produces four diploid daughter cells

7. **K/U** What can cause an individual to have too many chromosomes?
   A. inversion
   B. monosomy
   C. translocation
   D. deletion
   E. non-disjunction

8. **K/U** What are the two key outcomes of meiosis?
   _____
   _____
   _____
   _____

9. **K/U** List four errors that can be caused by changes in chromosome structure.
   _____
   _____
   _____
   _____

10. **K/U** Describe the key differences between the processes of mitosis and meiosis.
   _____
   _____
   _____
   _____

1. **A** How is the cell theory related to the study of genetics?

_____

_____

_____

_____

2. **C** Draw a diagram to illustrate how sperm are produced. Include the chromosomal changes in your diagram.

13. **A** What leads to the development of fraternal twins? Identical twins?

_____

_____

14. **T/I** Scientists have developed techniques for inserting DNA into plants and animals. What are the potential benefits and risks? Explain your answer.

_____

_____

_____

Self Study Guide

Question	If you answered this question incorrectly, see this Study Guide page for further review.	Question	If you answered this question incorrectly, see this Study Guide page for further review.
1	SG-60	8	SG-61, SG-62
2	SG-60	9	SG-62
3	SG-60	10	SG-60 to SG-62
4	SG-61	11	SG-59
5	SG-61	12	SG-61
6	SG-61, SG-62	13	SG-64
7	SG-62	14	SG-64

CHAPTER 5

Patterns of Inheritance

Self Assessment

1. Which scientist is known for his contributions to the modern theory of inheritance?

   A. Aristotle   **B.** Anthony van Leeuwenhoek

   C. Charles Darwin   **D.** Gregor Mendel

   E. Dmitri Mendeleev

2. In breeding, what is the name for the organisms that are initially crossed?

   A. monohyrids   **B.** dihybrids   **C.** F_1 generation

   D. P generation   **E.** genotypes

3. What determines inherited traits according to the law of segregation?

   A. single alleles that segregate during meiosis

   B. single alleles that segregate during mitosis

   C. pairs of alleles that segregate during meiosis

   D. pairs of alleles that segregate during mitosis

   E. random numbers of alleles that realign during meiosis

4. What is the name for an individual with two different alleles of a gene?

   A. heterozygous   **B.** heterozygous dominant

   C. homozygous dominant   **D.** homozygous recessive

   E. heterozygous recessive

5. What can a Punnett square be used to determine?

   A. phenotypes of P generation

   B. genotypes of P generation

   C. only the phenotypes of offspring

   D. only the genotypes of offspring

   E. phenotypes and genotypes of offspring

6. What ratio of F_2 phenotypes would two heterozygous parents produce?

   A. 1:2   **B.** 2:3   **C.** 3:1

   D. 2:2   **E.** 4:0

7. In a test cross, if any of the offspring have the recessive trait, what must be the unknown genotype of the parent?

   A. homozygous dominant   **B.** homozygous recessive   **C.** recessive

   D. dominant recessive   **E.** heterozygous

8. A dihybrid cross of individuals heterozygous for both traits yields offspring with what ratio?

   A. genotypic ratio of 1:3:3:9

   B. genotypic ratio of 9:3:3:1

   C. phenotypic ratio of 1:3:3:9

   D. phenotypic ratio of 3:3:3:3

   E. phenotypic ratio of 9:3:3:1

9. What is the name of the law that states that alleles for one gene segregate or assort independently during gamete formation?

   A. segregation

   B. independent assortment

   C. chromosome theory of inheritance

   D. genetic inheritance

   E. phenotypic expressions

10. In humans, autosomal inheritance refers to traits found on which chromosomes?

   A. X chromosomes only.   **B.** Y chromosomes only.

   C. X and Y chromosomes   **D.** chromosomes 1 to 22

   E. chromosomes 1 to 23

11. Which disease is classified as an autosomal dominant disorder?

   A. Huntington disease   **B.** Cystic fibrosis   **C.** Sickle cell anemia

   D. Tay-Sachs disease   **E.** Phenylketonuria (PKU)

12. In autosomal recessive inheritance, which parents will definitely produce an affected child?

   A. one homozygous recessive and one heterozygous

   B. one homozygous dominant and one heterozygous

   C. both heterozygous

   D. both homozygous dominant

   E. both homozygous recessive

13. Which genetic test could be used to detect extra copies of chromosomes?

   A. FISH (fluorescence in situ hydbridization)

   B. karyotype

   C. gene testing

   D. pedigree mapping

   E. biochemical testing

Self Study Guide

Question	If you answered this question incorrectly, see this Study Guide page for further review.	After completing your review, be sure to answer these questions in the Chapter 5 Practice Test.	Question	If you answered this question incorrectly, see this Study Guide page for further review.	After completing your review, be sure to answer these questions in the Chapter 5 Practice Test.
1	SG-70	2	8	SG-74	11
2	SG-70	4	9	SG-74	9
3	SG-70	9	10	SG-78	3
4	SG-70	3	11	SG-78	12
5	SG-72	4, 10	12	SG-78	3
6	SG-72	2, 4, 10	13	SG-79	13
7	SG-72	3			

Key Terms

trait
true breeding
cross
P generation
F$_1$ generation
monohybrid cross
F$_2$ generation
dominant
recessive
law of segregation
genotype
phenotype
homozygous
heterozygous
Punnett square
test cross
dihybrid cross
law of independent assortment
chromosome theory of inheritance
pedigree
autosomal inheritance
autosomal dominant
autosomal recessive
genetic counsellor
gene therapy

For more information about Mendel's research with pea plants, see pages 203–205 in your textbook.

Mendel's Crosses and the Law of Segregation (5.1)

In the mid 1800s genes and chromosomes had not yet been discovered. Nevertheless, Gregor Mendel formulated the basic laws of genetics by studying seven **traits** in pea plants.

Mendel crossed pairs of true breeding pea plants that had opposite traits, such as round seeds and wrinkled seeds. **True breeding** plants produce offspring with consistent traits generation after generation. He called this parental generation **P**. He called the offspring the first filial generation (F$_1$). All plants in the **F$_1$ generation** had round seeds. Mendel let the F$_1$ plants self pollinate. Most of the **F$_2$ generation** had round seeds, but some had wrinkled seeds.

Mendel determined that individuals have two alternative forms of each trait in their body cells. For each trait, one form is **dominant**. We now know that these two forms of a trait are two alleles of a gene. We show the dominant allele with a capital letter and the **recessive** allele with a lower case letter.

round

wrinkled

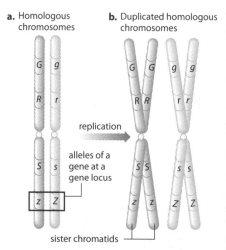

a. Homologous chromosomes **b.** Duplicated homologous chromosomes

replication

alleles of a gene at a gene locus

sister chromatids

For example, the round seed allele is dominant. A plant with round seeds has at last one copy of the dominant allele. It can have one of these **genotypes: homozygous dominant** (*RR*) or **heterozygous** for this trait (*Rr*). A plant with wrinkled seeds can only be **homozygous recessive** (*rr*).

Genes are found at specific locations (loci) on specific chromosomes. Alleles are alternative forms of a gene having the same position on a pair of homologous chromosomes. For example the "*R*" could represents allele for the dominant trait (round seeds) and the "*r*" represents the recessive allele (wrinkled seeds).

Genotype usually determines the **phenotype**, or physical appearance, of an individual. However, the expression of some genes in an organism can be influenced by the environment, such as in temperature-dependent sex determination.

Mendel's Law of Segregation

Mendel concluded that reproduction between two heterozygous individuals (*Tt*) resulted in both dominant and recessive phenotypes among the offspring. Approximately three offspring had the dominant phenotype for every one that had the recessive phenotype.

Mendel reasoned that these results were obtainable only if the alleles of each parent segregated, or separated, during meiosis. Based on his observations, Mendel formulated the **law of segregation**: Each individual has two alleles for each trait. The alleles segregate (separate) during the formation of the gametes. Each gamete contains only one allele from each pair of alleles. (See page 171 of your textbook for a review of gamete formation in meiosis.) When fertilization occurs, the new organism has two alleles for each trait, one from each parent.

Learning Check

1. **K/U** How do you know that a pea plant with wrinkled seeds does not have one copy of the round seed allele?

2. a. **K/U** Add labels to the diagram, which illustrates Mendel's first law.

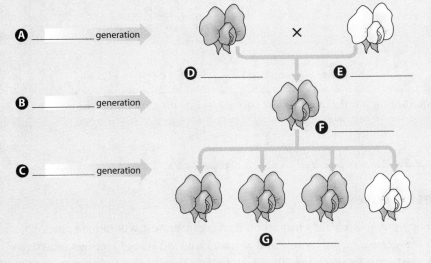

A _____ generation

B _____ generation

C _____ generation

D _____

E _____

F _____

G _____

b. Use the diagram to write Mendel's first law in your own words.

_____

_____

_____

3. **T/I** **a.** How can you remember what F_2 stands for?

_____

_____

b. How can you remember the difference between genotype and phenotype?

_____

_____

One-Trait (Monohybrid) Crosses and Test Crosses (5.1, 5.2)

For more information about using Punnett squares, see pages 208–211 of your textbook.

A **monohybrid cross** involves parent organisms with different forms of one trait. Use a pattern similar to the one shown below to solve single trait (monohybrid) genetic questions.

Sample Problem: In pea plants, tall stems are dominant (T) and short stems are recessive (t). Two heterozygous tall plants are crossed. Predict the probability that their offspring will be tall and the probability that their offspring will be short.

Step 1:	P phenotypes	Tall plant × Tall plant
Step 2:	P genotypes	$T\ t$ × $T\ t$
Step 3:	alleles in gametes	T t × T t
Step 4:	Use a **Punnett square** to predict possible genotypes for offspring and their probability. 	

	T	t
T	TT	Tt
t	Tt	tt

Probability of genotypes: TT: $\frac{1}{4}$ (25%), Tt: $\frac{2}{4}$ (50%), tt: $\frac{1}{4}$ (25%)

Step 5:	Add the probabilities of genotypes with the same phenotype to calculate the probability of possible phenotypes of this cross. Tall plants (TT or Tt): $\frac{1}{4} + \frac{2}{4} = \frac{3}{4}$ or 75% Short plants (tt): $\frac{1}{4}$ or 25%

Test Crosses

It is not possible to tell by inspection if an organism with a dominant phenotype is homozygous or heterozygous for that trait. Plant and animal breeders sometimes do a **test cross** in which the individual showing the dominant phenotype is crossed with one showing the recessive phenotype. The recessive phenotype is used because it has a known genotype. The results of the test cross can indicate the genotype of the parent with the dominant phenotype.

Sample Problem: In pea plants, green pods (G) are dominant to yellow pods (g). A plant breeder would like to know if the plants that produce green pods are pure bred for that trait. To determine the genotype of a plant with green pods, this plant breeder could perform a test cross as shown, and use the F_1 genotypes to determine the unknown allele in the parent plant with green pods.

P Green pods   ×   yellow pods
        G_   gg
(unknown genotype)   (recessive genotype)

Possibility 1   **Possibility 2**

	g	g
G	Gg	Gg
	Gg	Gg

	g	g
G	Gg	Gg
	gg	gg

Analyze the results:

If all the F_1 plants produce green pods, the unknown parent genotype is

If 50% of the F_1 plants produce yellow pods, the unknown parent genotype is

Learning Check

1. **A** Mendel crossed true breeding plants that produced round seeds (RR) with true breeding plants that produced wrinkled seeds (rr). Use Punnett squares to find the genotypes and phenotypes of the F_1 and F_2 generations. Predict the ratio of F_2 plants with round seeds to F_2 plants with wrinkled seeds.

Study Tip

Math skills are important in many areas of science. If you are unsure about the concept of **probability**, take the time to review it. Understanding probability will help you calculate patterns of inheritance.

2. **A** Black fur is dominant (B) and white fur is recessive (b) is guinea pigs. A black guinea pig with an unknown genotype is mated with a white guinea pig. Outline a procedure that could be used to determine if the black guinea pig is pure bred for hair colour. Include Punnett squares to illustrate your conclusions.

3. **T/I** Why can you calculate the probability of a phenotype by adding the probabilities of all genotypes that produce that phenotype? Use an analogy if it helps you explain.

_____

_____

The Law of Independent Assortment (5.2)

A **dihybrid cross** involves parent organisms with different forms of two traits. You can use a Punnett square with 16 cells to solve dihybrid (double trait) genetic problems.

Studying the inheritance of two traits will help you understand multi-trait inheritance. The genes for these traits are on different homologous chromosomes; therefore the alleles are not linked.

The **law of independent assortment** states:
- Each par of alleles segregates (assorts) independently of the other pairs during meiosis.

- All possible combinations of alleles can occur in the gametes.

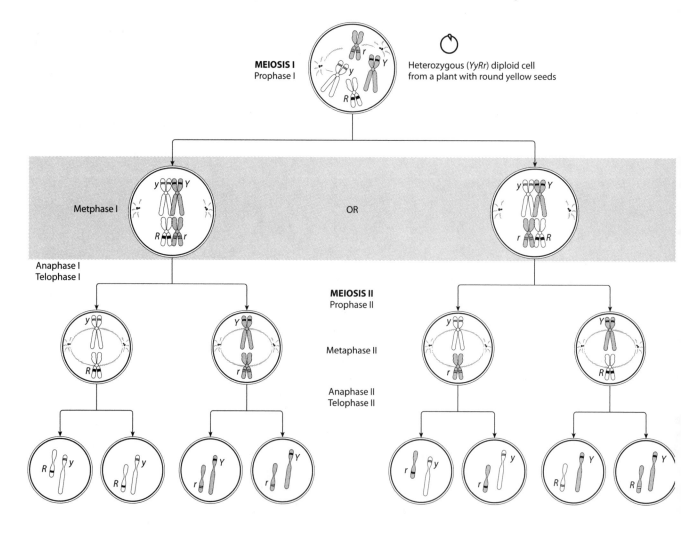

Each parent cell has four chromosomes: two alleles for seed colour (yellow or green) are on one set of homologous chromosomes and two alleles for seed shape (round or wrinkled) are on another pair of homologous chromosomes. When the homologous chromosomes separate during meiosis I, they segregate. Each cell beginning meiosis II has only one allele for each trait. Also, independent assortment occurs. The homologous chromosomes line up randomly at the metaphase plate; therefore, the homologous chromosomes, and the alleles they carry, segregate independently during gamete formation. Each gamete has two chromosomes: one allele for seed colour is on one chromosome and one allele for seed shape is on the other chromosome. All combinations of these two alleles are possible in the gametes: *ry*, *rY*, *Ry*, and *RY*.

1. **A** Mendel took true breeding pea plants that had purple flowers and were tall (*PPTT*) and crossed them with true breeding pea plants that had white flowers and were short (*pptt*).

a. Fill in the blanks to determine the genotype and phenotype of the F_1 generation of plants.

P phenotypes   purple flowers _____ × _____ short plant

P genotypes   _____ × _____

P gametes   *PT*   ×   *pt*

F_1 genotypes all *PpTt*

F_1 phenotypes all _____ flowers and _____ plants

b. Fill in the blanks to determine the genotypes of the gametes produced by the F_1 plants.

F_1 phenotypes _____ plants   × purple flowers _____

F_1 genotypes   *PpTt*   × _____

F_1 gametes _____   × *PT* *Pt* *pT* *pt*

c. Determine the genotypes and phenotypes of the F2 generation by completing the Punnett square.

	PT	*Pt*	*pT*	*pt*
PT	*PPTT*	*PPTt*	*PpTt*	
Pt		*PPtt*	*PpTt*	
pT	*PpTT*		*ppTT*	
		Pptt		

F_2 Ratio of phenotypes:

9 _____ : _____ purple short : 3 white tall : 1 _____

_____

2. **A** In maize, coloured seeds are dominant (*A*) and colourless seeds are recessive (*a*). Normal starch is a dominant trait (*W*) and waxy starch is a recessive trait (*w*). To determine the genotype of a plant with coloured seeds and normal starch, you perform a test cross. The resulting ear of corn has 350 coloured seeds with normal starch and 335 colourless seeds with normal starch. What is the genotype of the parent plant with coloured seeds and normal starch?

_____

_____

Using Pedigrees to Track Autosomal Recessive Disorders (5.3)

Autosomal recessive disorders are genetic disorders caused by recessive alleles on autosomes (chromosomes other than the sex chromosomes). These disorders follow the basic principles of Mendellian genetics: only individuals who inherit a recessive allele from each parent (genotype aa) are affected. Cystic fibrosis is the most common lethal genetic disease among Caucasians in North America. Individuals with this disorder produce very thick mucus that affects the function of the lungs and the pancreas.

When geneticists want to learn about the inheritance of autosomal disorders, they collect as much information about a family's history as they can and use this information to create a pedigree. A **pedigree** uses symbols that identify males and females, individuals affected by the trait being studied, and family relationships to represent genetic inheritance graphically.

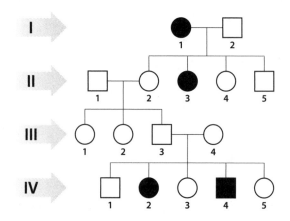

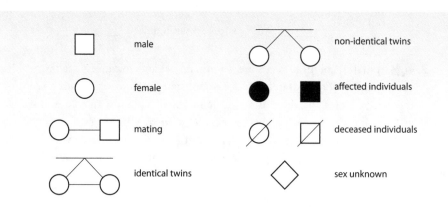

This pedigree shows the inheritance pattern of an autosomal recessive trait from generation to generation in one family.

Since individual II-5 in the pedigree has a sister who is homozygous recessive (*aa*), he knows that at least one of his parents is a heterozygous carrier. Since he inherited one allele from each parent, he has a 25% chance of being a heterozygous carrier if one of his parents is heterozygous (<u>*Aa*</u>), and a 50% chance if both of his parents are heterozygous (*Aa*).

Inheritance Pattern of Autosomal Recessive Disorders

- Affected children can have unaffected parents.
- Heterozygotes (*Aa*) have a normal phenotype but are carriers of the recessive allele.
- Two affected parents (*aa*) will always have affected children.
- Affected individuals (*aa*) with homozygous dominant mates (*AA*) will have unaffected children who will be carriers of the recessive allele (*Aa*).
- Both males and females are affected with equal frequency.

Learning Check

1. **A** Complete the paragraph and Punnett square to determine the genotypes of individuals I-1 and I-2 in the pedigree shown on the previous page.

   Individuals I-1 and I-2 had _____ girls and one boy. One of their children (II-3) displays the recessive phenotype and would have the genotype _____. The only way this child can display the phenotype of an autosomal _____ trait is if they have a _____ recessive genotype (*aa*). Individual II-3 would have to inherit one _____ allele from her father and one _____ allele from her mother. Since both parents have a normal phenotype, they must both be _____ (*Aa*). Based on this information, you can draw a _____ square for the mating of individuals I-1 and I-2 to prove that they are both heterozygous for this trait.

	A	a
A	AA	
a		

Study Tip

Pedigrees, like other **graphic organizers,** can help you organize and analyze relationships.

2. **A** If individual III-4 on the pedigree was homozygous dominant (*AA*), could she and individual III-3 have children affected by this autosomal recessive trait? Use a Punnet square to prove your answer. Assume the genotype of III-3 is heterozygous (*Aa*) for this trait.

3. **A** If male IV-4 and a female who displayed the phenotype of this autosomal recessive trait have children, what are the chances that their children will have the dominant phenotype? Use a Punnett square to prove your answer.

Autosomal Dominant Genetic Disorders (5.3)

Autosomal dominant disorders are controlled by dominant alleles on autosomal chromosomes. A single dominant allele inherited from one parent is all that is needed for a person to show this trait. Huntington's disease is a lethal genetic disorder caused by a rare dominant allele. It results in a breakdown of certain areas of the brain. No effective treatment exists.

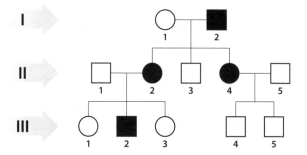

This pedigree shows the inheritance of Huntington's disease in one family.

Inheritance Pattern of Autosomal Dominant Disorders

- Heterozygotes (*Aa*) are affected.
- Affected children will have at least one affected parent.
- Two affected parents can produce an unaffected child if both parents are heterozygous (*Aa*).
- Two unaffected parents (*aa*) will not have an affected child.
- Both males and females are affected with equal frequency.

Learning Check

Use the pedigree for Huntington's disease above to answer the questions.

1. a. **A** What are the phenotypes of individuals I-1 and I-2?

_____

b. **K/U** What are the genotypes of individuals I-1 and I-2? How do you know? Draw a Punnett square if it helps you.

2. **A** Determine the genotypes and phenotypes for the remaining individuals in the pedigree.

Study Tip

Compare and **contrast** two related concepts to better understand them. How are the inheritance patterns of autosomal recessive disorders similar to the inheritance patterns of autosomal dominant disorders? How are they different, and why?

Genetic Testing and Gene Therapy (5.3)

Genetic tests look for signs of a disease or disorder in DNA taken from an individual's blood, other body fluids like saliva, or tissues. These tests can detect large changes, such as a chromosome that has a section missing or added. They can also detect mutations within the DNA strand itself.

Some genetic testing involves the direct examination of the DNA molecule. Other genetic tests include testing for gene products such as enzymes or using kayrotypes to examine stained or fluorescently-marked chromosomes.

Genetic tests are used for several reasons.

For more information about specific genetic testing techniques, see page 224 of your textbook.

- Carrier screening is used to identify individuals who carry an allele for an autosomal recessive disorder.

- Prenatal testing is performed during a pregnancy to assess the health of a fetus and to assist in family planning.

- Newborn screening is used to identify individuals who have an increased chance of having a specific genetic disorder so that treatment can be started as soon as possible.

- Predictive testing is used to determine if an individual is at risk for developing a genetic disorder later in life. These tests may be helpful for individuals with diseases that run in their family.

- Diagnostic testing is used to confirm or rule out a known or suspected genetic disorder.

- Preimplantation testing is performed on early embryos resulting from in vitro fertilization to decrease the probability of a particular genetic condition occurring in the fetus.

Genetic counsellors can estimate the risk of inheriting a particular genetic condition. As well, they can explain the symptoms of genetic conditions and the available treatments, provide other information, and give emotional support before, during, and after genetic testing.

Gene therapy is an experimental approach to treating genetic disorders in which the faulty gene is fixed, replaced, or supplemented with a healthy gene so that it can function normally. Most genetic diseases cannot currently be cured, but gene therapy research provides hope that one day a cure may be found.

In gene therapy, a substance called a DNA vector carries a healthy gene into target cells in the patient. Viruses are often used as DNA vectors because viruses have the ability to enter certain types of living cells and insert their DNA into the genomes of these cells. To use a virus as a vector, viral genes are removed and replaced with the new gene destined for the cell.

Read the article and answer the questions that follow.

Gene Therapy Frees "Bubble Babies"

The body's immune system protects us from pathogens that cause diseases and infections. Severe combined immunodeficiency disease (SCID) is an inherited disorder found on the X chromosome resulting in severe defects to the individual's immune system. White blood cells, which fight infection, are produced in the bone marrow by stem cells. The bone marrow stem cells are absent or defective in people affected by SCID leaving them very susceptible to pathogens. Usually, patients with SCID are forced to live in tightly-controlled, sterile plastic bubbles. The current treatment is bone marrow transplant from a matched sibling, which is not always possible or effective in the long term. Gene therapy holds great promise for treating this disease.

Researchers in England and France knew the disease was caused by a faulty gene on the X chromosome and conducted a clinical trial on 14 children. The researchers removed bone marrow cells from the patients' hipbones and cultured them in flasks. Genetically engineered viruses, containing a normal bone marrow stem cell production gene, were used to transfer the new gene into bone marrow cells. Once the transfer was complete, the cells were returned to the patient, where they continued to grow and produce the new gene product. Upon receiving the altered cells, the patients showed great improvements in their immune system functions.

Unfortunately, two of the children in this trial developed a form of leukemia several years after the treatment. Scientists determine the viral vector had inserted the therapeutic gene near a gene linked to leukemia. From this single trial, it is clear that gene therapy holds significant promise—and poses significant risks.

1. **K/U** Identify the main idea of the article.

   _____

2. **K/U** Explain why babies born with SCID are called "bubble babies."

   _____

3. **C** **T/I** a. Use a T-chart to evaluate the pros and cons of using gene therapy to treat SCID children.

   b. Based on your T-chart, would you allow this type of clinical trial to continue? Explain your reasoning.

   _____

   _____

Study Tip

T-charts (question 3) can be used to compare two ideas or evaluate the pros and cons of one idea.

Bringing It All Together

Add information and links to this web diagram to summarize current understandings of patterns of inheritance.

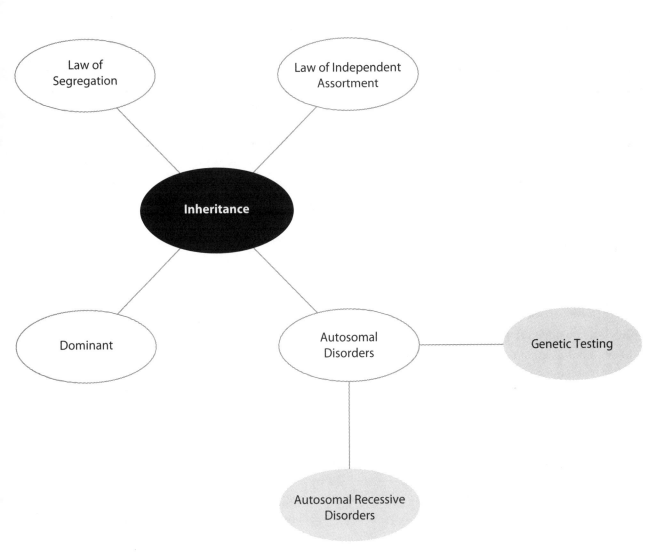

1. **K/U** Which is the best example of genotype?
   A. a short-haired cat
   B. *TT*
   C. physical appearance of an organism
   D. frequency of genes
   E. the length of stem in pea plants

2. **T/I** A homozygous tall plant is crossed with a homozygous short plant. If the tall gene is dominant, what will the offspring be like?
   A. all tall
   B. all short
   C. all purebred
   D. half tall, half short
   E. three quarters tall, one quarter short

3. **K/U** When is a recessive trait expressed?
   A. when one recessive gene is present
   B. when one dominant gene is present
   C. when two recessive genes are present
   D. when two dominant genes are present
   E. when one dominant and one recessive gene are present

4. **T/I** Which Punnett square shows a heterozygous-homozygous cross?

A.

	P	*P*
P	*PP*	*PP*
p	*pp*	*pp*

B.

	P	*P*
P	*pp*	*pp*
p	*pp*	*pp*

C.

	P	*P*
p	*Pp*	*Pp*
p	*Pp*	*Pp*

D.

	P	*P*
p	*Pp*	*Pp*
p	*pp*	*pp*

E.

	P	*P*
P	*PP*	*PP*
p	*PP*	*PP*

5. **K/U** How many squares are in a complete Punnett square for a dihybrid cross?
   A. 2   B. 4
   C. 8   D. 16
   E. 32

6. **T/I** In wolves, the allele for brown eyes (*B*) is dominant to the allele for blue eyes (*b*). The allele for grey coat (*G*) is dominant to the allele for black coat (*g*). Which genotype is for a wolf with brown eyes and a black coat?
   A. *bbgg*   B. *Bbgg*
   C. *bbGg*   D. *BbGG*
   E. *BBGG*

7. **K/U** In a pedigree diagram, which symbol represents an affected female?
   A. □   B. ○
   C. ■   D. ⊘
   E. ●

8. **T/I** In humans, the allele for brown eyes (*B*) is dominant while the allele for blue eyes (*b*) is recessive. What are the possible genotypes for offspring with brown eyes?
   _____

9. **K/U** Which theory in genetics supports Mendel's law of segregation?
   _____

10. **C T/I** Corn plants can be either tall or short. A homozygous tall corn plant is crossed with a heterozygous tall corn plant.
   a. Which trait is dominant?
   _____
   b. Complete the Punnett square for the cross.

   c. What percent of the offspring will be tall?
   _____
   d. What is the genotypic ratio of the offspring?
   _____

11. **C** **T/I** Complete the Punnett square for the cross *BbGg* × *BbGg*.

12. **A** Suppose the dominant allele *H* codes for Huntingdon disease. If one parent has the alleles *Hh* and the other parent has the alleles *HH*, explain the inheritance pattern for the next generation.

_____

_____

_____

_____

13. Describe three reasons why a person may want to undergo genetic testing.

_____

_____

_____

Self Study Guide

Question	If you answered this question incorrectly, see this Study Guide page for further review.
1	SG-70
2	SG-72
3	SG-70
4	SG-72
5	SG-74
6	SG-74
7	SG-76
8	SG-72
9	SG-70
10	SG-72
11	SG-74
12	SG-78
13	SG-79

CHAPTER 6 — Complex Patterns of Inheritance

Self Assessment

1. A true-breeding red-flowered plant and a true-breeding white-flowered plant produce offspring with pink flowers in the F_1 generation. What term best describes this?

A. autosomal recessive inheritance

B. heterozygous advantage

C. sex-linked trait

D. incomplete dominance

E. polygenic inheritance

2. Which best describes codominance?

A. One allele varies with each generation.

B. One allele is expressed and the other allele is not.

C. One allele is dominant and one allele is recessive.

D. Both alleles are recessive.

E. Both alleles are dominant.

3. What is the genotype for individuals who have inherited sickle cell anemia?

A. $Hb^A Hb^s$ **B.** $Hb^s Hb^s$ **C.** $Hb^A Hb^A$

D. $Hb^s Hb^a$ **E.** $Hb^s Hb^O$

4. What can polygenic traits explain?

A. Differences in gene expression due to environmental effects.

B. The occurrence of degrees of dominance.

C. The range in phenotypes among the offspring.

D. Autosomal inheritance patterns.

E. The heterozygous advantage of inheritance.

5. What is true about alleles of different genes that are on the same chromosome?

A. They display similar phenotypic patterns.

B. They display similar genotypic patterns.

C. They sort independent of each other.

D. They do not sort independently.

E. They produce increased frequencies of genetic disorders.

6. When does crossing over occur?

A. telophase II of mitosis   **B.** prophase I of meiosis

C. metaphase II of meiosis   **D.** anaphase I of mitosis

E. interphase

7. What is the name for traits that are controlled by genes on the X or Y chromosome?

A. sex-linked   **B.** polygenic   **C.** autosomal

D. codominant   **E.** multiple alleles

8. Females with an X-linked dominant allele pass the allele on to

   A. female offspring only.

   B. male offspring only.

   C. twenty-five percent of their offspring.

   D. fifty percent of their offspring.

   E. all their offspring.

9. What field of study uses computer technology to create and analyze large databases of information?

   A. epigenetics   **B.** bioinformatics   **C.** genomics

   D. protenomics   **E.** pharmacogenetics

10. How many DNA base pairs are found in the nucleus of a human cell?

   A. one million   **B.** three hundred million   **C.** three billion

   D. thirty billion   **E.** one trillion

11. What is the most common type of genetic variation?

   A. copy number variation   **B.** epigenetic markings

   C. clines   **D.** variable number tandem repeat

   E. single nucleotide polymorphisms

12. Epigenetic changes represent a response to

   A. new proteins being introduced into the genotype of the organism.

   B. a permanent change to the DNA sequence of the organism.

   C. a temporary change to the DNA sequence of the organism.

   D. an environmental condition that may not be reversed once the condition changes.

   E. an environmental condition that may be reversed once the condition changes.

Self Study Guide

Question	If you answered this question incorrectly, see this Study Guide page for further review.	After completing your review, be sure to answer these questions in the Chapter 6 Practice Test.	Question	If you answered this question incorrectly, see this Study Guide page for further review.	After completing your review, be sure to answer these questions in the Chapter 6 Practice Test.
1	SG-86	1	7	SG-91	5, 6
2	SG-86	2	8	SG-91	5, 6, 13
3	SG-86	2, 12	9	SG-93	7, 10
4	SG-88	3, 8	10	SG-93	10, 14
5	SG-90	4	11	SG-93	10
6	SG-90	4	12	SG-93	10

Summary

Key Terms

incomplete dominance

codominance

heterozygous advantage

continuous variation

polygenic trait

linked genes

sex-linked trait

bioinformatics

genomics

genetic profile

Incomplete Dominance and Codominance (6.1)

In **incomplete dominance,** neither allele is dominant. A heterozygote has an intermediate phenotype between that of its homozygote parents. For example, a red snapdragon ($C^R C^R$) crossed with a white snapdragon ($C^W C^W$) will produce pink offspring ($C^R C^W$). When representing incomplete dominance, many geneticists use all upper-case letters with superscripts to show the alleles.

In **codominance,** two alleles are both fully expressed (dominant). For example, a roan horse or cow is a heterozygote in which both the base colour and white are expressed in its phenotype. A blue-roan horse ($C^B C^W$) has both black hairs and white hairs. One allele is expressed in the black hairs and the other allele is expressed in the white hairs. The horse's body looks blue because the black and white hairs are thoroughly mixed.

Sickle-cell anemia is a human disorder controlled by codominant alleles. Individuals with the genotype $Hb^S Hb^S$ have C-shaped (or sickle-shaped) red blood cells that cannot transport oxygen effectively. Individuals with the genotype $Hb^A Hb^A$ have normally shaped red blood cells. Individuals with the genotype $Hb^S Hb^A$ have some of each, and are said to have the sickle-cell trait. These heterozygotes have blood cells that are able to transport oxygen normally, and are protected from contracting malaria.

The sickle-cell trait is an example of **heterozygous advantage.** This advantage keeps the Hb^S allele prevalent in populations exposed to malaria. If two individuals with sickle-cell trait ($Hb^S Hb^A$) reproduce, the phenotypic ratio of their children is 1:2:1. Each child has 50% chance of having the sickle-cell trait and a 25% chance of having sickle-cell anemia.

Study Tip

Genotypes are often represented with **symbols**, such as $Hb^S Hb^A$. Whenever you read a genotype symbol, remind yourself of what it means.

Learning Check

1. Ⓐ Use the information above about snapdragons to complete the table.

Snapdragon Genotype	Homozygous or Heterozygous	Snapdragon Phenotype (colour of flowers)
$C^R C^R$		
	heterozygous	
		white flowers

2. **K/U** **a.** Explain how incompletely dominant and co-dominant alleles differ from dominant and recessive alleles.

_____

_____

b. What type of observations would indicate that alleles are co-dominant?

_____

_____

3. **A** Complete the Punnett square to predict the genotype and phenotype ratios for the children of two individuals who have the sickle cell trait (heterozygous).

P phenotypes   normal hemoglobin   ×   normal hemoglobin
                 (sickle-cell trait)   ×   (sickle-cell trait)
P genotypes Hb^A _____   ×   _____ Hb^S
P gametes   _____ Hb^S × Hb^A _____

Predicted genotype of children

		Hb^S
Hb^A		$Hb^A Hb^S$
	$Hb^A Hb^S$	

Predicted phenotypes:

If two individuals with sickle-cell trait reproduce, the phenotypic ratio is 1:2:1 and each child has a _____ chance of having the sickle-cell trait and a 25% chance of having sickle-cell disease.

4. **A** Use the key to complete the Punnett square. Predict the genotype and phenotype ratios for offspring of a pure bred black-horse and a pure-bred white horse.

P phenotypes   black horse   ×   white horse
P genotypes $C^B C^B$ × $C^W C^W$
P gametes C^B _____   ×   _____ C^W
Predicted genotypes of offspring

Key

$C^B C^B$ - pure bred black horse
$C^B C^W$ – blue-roan horse
$C^W C^W$ – pure bred white horse

		C^B
C^W	$C^B C^W$	

Genotype ratio of the offspring: all _____ _____
Phenotype ratio of the offspring: all _____ colour

Polygenic Traits (6.1)

The length of ears of corn varies over a wide range. In corn, ear length is a continuous trait controlled by more than one gene.

Traits that are controlled by two or more pairs of alleles are called polygenic traits. These pairs of alleles can be located on many different parts of different chromosomes. The dominant allele of each pair has a quantitative effect on the phenotype, and these effects are additive.

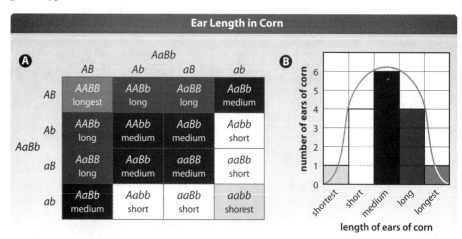

Phenotypic ratio = 1 shortest : 4 short : 6 medium : 4 long : 1 longest

Ear length in corn is a polygenic trait. In this example it is controlled by two genes. The Punnett square (**A**) shows the results of a cross between corn with medium-length ears (*AaBb*). The offspring phenotype ratio of 1:4:6:4:1 shows a bell-shaped curve as shown in graph (**B**).

See Chapter 3, page 120, of your textbook to learn how the temperature that eggs are incubated at determines the gender of many species of reptiles.

A change in the environment can also affect the phenotype. Environmental conditions such as temperature, precipitation, and soil composition all influence ear length in corn. Many human disorders, such as cleft lip and palate, clubfoot, and diabetes are most likely due to the combined action of many genes plus environmental factors.

Multiple Alleles

When a trait is controlled by **multiple alleles,** the gene exists in several allelic forms. Each individual, however, normally has only two of the possible alleles (one allele on each homologous chromosome).

In humans, there are three alleles for the same gene related to blood type. These alleles determine the presence or absence of antigens on red blood cells. The gene is designated I and has three common alleles: I^A, I^B, and i. Possible genotypes, phenotypes, and antigens on the red blood cell are shown in the table in question 3 below.

1. **K/U** **a.** What is a polygenic trait?

_____

_____

  b. In the example of the length of an ear of corn, identify the phenotypes and genotypes of the two extremes.

_____

_____

2. **K/U** **a.** Describe how the inheritance of blood type in humans is an example of a trait that is controlled by multiple alleles.

_____

_____

_____

  b. Identify two genotypes that would result in an individual having blood type A.

_____

3. **K/U** Complete the table identifying the genotypes, phenotypes, and antigens found on the surface of red blood cells in humans.

Genotype	Phenotype (blood type)	Antigen(s) on Red Blood cells
ii	type O	none
$I^A i$		A
$I^A I^A$		
$I^B i$	type B	
$I^B I^B$		B
$I^A I^B$		

4. **A** Use the table from question 3 to complete the Punnett square. Predict the genotype and phenotype ratios for offspring of individuals with type A blood and type B blood. Both individuals are heterozygous for blood type.

P phenotypes   type A   ×   type B
P genotypes I^A _____   ×   _____ i
P gametes   _____ i × I^B _____

Predicted genotypes of offspring

		i
I^B	$I^A I^B$	
		ii

Genotypic ratio: 1 $I^A I^B$: 1_____: 1 $I^A i$: 1 _____

Phenotypic ratio: 1 type _____: 1 type B: 1 type _____: 1 type _____

Linked Genes (6.2)

The law of independent assortment states that genes sort independently of one another in meiosis. This is true when the genes are on different chromosomes. Alleles of two different genes on the same chromosome do not assort independently. Genes that are found on the same chromosome are sometimes called linked genes.

Linked genes do segregate, or separate, on a regular basis. Recall that in meiosis I, crossing over can take place when the non-sister chromatids in a tetrad exchange pieces of a chromosome. If the point at which a crossover occurs is between two genes, the previously linked alleles will end up on separate chromosomes and will therefore migrate into different gametes.

Crossing over is a random event and occurs with equal probability at nearly any point on the sister chromatids except near the centromere. A crossover is more likely to occur between genes that are far apart on a chromosome than between genes that are close together. Geneticists can use this difference in probabilities to determine the relative positions of genes on a chromosome in a process known as chromosome mapping.

See page 252 of your textbook to review crossing over in meiosis I.

Learning Check

1. **K/U** This diagram represents the location of three genes found on a chromosome from a fruit fly. What are linked genes and how does the diagram help explain this concept?

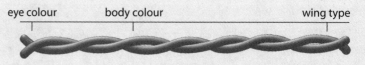

eye colour   body colour   wing type

_____

_____

2. **C** In this diagram, genes *A* and *B* are linked on one chromosome while genes *a* and *b* are linked on another chromosome. Normally, you would expect the gametes to have only two combinations, *AB* or *ab*. However, four different combinations of genes can be found in the gametes: *AB*, *ab*, *Ab*, or *aB*. Use a diagram to help explain why there are four possible combinations of these genes in the organism's gametes.

Study Tip

To understand or review the results of crossing over (**question 2**), you can create **models** of chromosomes with coloured clay and use them to act out the process.

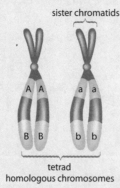

sister chromatids

A A   a a

B B   b b

tetrad
homologous chromosomes

Sex-linked Traits (6.2)

The sex chromosomes contain genes just as the autosomal chromosomes do. Some of these genes determine whether the individual will be male or female. Other traits controlled by genes on the sex chromosomes are said to be sex-linked.

The X chromosome carries alleles that are not found on the Y chromosome. Because of this, a single recessive allele on a male's X chromosome is expressed in his phenotype.

X-linked Recessive Disorders

Disorders caused by X-linked recessive alleles can be recognized in several ways:

- More males than females are affected.
- An affected son can have parents who have the normal phenotype.
- For a female to have the disorder, her father must also have it. Her mother must have the disorder or be a carrier.
- The disorder often skips a generation. For example, a man has the trait, his daughter is normal but is a carrier, and his grandson has the trait.
- If a woman has the disorder, all her sons will also have it.

Learning Check

1. **K/U** Why are males more affected than females by X-linked recessive alleles?

_____

_____

Study Tip

Pedigrees are a visual way to show phenotypes of several generations in a family. Review the meanings of the **symbols** used in pedigrees in Chapter 5, page 219, of your textbook.

Use this pedigree to complete the questions on the following page.

The pedigree represents the typical inheritance pattern for red-green colour vision deficiency in humans (colour-blindness). The alleles for red and green pigments in the cones of the human eye are X-linked and recessive. About 8% of Caucasian men have red-green colour vision deficiency.

Pedigree – Human Colour Vision Deficiency

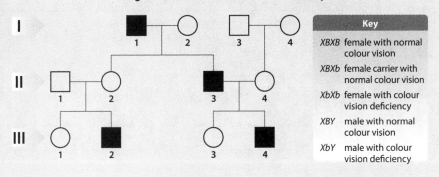

Key	
XBXB	female with normal colour vision
XBXb	female carrier with normal colour vision
XbXb	female with colour vision deficiency
XBY	male with normal colour vision
XbY	male with colour vision deficiency

2. (A) Use the key in the pedigree to complete this table.

Mother Phenotype	Father Phenotype	Mother Genotype	Father Genotype	Offspring Phenotype	Offspring Genotype
normal vision	normal vision			colour vision deficient son	$X^b Y$
		$X^B X^B$	$X^b Y$		$X^B Y$
normal vision				colour vision deficient daughter	
colour vision deficient	normal vision			all sons colour vision deficient	

See page 256 of your textbook to review how to use Punnett squares to analyze sex-linked inheritance patterns.

3. (A) **a.** Use the key to complete the Punnett squares.

Parents	I-1	×	I-2
Genotype	$X^b Y$	×	$X^B X^b$
Gametes	X^b	Y ×	X^B	X^b

Parents	II-1	×	II-2
Genotype	$X^B Y$	×	$X^B X^b$
Gametes	X^B	Y ×	X^B	X^b

Predicted genotypes of offspring

	X^b	Y
X^B		
X^b		$X^b Y$

Predicted genotypes of offspring

	X^B	Y
X^B		
X^b	$X^B Y^b$	

b. Identify the genotypes and phenotypes of the individuals in the pedigree.

Individual	Genotype	Phenotype
I-1	$X^b Y$	male, colour vision deficient
I-2	$X^B X^b$	female, carrier, normal (she must be a carrier to pass the X-chromosome to her son, II-3.]
I-3		
I-4	$X^B X^b$	female, carrier, normal
II-1	$X^b Y$	
II-2		
II-3		
II-4	$X^B X^b$	
III-1		
III-2		
III-3		female, carrier, normal
III-4		

Genetic Research (6.3)

The Human Genome Project (HGP) was an international research effort to sequence and map all the genes in human chromosomes (genome). Each chromosome contains hundreds or thousands of genes, which carry the instructions for making proteins. There are approximately 25 000 genes in the human genome.

Discovering the sequence of the human genome is only one step in understanding how the instructions coded in DNA lead to a functioning human being. Current **genomics** uses a variety of technologies and scientific methods to derive meaningful knowledge from the DNA sequence. Five examples are described below. Goals of genomics include finding the location of variations in the DNA sequence among people and determining the significance of those variations.

1. **Bioinformatics** uses computer technology to create and analyze large databases of information in a comparatively short time period. The first bioinformatics project, by the chemist Margaret Dayhoff, involved creating a computerized protein and DNA sequence database. Now, online genetics databases allow scientists and the public to access vast amounts of genetic information.

2. **Proteomics** focuses on studying the shape of human proteins to determine their function. Each gene serves as a recipe for how to build protein molecules. The 25 000 genes in the human genome can code for at least ten times as many proteins, and the proteins made differ between cells and time periods. Proteomics is more complicated than genomics because a single gene can create a number of different proteins.

3. **DNA microarray technology** allows scientists to study differences in gene activity. Although all the cells in the human body contain identical genetic material, the same genes are not active in every cell. Studying which genes are active and which are inactive in different cell types helps scientists understand how these cells function normally and how they are affected when various genes do not perform properly.

4. **Epigenetics** is the study of changes in gene activity that do not involve alterations to the genetic code but are still passed on to at least one successive generation. Epigenetic "marks" sit on top of the genome, just outside it, and tell your genes to turn on or off. It is through epigenetic marks that environmental factors like diet, stress, and prenatal nutrition can make an imprint on genes that are passed from one generation to the next.

5. **Single nucleotide polymorphism (SNPs)** are DNA sequence variations that occur when a single nucleotide (A, T, C, or G) in the genome sequence is altered. For example, one person might have the DNA sequence AAGG*C*TAA where another person has AAGC*T*TAA. SNPs occur normally throughout a person's DNA. Alleles of SNPs that are close together tend to be inherited together. These regions of genetically linked variations are called haplotypes. Certain tag SNPs can uniquely identify these haplotypes and can be used as a basis for comparing genetic variations. Applications include predicting an individual's response to drugs, susceptibility to environmental factors such as toxins, and risk of developing diseases. SNPs can also be used to track the inheritance of disease genes within families. SNP studies will serve as the foundation of pharmacogenomics, the emerging field of personalized medicine: the right drug, in the right dose, to the right person, at the right time.

Social Issues

The Human Genome Project and the many other genomic and proteomic studies currently underway promise to bring unprecedented scientific rewards in the discovery of disease-causing genes, the design of new drugs, a better understanding of developmental processes, and a new way to determine the origin and evolution of the human race.

But these studies also raise many ethical issues surrounding the ownership and use of genetic information. Some fear genetic profiles that indicate a risk of disease might be used to deny people insurance coverage or employment. Patenting genes, using prenatal testing to select for nonmedical traits or to terminate a pregnancy based on undesirable traits, and the psychological consequences of knowing your genetic predisposition to disease well before developing any condition are other issues.

Learning Check

1. **K/U** Describe how each tool is related to human genomics.

a. bioinformatics _____

_____

b. proteomics _____

_____

c. DNA microarrays _____

_____

d. epigenetics _____

_____

e. studying single nucleotide polymorphism (SNP)

_____

_____

2. **T/I** In fruit flies, white eye colour is an X-linked, recessive trait. A cross between two white-eyed flies produces only white-eyed offspring if the larvae are nurtured at 25°C. When the surrounding temperature is briefly raised to 37°C, some red-eyed offspring are produced. If the red-eyed flies are crossed, without further heat treatment, the next generation will include red-eyed and white-eyed flies. The DNA sequence for the gene responsible for eye colour remains the same for white-eyed parents and red-eyed offspring. Explain why this is an example of an epigenetic study.

_____

_____

3. **C** Use a T-chart to show the pros and cons of genomic and proteomic studies such as the ones identified in this section.

Study Tip

A **T-chart** (**question 3**) can help you compare pros and cons of issues such as genetic research.

Bringing It All Together

Add information and links to this web diagram to summarize current understandings of more complex patterns of inheritance.

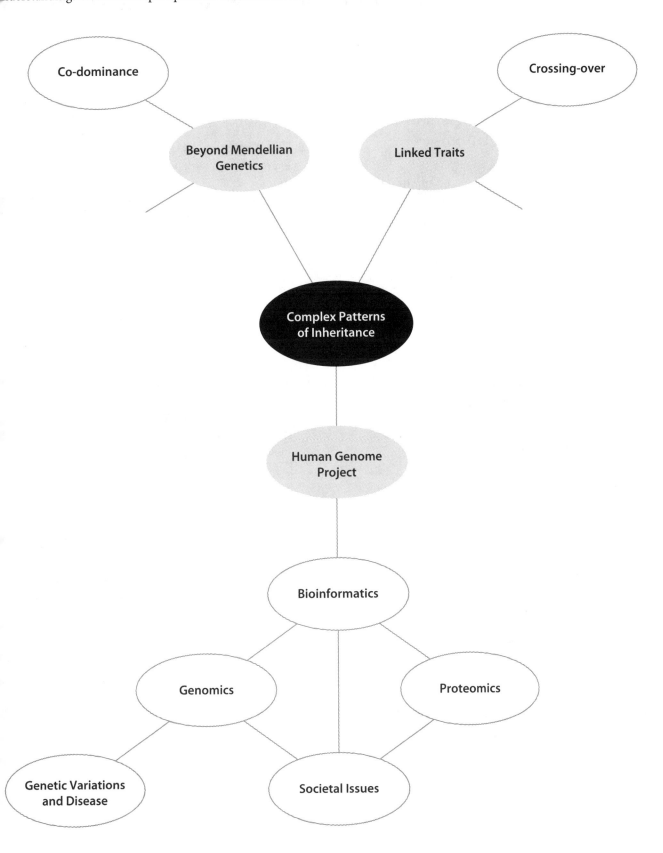

Practice Test

1. **T/I** What pattern of inheritance is demonstrated by a red-flowered plant and a white-flowered plant producing all pink-flowered plants in the F^1 generation?

   A. dominance
   B. incomplete dominance
   C. multiple alleles
   D. recessive traits
   E. polygenic traits

2. **T/I** Which blood types are possible for the children of a female with genotype $I^B i$ and a male with genotype $I^A I^B$?

   A. AB
   B. B
   C. O
   D. O and AB
   E. A, B, and AB

3. **K/U** What controls polygenic traits?

   A. many recessive alleles
   B. many dominant alleles
   C. one dominant and one recessive allele
   D. a recessive allele controlling a dominant allele
   E. multiple recessive alleles controlling a dominant allele

4. **K/U** Which statement is true about crossing over?

   A. It increases genetic diversity.
   B. It decreases genetic diversity.
   C. It has no effect on the genotype of the organism.
   D. It occurs during prophase of mitosis.
   E. It affects the phenotype of the parent.

5. **K/U** **T/I** Which condition is more likely to be inherited by males than females?

   A. Down's syndrome
   B. familial hypercholesterolemia
   C. hereditary deafness
   D. hemophilia
   E. sickle cell anemia

6. **T/I** What is the chance of a female carrier for colour vision deficiency and a male with normal colour vision having a colour vision deficient daughter?

   A. 0%
   B. 25%
   C. 50%
   D. 75%
   E. 100%

7. **K/U** According to the Human Genome Project, what i the estimated total number of genes in human DNA?

   A. 10 000
   B. 25 000
   C. 100 000
   D. 140 000
   E. 1 000 000

8. **K/U** Why can rabbits have four different phenotypic expressions for the colour of their coats?

   _____

   _____

9. **K/U** What is a Barr Body?

   _____

   _____

10. **K/U** What is genomics?

    _____

    _____

11. **T/I** Describe the genetic difference that exists betweer the two individuals.

	Section of haplotype map of genome
Individual A	AACACGCCA....... TTCGGGTC
Individual B	AACACGCCA....... TTCGAGTC

    _____

    _____

12. **C** **A** A mother has type A blood and her son has Type B blood. Is it possible for the father to have Type O blood? Prove your answer.

13. **C** **A** The brother of a woman's father has hemophilia. Her father is unaffected, but she worries that she may have an affected son. Should she worry? Explain.

14. **C** **A** Should companies that use DNA in medical research be required to share the results with the individuals whose genetic information was used? Justify your response.

_____

_____

_____

Self Study Guide

Question	If you answered this question incorrectly, see this Study Guide page for further review.	Question	If you answered this question incorrectly, see this Study Guide page for further review.
1	SG-86	8	SG-88
2	SG-86	9	SG-91
3	SG-88	10	SG-93
4	SG-90	11	SG-93
5	SG-91	12	SG-86
6	SG-91	13	SG-91
7	SG-93	14	SG-93

Add information and links to this web diagram to summarize current understandings of genetic processes.

Unit 2 Practice Test

1. **K/U** What happens during the S phase of mitosis?
   - **A.** New molecules are synthesized.
   - **B.** Cellular DNA is replicated.
   - **C.** Chromatin condenses into chromosomes.
   - **D.** Spindle fibres form.
   - **E.** Centromeres split apart.

2. **K/U** What are different forms of the same gene called?
   - **A.** homologous chromosomes
   - **B.** karyotypes
   - **C.** autosomes
   - **D.** alleles
   - **E.** genes

3. **K/U** **T/I** When human gametes combine
   - **A.** 23 individual homologous chromosomes are formed.
   - **B.** 23 pairs of homologous chromosomes are formed.
   - **C.** 23 pairs of autosomal chromosomes are formed.
   - **D.** 46 pairs of homologous chromosomes are formed.
   - **E.** 46 individual somatic chromosomes are formed.

4. **K/U** The process of oogenesis produces
   - **A.** one haploid mature egg cell and one haploid polar body.
   - **B.** one diploid mature egg cell and one haploid polar body.
   - **C.** one diploid mature egg cell and one diploid polar body.
   - **D.** one haploid egg cell and one mature diploid polar body.
   - **E.** one diploid egg cell and one immature haploid polar body.

5. **K/U** Which reproductive technology has allowed scientists to program cells to become certain cell types?
   - **A.** artificial insemination   **B.** gene cloning
   - **C.** stem cell research   **D.** in vitro fertilization
   - **E.** embryo transfer

6. **T/I** The P generation of plants are true-breeding plants with opposite forms of a trait. In what ratio will traits appear in the F^2 generation?
   - **A.** 1:1   **B.** 2:2
   - **C.** 1:3   **D.** 3:1
   - **E.** 4:0

7. **K/U** A gene exists in two different forms, B and b. Which type of gamete can a homozygous dominant individual produce?
   - **A.** Bb **B.** BB
   - **C.** B and b **D.** B
   - **E.** b

8. **T/I** A homozygous, long-tailed cat is mated with a homozygous, short-tailed cat. If long tails are the dominant trait, what would be expected in the offspring?
   - **A.** all short-tailed
   - **B.** all long-tailed
   - **C.** 50% long-tailed, 50% short-tailed
   - **D.** 75% long-tailed, 25% short-tailed
   - **E.** 25% long-tailed, 75% short-tailed

9. **K/U** Which genotypes are possible for a person with blood type B?
   - **A.** $I^B I^B$ **B.** $I^B I^B$ or $I^B i$
   - **C.** $I^A I^B$ or $I^B I^B$ **D.** $I^A I^A$
   - **E.** ii

10. **K/U** What term describes the inheritance of characteristics such as skin colour in humans?
    - **A.** multiple alleles   **B.** heterozygous advantage
    - **C.** codominant   **D.** incomplete dominant
    - **E.** polygenic traits

11. **K/U** In humans, who do X-linked recessive traits affect?
    - **A.** females only
    - **B.** males only
    - **C.** males and females equally
    - **D.** more males than females
    - **E.** more females than males

12. **K/U** Which area of research examines how environmental changes can turn a gene "on" or "off"?
    - **A.** genomics   **B.** epigenetics
    - **C.** bioinformatics   **D.** proteomics
    - **E.** genetic engineering

13. (K/U) Why is meiosis important?

_____

14. (K/U) What is a plasmid?

_____

15. (K/U) Name one type of test geneticists can use to detect changes in the structure or number of chromosomes.

_____

16. (T/I) A man with X-linked severe combined immunodeficiency (SCID) passes this trait onto all of his female offspring. Explain why.

_____

17. (C) Draw a model of DNA. Label the nucleotides, sugar, phosphates, and bonding interaction between the pairs.

18. (A) Manx cats are heterozygous for a dominant mutation that results in no tails or very short tails, large hind legs, and a distinctive gait. Mating two Manx cats yields two Manx kittens for each normal, long-tailed kitten.

  a. Use a Punnett square to illustrate the genetic inheritance of the kittens.

  b. Suggest some reasons for the 2:1 ratio of the kittens rather than the Mendelian ratio that would be expected from this cross.

_____

_____

_____

19. (A) This is a pedigree of a family affected by Huntington disease.

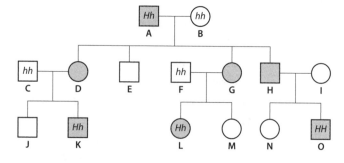

  a. What is the genotype of individual D? _____

  b. What are the genotypes of individuals H and I? _____

  c. What is the probability of individual N inheriting Huntington disease?

_____

20. **C** Create a T-chart to compare the processes of Mitosis and Meiosis.

_____

_____

_____

_____

_____

21. **A** Genetic testing has long been part of Canada's health system, but the scope of genetic testing is growing. Who should have access to the results of these tests? Justify your answers.

_____

_____

_____

_____

_____

_____

_____

_____

Self Study Guide

Question	If you answered this question incorrectly, see this Study Guide page for further review.	Question	If you answered this question incorrectly, see this Study Guide page for further review.
1	SG-60	12	SG-93
2	SG-56	13	SG-61
3	SG-61	14	SG-79
4	SG-61	15	SG-79
5	SG-63	16	SG-91
6	SG-70, SG-72	17	SG-56
7	SG-70, SG-72	18	SG-72
8	SG-74	19	SG-79
9	SG-86	20	SG-60, SG-61
10	SG-88	21	SG-79
11	SG-91		

Unit 3 Evolution

Chapter 7 Introducing Evolution

There is variation among the individuals in almost any population. The initial cause of all variation is mutations—random changes to the base sequence of one or more genes. If mutations occur in a sex cell, they can be passed on to offspring and increase the variation of the population. Variation is further increased by the vast number of possible combinations of genes that offspring can inherit from their parents.

- In a given environment, some characteristics provide a selective advantage. Individuals with those characteristics are more likely to survive and reproduce. For example, in a drought an individual that requires less water has a selective advantage. Because individuals with a selective advantage are more likely to survive, they are also more likely to pass their advantage on to their offspring.

- Natural selection is the process by which genetic mutations that lead to selective advantages and increased fitness become, and remain, more common in successive generations of a population. Natural selection is a result of selective environmental pressures, and results in a population that includes more individuals that are well adapted to their environment.

- An adaptation is a structure, behaviour, or physiological process that helps an organism survive and reproduce in a particular environment. Adaptations are the result of gradual, cumulative changes in a population.

- Artificial selection is the selective breeding carried out by humans to alter the phenotype of a population. It is used to describe the breeding of plants and animals for desirable traits and not necessarily those that would allow the offspring to better survive in the wild.

- Historically, biotechnology has been the basis of traditional animal and plant breeding techniques, such as the selection of plants and animals with specific characteristics and hybridization. Today, modern biotechnology techniques allow researchers to take a single gene from a plant or animal cell and insert it into another plant or animal cell to introduce particular characteristics directly.

- Artificial selection and other forms of biotechnology provide many advantages to agriculture. They also introduce some significant disadvantages.

Chapter 8 Developing a Theory of Evolution

Scientific theories explain observations and tie them together in a comprehensive way, enabling scientists to make predictions about new situations and experimental outcomes. Theories are supported by a large body of evidence from many sources.
- Contributions by Buffon, Cuvier, Lamark, Lyell, and others helped to develop the hypotheses that have led to the theory of evolution by natural selection. Charles Darwin and Alfred Russel Wallace both developed hypotheses to explain natural selection based on their own observations and on data that had been gathered by others.

- The fossil record, including transitional fossils and evidence of vestigial structures, provides evidence supporting the theory of evolution by natural selection.

- Biogeography, or the study of the past and present distribution of species around the world, provides evidence of evolution by natural selection.

- Further evidence supporting the theory of evolution by natural selection comes from anatomy (homologous and analogous structures), embryology, and molecular biology.

Chapter 9 Evolution and Speciation

Over time, the process of evolution changes the gene frequencies within the gene pool of a population.

The agents of evolutionary change are:
- mutations
- gene flow
- non-random mating
- genetic drift
- natural selection

Of these, only natural selection involves adaptation to the environment.

- Speciation describes the formation of new species from existing species. It is a result of evolution by natural selection and geographic isolation or reproductive isolation. Speciation as a result of geographic isolation is called allopatric speciation. Speciation as a result of reproductive isolation in the same geographical area is called sympatric speciation.

- Reproductive isolation can be a result of geographic isolation. Geographically isolated populations often differentiate as they adapt to their new environment. Eventually, they are so distinct from other populations they are unable to interbreed. Adaptive radiation is an example of allopatric speciation that is easily observable.

- Isolating mechanisms—mechanisms that lead to reproductive isolation—prevent viable, fertile offspring. Prezygotic isolating mechanisms prevent hybrid offspring formation. Post-zygotic isolating mechanisms prevent hybrid offspring from surviving and reproducing.

- Currently, there are two hypotheses about the pace of speciation. One hypothesis, gradualism, describes slow, steady changes leading to speciation. A new model, punctuated equilibrium, argues that speciation occurs relatively quickly in rapid bursts, with long periods of genetic equilibrium in between.

- Mass extinctions have occurred in the past and shape the overall pattern of evolution. Human alteration of the biosphere is currently causing a global mass extinction. Habitat loss is one of the most important causes of species extinction.

Introducing Evolution

Self Assessment

1. Which statement best describes the process of adaptation?
   A. It causes changes to organisms over time.
   B. It stabilizes behavioural characteristics of organisms.
   C. It reduces an organism's chance of survival.
   D. It helps an organism to survive and reproduce.
   E. It allows organisms to exist in any environment.

2. Hibernation is an example of what type of adaptation?
   A. structural **B.** physiological **C.** behavioural
   D. mimicry **E.** artificial

3. Which example shows how variation within a species can lead to adaptation due to environmental changes?
   A. colour variation of the English peppered moth
   B. interbreeding between domestic cat populations
   C. genetic modification of the wild mustard plant
   D. selective breeding of English bulldogs
   E. monoculture practices in agriculture

4. What term describes an adaptation in which a harmless species resembles a harmful species in colouration or structure?
   A. somatic mutation **B.** germinal mutation **C.** variation
   D. mutagen **E.** mimicry

5. What causes genetic variation within a population?
   A. behavioural responses to environmental changes that affect the population
   B. a sequence of environmental changes that affect the population
   C. random events that affect individuals in the population
   D. the variety of genetic information in all the individuals in the population
   E. the variety of genetic information from some individuals in the population

6. What is selective advantage?
   A. a behavioural response to environmental changes
   B. a defence mechanism that increases an organism's survival
   C. the genetic advantage of one organism over its competitors
   D. a physiological change that occurs to an organism
   E. a structural adaptation that reduces the survival rate of the organism

7. Why are bacteria often used for researching genetic variation?
   A. They have a range of metabolic activities.
   B. They have short reproduction cycles.
   C. They can exist in anaerobic conditions.
   D. They can form plasmids.
   E. They have a protective capsule.

8. What happens when a random genetic mutation occurs?

    A. Individuals change but not populations.

    B. Individuals do not contribute to these changes.

    C. Populations change but not individuals.

    D. Populations level out to a point of equilibrium.

    E. Population levels decrease to a point of extinction.

9. Which term best describes environmental conditions that select for certain characteristics of individuals and select against other characteristics?

    A. natural selection   **B.** selective pressure   **C.** variation

    D. mutation   **E.** artificial selection

10. The ability of some bacteria in a population to survive exposure to an antibiotic is an example of which phenomenon?

    A. natural selection   **B.** positive mutation   **C.** negative mutation

    D. mimicry   **E.** selective pressure

11. When discussing natural selection, a high degree of fitness is linked to an organism's

    A. metabolic rate   **B.** mobility mode   **C.** reproductive rate

    D. ability to adapt   **E.** genetic inheritance

12. What caused the modification of the wild mustard plant to produce broccoli and cauliflower?

    A. abiotic factors   **B.** natural selection   **C.** biotic factors

    D. selective breeding   **E.** environmental changes

13. Why is monoculture risky?

    A. Crop yields increase.

    B. Crops compete genetically with each other.

    C. Crops react to abiotic factors.

    D. Crops produce more greenhouse gases.

    E. Crops could be killed or damaged by a new pest.

Self Study Guide

Question	If you answered this question incorrectly, see this Study Guide page for further review.	After completing your review, be sure to answer these questions in the Chapter 7 Practice Test.	Question	If you answered this question incorrectly, see this Study Guide page for further review.	After completing your review, be sure to answer these questions in the Chapter 7 Practice Test.
1	SG-106	1, 5, 8	8	SG-108	2
2	SG-106	2	9	SG-110	8, 9
3	SG-108	3, 4	10	SG-110	4, 12
4	SG-107	1	11	SG-110	10
5	SG-106	2	12	SG-112	6
6	SG-108	3, 11	13	SG-112	14
7	SG-108	4			

Summary

Key Terms

extinct

adaptation

mimicry

variation

mutation

selective advantage

natural selection

selective pressure

fitness

artificial selection

biotechnology

monoculture

Adaptation and Variation (7.1)

An **adaptation** is a process that helps an organism survive and reproduce in a particular environment. Organisms that survive long enough to reproduce have the opportunity to pass along their genetic information to their offspring.

- A structural adaptation affects a specific part or feature of the organism's body. Humans' opposable thumbs are a structural adaptation.

- Behavioural adaptations affect the way an organism acts. Behavioural adaptations can include hunting strategies, migration, hibernation, and other behaviours that help an organism survive in a particular environment.

- Physiological adaptations permit an organism to perform special functions such a producing slime or venom.

The eastern Massasauga rattlesnake (*Sistrurus catenatus catenatus*)—Ontario's only venomous snake—has developed several adaptations that help it survive in its environment.

Structural Adaptations	Behavioural Adaptations	Physiological Adaptations
• The dark, saddle-shaped blotches on its brown to greyish-brown body help the snake blend into its environment. • The snake has a rattle at the end of its tail to frighten potential predators. • The snake's main diet is small mammals. It uses a small hole on each side of its head called a *heat-sensitive pit* to detect warm-blooded animals up to 70 cm away, even in complete darkness.	• Snakes are ectothermic. The snake uses the temperature of its surrounding environment to maintain an optimal body temperature. • The snake hibernates to avoid freezing during the Ontario winter.	• The snake injects venom into its prey through two hollow fangs. The venom is a combination of hemotoxins and cytotoxins. Hemotoxins attack the blood and cause massive haemorrhaging. (bleeding). Cytotoxins attack the tissues, making it easier for the snake to digest its prey.

Mimicry is a special type of adaptation. The eastern Massasauga rattlesnake has a blotched pattern, but so do other snakes including the eastern fox snake. Fox snakes, like many other harmless snakes, sometimes mimic rattlesnakes by vibrating their tails. Unfortunately, this defensive strategy backfired when humans began killing rattlesnakes and, with them, fox snakes. False cobra snakes are harmless, but have a hood similar to that of a poisonous Indian cobra. Ash borers cannot sting, but their physical appearance resembles wasps.

Learning Check

1. **K/U** What advantages does a fox snake get by mimicking rattlesnake behaviour?

   _____

2. **K/U** **T/I** Like most other snakes, rattlesnakes do not need to eat daily, and can go weeks or even months without food. A rattlesnake re-absorbs a large part of the mass of its digestive tract in between feedings. Once prey is consumed, the snake rebuilds its digestive system. This adaptation is related to the consumption of large, infrequent meals.

   a. What type of adaptation is this?

   _____

   b. Why would this practice be advantageous to the rattlesnake?

   _____

   _____

3. **K/U** A xerophyte describes a plant that has structural and physiological adaptations that enables it to survive in areas with very little free moisture. One adaptation found in some xerophyte plants is the ability to fold their leaves, especially during the day, reducing the rate of water loss by the plant. What type of adaptation is this?

   _____

4. **K/U** The eastern white pine (*Pinus strobus*) is the provincial tree of Ontario. Eastern white pine is moderately fire resistant. Mature trees survive most surface fires because they have thick bark, very few branches on their trunks, and moderately deep root systems.

   a. Identify the adaptations of the eastern white pine that would help this species of tree survive and be successful in Ontario.

   _____

   _____

   b. What types of adaptations did you describe in Part a?

   _____

5. **A** Think of an animal or plant and identify the adaptations it has that help it survive and reproduce.

   _____

   _____

Study Tip

Thinking of **real life examples** (**question 5**) can help you understand abstract ideas.

Variations, Mutations, and Selective Advantage (7.1)

The offspring of sexually reproducing organisms inherit a combination of genetic material (genes) from both biological parents. The number of possible combinations of genes that offspring inherit from their parents results in genetic **variation** among individuals within a population.

A change in the content of the genetic message–the base sequence of one or more genes–is referred to as a **mutation**. Some mutations alter the identity of a particular nucleotide, while others remove or add nucleotides to a gene. Mutations that occur in somatic tissue can have significant effects on an individual, but will not be passed on to offspring. Some mutations have negative effects, some have neutral effects, and some have positive effects for the individual. Mutations that occur in gametes can have significant effects on offspring and on the entire species.

Mutations result in new alleles and therefore underlie all other mechanisms that produce variation, the raw material for evolutionary change.

Selective advantage is the genetic advantage of one organism over its competitors that causes it to be favoured in survival and reproduction rates over time. For example, some flies have a mutation that makes them immune to the effects of the insecticide DDT. This mutation, however, reduces the flies' growth rate. Before the introduction of DDT to their environment, this mutation was a disadvantage to the flies. When DDT was introduced, however, this mutation enabled the individuals that possessed it to survive. These flies had a selective advantage in the population. They were more likely to survive and reproduce, potentially passing on this now-helpful mutation to their offspring. Adaptations are the result of gradual, accumulative changes that help an organism survive and reproduce.

Mutations like the one that allows some flies to survive DDT exposure come about completely by chance. Organisms do not alter their genetic information so they can exist in new environments. When an environment changes, some individuals in a population may have mutations that allow them to take advantage of the change. If so, they may survive and pass their beneficial genes on to their offspring. Organisms that do not have this mutation may not survive or may not be healthy enough to reproduce. The rate at which resistance develops in a population is influenced by genetics and also by other biological properties, such as the organisms' rate of reproduction.

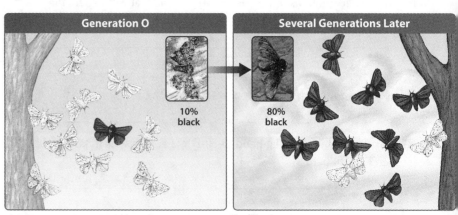

Mutations cause genetic variation, such as colour differences. Environmental changes lead to selective advantage and adaptations.

Use this information for question 1.

Eastern massasaugas rattlesnakes are members of the Pygmy rattlesnake family, *Sistrurus*. They are approximately 50 to 70 cm in length. Their bodies are brown, grey, or even black with 25 to 50 dark saddles that run down the middle of their backs and two or three rows of dark blotches on their sides. Their bellies are dark grey or black and the underside of their chins is white. They have a characteristic dark band that runs diagonally across their eyes to the back of their jaws. This band is usually bordered by a lighter colour.

1. **K/U** Identify the variations in the eastern Massasauga rattlesnakes.

   _____

   _____

   _____

2. **K/U** **C** Draw a flowchart or a cause-and-effect map to show the factors that lead to selective advantage.

Study Tip

Flowcharts and **cause-and-effect maps** (**question 2**) can help you show and understand relationships among concepts.

Use this information for questions 3 and 4.

The insecticide DDT was banned by many countries, including Canada, in the 1970s. It is still used in some parts of Africa, Asia, and South America.

An area infested with mosquitoes was sprayed weekly with DDT over several months. The graph shows the mosquito count during the spraying.

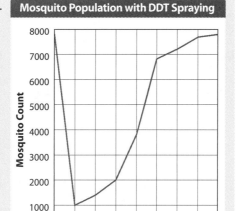

Mosquito Population with DDT Spraying

3. **A** Why did some mosquitoes survive the first spraying?

   A. More mosquitoes moved into the area.

   B. The summer weather was cool and wet.

   C. There was natural variation in the population.

   D. Environmental factors changed as the summer progressed.

   E. Most of the mosquitoes were old enough to reproduce.

4. **A** **T/I** Why did the DDT become less effective?

   A. Individual mosquitoes were able to change their genes in response to the presence of DDT.

   B. DDT caused mutations in the mosquitoes, which resulted in immunity.

   C. The DDT reacted chemically with the mosquito's DNA.

   D. The DDT was only sprayed once.

   E. Mosquitoes that had a pre-adaptive resistance to DDT lived and passed their beneficial genes onto their offspring.

Natural Selection (7.2)

An individual that has a selective advantage is more likely to survive, reproduce, and pass its characteristics on to its offspring. Offspring with the selective advantage are more likely than other members of the population to survive and reproduce, passing on their characteristics. Eventually, the selective advantage is likely to become a common characteristic of the population. This process is known as **natural selection.**

- Natural selection is a result of **selective pressures** in the environment.
- It produces populations of individuals that are well adapted to their environment.
- It is the process by which genetic mutations that enhance reproduction become, and remain, more common in successive generations of a population.
- It is situational. Selective advantages are different in different environments. A selective advantage in one environment may be a disadvantage in another.
- It can only take place when there is variation in the population.
- Natural selection does not cause change in individuals.

To describe natural selection, scientists talk about the *fitness* of individuals in a population. In this sense, **fitness** is measured by the number of fertile offspring produced in the next generation. A high degree of fitness means that an organism is more likely to survive and reproduce, thereby passing on its advantageous genes to its offspring.

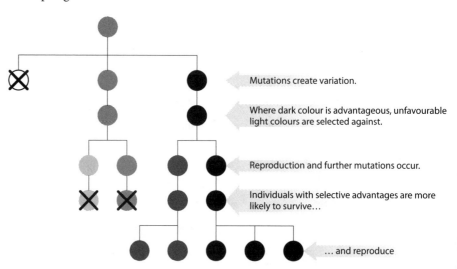

Mutations create variation.

Where dark colour is advantageous, unfavourable light colours are selected against.

Reproduction and further mutations occur.

Individuals with selective advantages are more likely to survive…

… and reproduce

This diagram illustrates the natural selection of darker colouration in an insect species over several generations.

Learning Check

1. **K/U** Fill in the blanks to complete this paragraph.

   Mutations cause _____ in a population. In some environments, certain individuals will have characteristics that give them a _____ _____. These individuals are more _____.

   They are more likely to survive and _____, passing their genes on to their _____. Over time, through the process of _____ _____, more and more members of the population will have the characteristic that provides a _____ _____. _____ members of the population will have characteristics that are not suited to the environment.

2. **C** Explain how the term *fitness* can have different meanings in different contexts.

   _____

   _____

   _____

3. **K/U** Define the term *selective pressure* in your own words.

   _____

   _____

   _____

4. **K/U** Summarize the main ideas of natural selection.

   _____

   _____

   _____

   _____

   _____

5. **T/I** If you have completed the unit on genetics, explain natural selection in terms of phenotype and genotype.

   _____

   _____

   _____

   _____

   _____

Study Tip

Use the **glossary** in your textbook to look up words you are not sure about. Many words have a slightly different meaning in biology than in everyday speech.

Artificial Selection (7.2)

Natural selection describes changes to a population caused by environmental pressures and selective advantages. **Artificial selection** describes changes to a population caused by deliberate, selective breeding by humans. It involves breeding plants and animals for traits desirable to humans—which are not necessarily traits that would increase a population's fitness to survive in the wild.

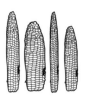 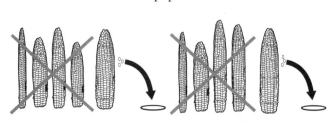 

❶ Natural variation occures in the wild population. For example, some ears of corn have juicier kernels.

❷ Seeds for the next generation are chosen only from individuals with the most desireable traits.

❸ Repeat this process for several generations.

❹ Over time, the quality of the crop increases.

Artificial selection is a form of **biotechnology**—the use of technology and organisms to create or modify a product for a specific use.

Historically, biotechnology has been used to modify fermentation techniques and make bread, cheese, and alcoholic beverages. It has also been the basis of artificial selection and hybridization used to create the plants and animals raised on farms today. Modern biotechnology techniques allow researchers to take a single gene from a plant or animal cell and insert it into another plant or animal cell to alter the plant's or the animal's characteristics in a process known as transgenics.

Pros and Cons of Artificial Selection

Pros	Cons
Used to produce all our major crop plants, livestock, and pets from their wild ancestors.	The original forms of the organisms have been artificially selected against, and in some cases, no longer exist
Produces organisms with traits that benefit humans, such as high crop yields, resistance to disease, and fast growth rate.	Traits that benefit humans do not always benefit the organisms and might threaten their ability to survive if environmental conditions change.
Genetic uniformity (monoculture) makes farming easier and ensures a uniform product.	Genetic uniformity leaves populations vulnerable to even minor environmental changes. It also leaves humans who depend on monoculture crops vulnerable to famine if the crops fail.
Transgenics can be used to modify a species' genetic makeup, such as increasing resistance to a specific pest, disease, or herbicide. This can reduce the use of pesticides and herbicides, which lowers production costs and has important environmental advantages.	Transgenics is a new science and lacks the checks and balances that are imposed by nature in traditional breeding. The full effect of transgenic species on our environment and our health is difficult to predict.

Gene banks have been established to protect against some of the disadvantages of artificial selection, primarily the lack of genetic diversity. They store genetic material from the early ancestors of modern plants. However, they are unable to conserve the full range of crop genetic diversity because of the sheer number of seed samples that would be involved.

Artificial selection and natural selection have some similarities.
- Far more offspring are born than will reproduce.
- There is variation among individuals. They have different genotypes and phenotypes.
- Individuals with certain characteristics have a better chance of surviving and reproducing than individuals with other characteristics.
- Some characteristics that result in increased survival and reproduction are inherited by offspring.
- Differential reproduction, or selection, occurs causing some inherited characteristics to become more frequent and prominent in the population and others to become less frequent as generations pass.
- A population changes over time so that certain traits become more common.

Learning Check

1. **K/U** **C** Natural selection and artificial selection have many similarities but many differences as well. Create a T-chart to contrast natural selection and artificial selection. Include information about
   - the speed of change
   - the role of the environment
   - the role of humans
   - the diversity of the resulting population

Study Tip

Graphic organizers such as **T-charts (question 1)** or **Venn diagrams** can help you organize your notes and make studying easier.

2. **A** Identify whether each change occurred through natural selection or artificial selection.

   a. One of the ancestors of the modern horse was *Eohippus*, a small animal with four toes.

   _____

   b. Since 1949, Warren Barheim's goal has been to develop inbred lines of plants with specific characteristics. For example, when crossed, the appropriate parents produce seeds for plants that produce seedless fruits, such as seedless watermelons.

   _____

c. The GT73 line of canola (*Brassica napus*) was developed through a specific genetic modification to be resistant to the activity of glyphosate herbicides. This novel variety was developed from the Westar canola variety by insertion of two genes.

_____

d. Deer mice with dark fur are widespread across North America. They can blend into dark soils and stay hidden from predators. Over a period of several thousand years the deer mouse populations inhabiting lighter coloured, sandy soils evolved a pale coat that helped them evade predators.

_____

3. **T/I** The Cavendish is the best known and most profitable species of banana grown today. This seedless variety must be propagated by cutting and rooting a section of the mature plant, making all generations genetically identical. Thousands of banana plantations grow fruit of genetically identical plants. List the advantages and disadvantages of this practice.

_____

_____

_____

_____

4. **T/I** **a.** What are gene banks?

_____

_____

b. Provide two reasons why gene banks are being established around the world.

_____

_____

Bringing It All Together

Add information and links to this web diagram to summarize current understandings of the processes that can result in the appearance of a new trait in a population (evolution).

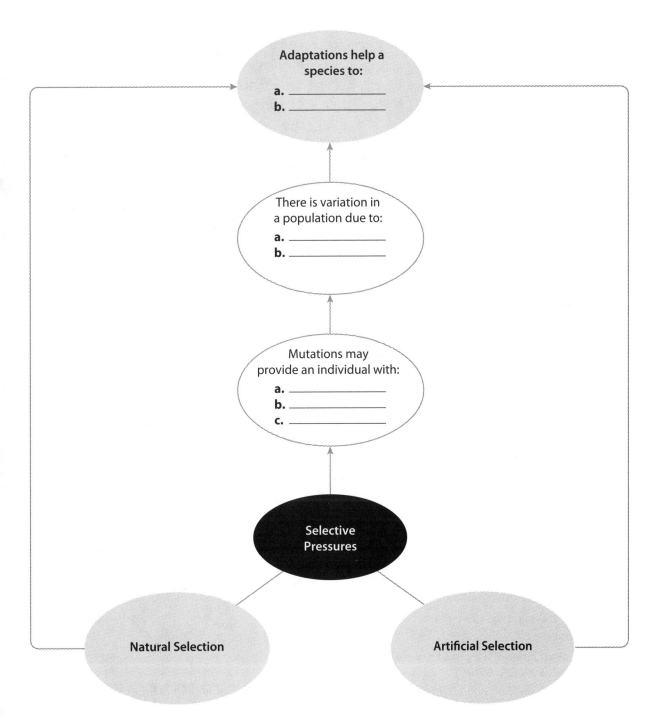

1. **K/U** The colouring and structure of a stick insect that allows it to blend into its environment are examples of what adaptation?

   A. behavioural adaptation

   B. physiological adaptation

   C. structural adaptation

   D. selective adaptation

   E. adaptive pressure

2. **T/I** Which statement is true about somatic mutations?

   A. They disappear when the organism dies.

   B. They are present in the parent cell.

   C. They produce new alleles.

   D. They lead to genetic variation in populations.

   E. They affect only germinal cells.

3. **T/I** Individuals with sickle cell trait who display some resistance to malaria have what adaptation?

   A. negative mutation

   B. selective advantage

   C. natural selection

   D. selective pressure

   E. structural adaptation

4. **K/U** What causes bacteria to build resistance to certain antibiotics?

   A. a random mutation of individual bacteria

   B. groups of bacteria resisting the antibiotic

   C. clusters of bacteria producing antigens

   D. colonies of bacteria releasing enzymes

   E. random reorganization of bacterial RNA

5. **T/I** In genetics, what does fitness measure?

   A. the quality of the genes passed into the next generation

   B. the phenotypic ratios of the parent generation

   C. the quality and quantity of chromosomes passed to the next generation

   D. the quantity of the copies of genes of an individual in the next generation

   E. the genotypic ratios of the parent and offspring

6. **K/U** What is an effect of the agricultural practice of selective breeding?

   A. infertile hybrids

   B. decreased biodiversity

   C. decreased variation within crops

   D. increased variation within crops

   E. reduction in viable offspring

7. **K/U** Which term describes the practice of planting fields with uniform varieties of the same species?

   A. biotechnology

   B. artificial selection

   C. transgenic agriculture

   D. companion planting

   E. monoculture

8. **K/U** What can lead to the development of an adaptation?

   _____

   _____

9. **K/U** Give three examples of biotic factors that can exert selective pressure on a population.

   _____

   _____

   _____

10. **K/U** In natural selection, what determines which individuals in a population are the fittest to survive and reproduce?

    _____

11. **A** What adaptations allow polar bears to survive in the Artic?

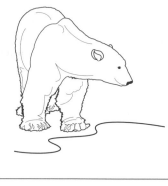

    _____

    _____

    _____

12. (A) Research scientists found that the resistance of normal human intestinal flora to the antibiotic tetracycline has risen from 2% in the 1950s to 80% in the 1990s. Describe what could account for this rise in resistance levels.

_____

_____

_____

13. (T/I) (C) Use the Venn diagram to illustrate the similarities and differences between artificial selection and natural selection.

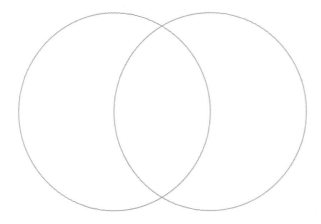

14. (A) What are some of the consequences when breeders purposely breed "the best to the best"? Give an example.

_____

_____

_____

Self Study Guide

Question	If you answered this question incorrectly, see this Study Guide page for further review.	Question	If you answered this question incorrectly, see this Study Guide page for further review.
1	SG-106	8	SG-106, SG-108
2	SG-106	9	SG-110
3	SG-106	10	SG-110
4	SG-108	11	SG-106, SG-110
5	SG-110	12	SG-108, SG-110
6	SG-112	13	SG-113
7	SG-112	14	SG-112

Self Assessment

1. What is the term for a general statement that explains and makes successful predictions about a broad range of observations?
   A. a conclusion   **B.** an experiment   **C.** a prediction
   D. a scientific theory   **E.** a scientific hypothesis

2. Which scientist is created with developing the science of paleontology?
   A. Charles Darwin   **B.** Georges Cuvier   **C.** Carolus Linnaeus
   D. Charles Lyell   **E.** Jean-Baptiste Lamarck

3. What is the term for the idea that a flood could destroy species in a particular region, which would allow species from neighbouring regions to repopulate an area?
   A. evolution   **B.** descent with modification
   C. survival of the fittest   **D.** catastrophism
   E. uniformitarianism

4. What is Charles Lyell's theory?
   A. Organisms alter their reproductive patterns when stressed.
   B. Revolutions can lead to new species repopulating an area.
   C. Organisms change to adapt to their environment.
   D. Geological changes must be rapid and destructive.
   E. Geological processes are slow and continuous.

5. Who proposed the idea of the inheritance of acquired characteristics?
   A. Charles Darwin   **B.** James Hutton
   C. Jean-Baptiste Lamarck   **D.** Mary Anning
   E. Georges-Louis Leclerc

6. What is another name for natural selection?
   A. common descent   **B.** adaptive radiation   **C.** divergent evolution
   D. convergent evolution   **E.** survival of the fittest

7. What is Darwin's theory of natural selection?
   A. Individuals that are better suited to local conditions survive to produce more offspring.
   B. Some animals' body parts that are not used will eventually disappear.
   C. Different species of fossilized organisms can be found in different sedimentary rock strata.
   D. Humans and apes have a common ancestor.
   E. Plants and animals can be classified based on anatomy and physiology.

8. When did the first land plants appear in fossil records?
   A. 520 million years ago   **B.** 300 million years ago   **C.** 225 million years ago
   D. 135 million years ago   **E.** 7 million years ago

9. Which organism is the oldest type of vertebrate?

    A. amphibians   **B.** birds   **C.** fish

    D. mammals   **E.** reptiles

10. Which is an example of a transitional fossil?

    A. Archaeopteryx   **B.** Atrociraptor   **C.** Gondwana

    D. Cynognathus   **E.** Dorudon

11. Which branch of science would study vertebrate forelimbs?

    A. biogeography

    B. genetics

    C. comparative biochemistry

    D. comparative anatomy

    E. embryology

12. Homologous structures have

    A. similar origins but different elements and functions.

    B. similar structural elements and origins.

    C. different structural elements but similar origins.

    D. different structural elements and origins but similar functions.

    E. similar structural elements and origins but may have a different function.

13. Which is an example of analogous structures?

    A. legs of a human and wings of an insect

    B. wing of a bird and arms of a human

    C. webbed toes of a frog and webbed toes of a duck

    D. legs of a horse, and legs of a cat

    E. wings of a bird and wings of a butterfly

14. One of the main stages of embryonic evidence that links vertebrates with each other is the development of

    A. forelimbs.   **B.** gills.   **C.** scales.

    D. paired pouches.   **E.** embryonic shells.

Self Study Guide

Question	If you answered this question incorrectly, see this Study Guide page for further review.	After completing your review, be sure to answer these questions in the Chapter 8 Practice Test.	Question	If you answered this question incorrectly, see this Study Guide page for further review.	After completing your review, be sure to answer these questions in the Chapter 8 Practice Test.
1	SG-120	3	8	SG-123	6
2	SG-120	1, 2	9	SG-123	6
3	SG-120	4	10	SG-123	9
4	SG-120	1, 4	11	SG-125	14
5	SG-120, SG-121	4	12	SG-125	9, 14
6	SG-121	10, 11	13	SG-125	9, 14
7	SG-121	11, 12	14	SG-125	14

Key Terms

paleontology

catastrophism

uniformitarianism

inheritance of
acquired characteristics

theory of evolution by
natural selection

evolution

survival of the fittest

descent with modification

fossil record

transitional fossil

vestigial structure

biogeography

homologous structures

analogous structures

embryology

Developing the Theory of Evolution by Natural Selection (8.1)

Scientific theories are the result of hard work by many people gathering and analyzing data. The general process follows steps similar to these:

1. A scientist observes certain patterns and states a hypothesis—an idea that may explain the pattern but has not yet been proved.

2. Experiments are done and more data is gathered and analyzed to see if it supports or refutes the hypothesis.

3. If significant data from several groups of researchers supports the hypothesis, then it becomes a theory—a coherent explanation for observations about the natural world.

If data refutes the hypothesis, then the hypothesis is often revised to take the data into account. In this way, many people over many centuries work together to advance our understanding of the natural world.

Today's theory of evolution is the result of centuries of research by many scientists, each one building on the work of others.

Traditional scientific thought, as expressed by early philosophers such as Plato and Aristotle, was that life was unchanging because it was already perfected. In 1707–1708, George-Louis Leclerc published *Histoire Naturelle*, in which he included the hypothesis that similarities between humans and apes might mean they had a common ancestor.

Georges Cuvier is credited with helping to develop the science of **paleontology**, the study of ancient life through the examination of fossils, in the early 1800s. He found different fossils in each layer of rock or soil and proposed that some species disappeared, or became extinct, over time and new ones appeared. Cuvier suggested that his observations were caused by catastrophes, which he called "revolutions"— violent shifts in the environment that caused numerous species to become extinct.

In 1830 Charles Lyell rejected **catastrophism** and developed the theory of **uniformitarianism**, which stated that geological processes operated at the same rate in the past as they do today. His idea also suggested that the Earth was older than the previously thought 6000 years. He believed that slow, continuous change would amount to large changes over time.

Around the same time, Jean-Baptiste Lamarck developed a hypothesis to explain how offspring might inherit characteristics from its parents. He called it the *inheritance of acquired characteristics*. Acquired characteristics are those changes in the structure or function of an organism that are the result of use, environmental influences, disease, mutilation, and so forth. For example, a muscle becomes enlarged through use or mice may lose their tails while escaping from a predator. Lamarck proposed that changes acquired during an organism's lifetime could be passed on to its offspring. Genetic evidence has since shown that this is not an actual mechanism of inheritance or of evolution.

Charles Darwin used the ideas, readings, and works of Jean-Baptiste Lamarck, Charles Lyell, and Thomas Malthus, as well as his own observations, to create his theory of evolution by natural selection, which is accepted today as a guiding theory to explain evolutionary pathways and forces. Alfred Russell Wallace developed similar theories during the same time period. Their combined paper was published in 1858.

Darwin based his theory of evolution by natural selection on two pillars:
• an analysis of data gathered by many other scientists that showed life had changed in specific ways over time
• his own observations of the distribution of species around the world

For detailed examples of Darwin's observations about the global distribution of species, see page 329 of your textbook.

These are the main points of the theory of evolution by natural section.

1. Members of a population vary (differ from one another). The traits that vary are inheritable.

2. Most populations have more offspring each year than local resources can support, leading to a struggle for resources. Since the environment cannot support unlimited population growth, not all individuals get to reproduce to their full potential. The fittest individuals will contribute more offspring to the next generation. This is the idea of survival of the fittest, and Darwin called this natural selection.

3. Natural selection acts on traits that can be passed on from one generation to the next.

4. The process for change is slow and gradual.

Learning Check

1. (K/U) Why is evolution by natural selection considered a theory and not a hypothesis?

_____

_____

2. (K/U) Explain how these three ideas relate to one another, according to Darwin's theory of evolution by natural selection.
  • survival of the fittest   • natural selection   • evolution

_____

_____

_____

Study Tip

As you read about the contributions of each scientist to today's understanding of evolution, look for the **main ideas**—the observations that were made and the hypothesis that were developed as a result.

3. **C** Create a time line summarizing how the scientists listed above contributed to the theory of evolution by natural selection.

4. Draw a four-part storyboard to summarize Darwin's theory of evolution by natural selection. Write a caption for each diagram.

1	2
Caption	Caption

3	4
Caption	Caption

Evidence for Evolution: Fossils and Biogeography (8.2)

Since Darwin's time, information from many different areas of science, including the fossil record and biogeography, has been gathered to support the theory of evolution by natural selection.

Fossils are the preserved remains or traces of animals, plants, and other organisms from the remote past. The **fossil record** shows the kinds of organisms that were alive in the past, where they lived, when they became extinct, and the order that they appeared in history.

In sedimentary rock, fossils are found in layers. Older fossils are found in the deeper rocks and younger fossils are closer to the surface. If different fossils exist at different levels, it is evidence that not all life forms came into existence at the same time.

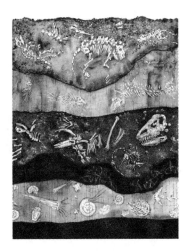

Transitional fossils show organisms with similarities to two groups. They provide evidence that the two groups are related. For example, Archaeopteryx fossils show a bird-like animal with feathers, but also with teeth, scales, claws on its wings, and a bony tail—like most reptiles including dinosaurs. It provides evidence that modern birds had reptile ancestors.

Vestigial structures in fossils also provide evidence for evolution. Scientists believe that vestigial structures once functioned in a common ancestor.

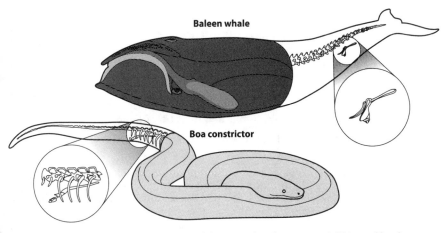

Baleen whales and snakes do not have back legs yet they have vestigial hip and leg bones where legs existed in their ancestors.

The fossils found within the sedimentary rock layers are just a fraction of what used to occupy Earth; many species' remains were simply destroyed. For example, marine animals are most often soft-bodied masses, and their remains are unlikely to be preserved. The evolutionary tree that we try to create is missing many branches because fossils of many species have not survived.

Biogeography is the study of how organisms are distributed throughout the world. Biogeography supports the hypothesis that species evolve in one location and then spread out to other locations. Examples include the following:

- Geographically close environments are more likely to be populated by related species than are locations that are geographically separate but environmentally similar.

- Animals found on islands often closely resemble animals found on the nearest continent.

- Fossils of the same species can be found on the coastlines of neighbouring continents.

- Closely related species are almost never found in exactly the same location or habitat.

See page 335 of your textbook for more details about how these examples support the theory of evolution.

Learning Check

1. Explain these two apparently contradictory statements.

   Statement 1: Evidence from the fossil record is unique, because it provides a time perspective for understanding the evolution of life on Earth.

   Statement 2: The fossil record is incomplete and working with it is like trying to put together a jigsaw puzzle with missing pieces.

   _____

   _____

   _____

2. The human appendix is the small organ that represents the caecum. In most vertebrates, the caecum is a large, complex organ of the digestive system. In herbivorous mammals such as mice, the caecum is the largest part of the large intestine and functions in the storage and digestion of plant material.

   a. In evolutionary terms, what is the human appendix?

   _____

   b. How can the appendix provide evidence of human evolution?

   _____

   _____

3. The plains of North and South America and the plains of Africa have similar environmental conditions but different mammals. Use what is written in this study guide and your textbook, as well as what you know about geology and the movement of the continents, to infer why there are zebras in Africa but not in North or South America.

   _____

   _____

   _____

Study Tip

Inference—using evidence to draw conclusions—is a useful skill in science. As you read your textbook, use **inference** to decide how each piece of evidence is connected to the conclusion (**question 3**).

More Evidence for Evolution: Anatomy, Embryology, and DNA (8.2)

The theory of evolution is a very powerful one. It provides a framework for understanding the diversity of life. Many observations from a wide variety of fields of biology simply cannot be understood in any meaningful way except as a result of evolution. Since Darwin's time, evidence in many areas has continued to support the theory of evolution by natural selection.

As vertebrates evolved, the same bones were sometimes put to different uses. Yet the structure of the bones gives away their evolutionary past. For example, the forelimbs of vertebrates are **homologous structures**—they serve different functions but still show a similar structure.

Analogous structures perform similar function in different species even though the organisms do not have a common evolutionary origin and the structure of the body part is often different. The functional similarities of analogous structures are evidence of environmental pressures selecting for the same function in different species.

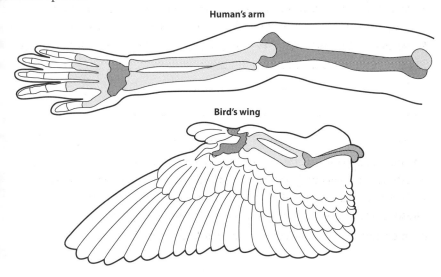

Human's arm

Bird's wing

A human arm and a bird wing are homologous structures. Notice the similar shapes and arrangement of bones. This similar structure shows humans and birds evolved from a common ancestor.

The study of embryos—**embryology**—also provides evidence for evolution. At some time during development, all vertebrates have a supporting dorsal rod, called a notochord, and paired pouches of the throat. In fish and some amphibians these pouches develop into gills. In humans, the first pair of pouches becomes the cavity in the middle ear and auditory tube.

Although vertebrates, from fish to humans, look very different as adults, the similarity of their embryos provides evidence of their common ancestry.

Recent genetic and biochemical research has also provided evidence that supports evolution. Almost all living organisms use the same basic biochemical molecules, including DNA, ATP, and many identical or nearly identical enzymes. The degree of similarity between DNA base sequences and amino acid sequences in two organisms is thought to indicate their degree of relatedness. For example, the protein cytochrome c is found in almost all organisms. The table on the next page shows that the amino acids in this protein in humans are almost identical to those in rhesus monkeys, but quite different from those in yeast.

See examples of similarities in the embryos of different species on page 338 of your textbook.

Molecular Similarities in Cytochrome c	
Organism	Number of amino acid differences from humans
chimpanzee	0
rhesus monkey	1
rabbit	9
cow	10
pigeon	12
bullfrog	20
fruit fly	24
wheat (wheat germ)	37
yeast	42

Learning Check

1. Are the paired throat pouches in vertebrate embryos homologous or analogous structures? Justify your choice.

_____

_____

_____

2. Are a bird wing and an insect wing homologous or analogous structures? Explain.

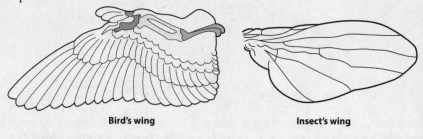

Bird's wing   Insect's wing

_____

3. All vertebrates have the protein hemoglobin. Like all proteins, hemoglobin is composed of a series of amino acids. Which vertebrate would you expect to have hemoglobin most similar to human hemoglobin: macaques (monkeys) or frogs? Explain why.

_____

4. Create a concept map to show how anatomy, embryology, and DNA evidence support the theory of evolution.

Bringing It All Together

Complete this web diagram to summarize the evidence supporting the theory of evolution. Add specific information to each circle to show how the evidence supports the theory. Add more circles as required.

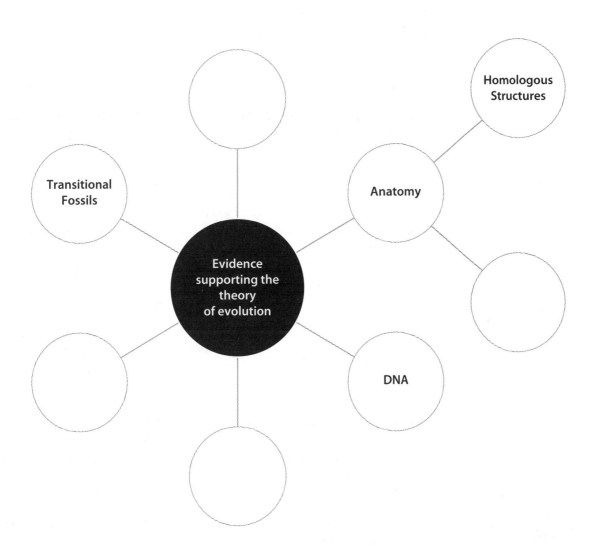

1. **K/U** Who first noted the common ancestry between humans and apes?
   - **A.** Wallace
   - **B.** Cuvier
   - **C.** Lcclerc
   - **D.** Darwin
   - **E.** Lamarck

2. **K/U** In the study of paleontology, what is true as you go deeper in the stratum?
   - **A.** The species are more similar to modern life.
   - **B.** The species are less similar to modern life.
   - **C.** The diversity of species increases.
   - **D.** The diversity of species decreases.
   - **E.** The fossil-laden rocks have younger fossils.

3. **T/I** What key idea did Darwin support from Thomas Malthus's *Essay on the Principles of Population*?
   - **A.** The surface of the Earth changes slowly and gradually over time.
   - **B.** Populations produced far more offspring than their environments could support.
   - **C.** The formation of the Galapagos Islands led to more species evolving.
   - **D.** All life descended from some unknown organism.
   - **E.** As organisms spread over different habitats, they develop adaptations.

4. **K/U** Which statement is **not** part of Darwin's theory of natural selection?
   - **A.** Individuals in a population vary extensively, and this variation is passed on to offspring.
   - **B.** Processes for change are slow and gradual.
   - **C.** Individuals that are better suited to local conditions survive to produce more offspring.
   - **D.** Organisms produce more offspring than can survive.
   - **E.** Individual organisms develop characteristics that they subsequently pass on to their offspring.

5. **T/I** What is true about functional similarity in anatomy?
   - **A.** It explains the diversity of the Galapagos finches.
   - **B.** It supports Lamarck's "line of descent" theory.
   - **C.** It occurs rarely in nature.
   - **D.** It shows that the species are closely related.
   - **E.** It does not mean that the species are closely related.

6. **T/I** Using the geological time scale, what is the correct order for the evolution of organisms from youngest to oldest?
   - **A.** first vertebrates, seed plants, birds, hominids
   - **B.** dinosaurs, hominids, bilateral invertebrate animals
   - **C.** mammals, insects, reptiles, shelled animals
   - **D.** flowering plants, reptiles, insects, multicellular eukaryotic organisms
   - **E.** eukaryotic cells, first vertebrates, seed plants, flowering plants

7. **K/U** What does the study of biogeography show?
   - **A.** The same species of plants and animals are found on different continents whenever the environment is the same.
   - **B.** The structure and function of organisms bear no relationship to the environment.
   - **C.** Barriers do not prevent the same species from spreading around the world.
   - **D.** One species can spread out and give rise to many species, each adapted to varying environments.
   - **E.** Geographically close environments are less likely to be populated by related species.

8. **K/U** What was the name of the southern supercontinent that broke apart about 150 million years ago?
   _____

9. **K/U** Describe an example of a vestigial structure.
   _____
   _____
   _____

10. **K/U** What is the name of the book in which Darwin presented the process of natural selection?
    _____

11. **K/U** Summarize the key points from Darwin's theory of natural selection.
    _____
    _____

12. **A** How could the work of Gregor Mendel helped Darwin explain parts of his theory of natural selection?
    _____

3. (A) Explain how the variety of finches found by Darwin in the Galapagos illustrates the process of evolution by natural selection.

_____

_____

_____

_____

woodpecker finch
(Cactospiza pallida)

small ground finch
(Geospiza fuliginosa)

cactus ground finch
(Geospiza scandens)

vegetarian tree finch
(Platyspiza crassirostris)

4. (T/I) List examples of how each field of science has contributed to our understanding of the process of evolution.

Field of Science	Examples
Fossils	
Biogeography	
Evidence from anatomy	
Evidence from embryology	
Evidence from DNA	

Self Study Guide

Question	If you answered this question incorrectly, see this Study Guide page for further review.	Question	If you answered this question incorrectly, see this Study Guide page for further review.
1	SG-120	8	SG-123
2	SG-120, SG-123	9	SG-125
3	SG-121	10	SG-121
4	SG-121	11	SG-121
5	SG-125	12	SG-70, SG-121
6	SG-123	13	SG-121
7	SG-123	14	SG-120, SG-121, SG-123, SG-125

Self Assessment

1. Which term describes the occurrence of small-scale changes in allele frequencies in a population?

   A. adaptive radiation   **B.** divergent evolution   **C.** gradualism

   D. microevolution   **E.** allopatric speciation

2. Which phrase best describes gene flow?

   A. introduction of new alleles into a population due to mutations

   B. random change in genetic variation from generation to generation due to chance

   C. net movement of alleles from one population to another

   D. caused by individuals selecting mates based on their phenotype

   E. the process that produces adaptive changes within populations

3. Which factor does not affect the relative frequencies of existing alleles?

   A. non-random mating   **B.** gene flow   **C.** genetic drift

   D. natural selection   **E.** mutation

4. The competition that occurs between the males in a caribou herd to mate with a female is an example of what mechanism of evolution?

   A. genetic drift   **B.** non-random mating   **C.** disruptive selection

   D. bottleneck effect   **E.** founder effect

5. Which is an example of the founder effect?

   A. loss of an allele in the F_2 generation of a flowering plant

   B. colonization of the Hawaiian and Galapagos Islands

   C. increase in the genetic diversity of a wolf population

   D. advantages for access to females eggs for different sizes of adult coho salmon

   E. courtship displays and mating behaviours of mallard ducks

6. What phenotypes does stabilizing selection favour?

   A. dominant phenotypes only

   B. the phenotypes at one extreme over the other

   C. intermediate phenotypes

   D. phenotypes at both extremes

   E. a range of phenotypes

7. Which is an example of a pre-zygotic isolating mechanism?

   A. chemical signals of insects

   B. production of a sterile hybrid offspring

   C. F_2 generation that is sterile or weak

   D. development of a polyploidy organism

   E. production of a hybrid offspring that does not survive

8 The production of a mule from a female horse and male donkey is an example of

   A. mechanical isolating mechanisms.

   B. gametic isolating mechanisms.

   C. hybrid breakdown.

   D. hybrid inviability.

   E. hybrid sterility.

9. In what group is sympatric speciation more common?

   A. animals   **B.** bacteria   **C.** fungi

   D. plants   **E.** protists

10. What type of speciation occurs when a population is split into two or more isolated groups by a geographical barrier?

   A. sympatric   **B.** allopatric   **C.** adaptive

   D. convergent   **E.** polyploidic

11. Which is an example of adaptive radiation?

   A. speciation of finches in Galapagos Islands

   B. hybridization of wheat

   C. near extinction of northern elephant seals

   D. inbreeding of purebred farm animals

   E. rapid increase in frequency of colour vision deficiency

12. The ability of spiders, silk moths, and weaver ants to produce silken threads is an examples of which phenomenon?

   A. gene flow   **B.** genetic drift   **C.** convergent evolution

   D. gradualism   **E.** divergent evolution

13. Which model describes evolutionary history as long periods of equilibrium that are interrupted by periods of divergence?

   A. genetic evolution   **B.** natural selection   **C.** gradualism

   D. punctuated equilibrium **E.** speciation

Self Study Guide

Question	If you answered this question incorrectly, see this Study Guide page for further review.	After completing your review, be sure to answer these questions in the Chapter 9 Practice Test.	Question	If you answered this question incorrectly, see this Study Guide page for further review.	After completing your review, be sure to answer these questions in the Chapter 9 Practice Test.
1	SG-132	6, 7	8	SG-136	4, 10
2	SG-132	1	9	SG-137	4, 12
3	SG-132, SG-133	1, 3	10	SG-136	4
4	SG-133, SG-135	3, 9	11	SG-139	7, 8, 13
5	SG-133	1, 2, 9	12	SG-139	13
6	SG-135	11	13	SG-137	6
7	SG-136	4, 10			

Key Terms

gene flow

non-random mating

genetic drift

founder effect

bottleneck effect

stabilizing selection

directional selection

disruptive selection

sexual selection

speciation

pre-zygotic isolating mechanism

sympatric speciation

allopatric speciation

ecological niche

adaptive radiation

divergent evolution

convergent evolution

gradualism

punctuated equilibrium

How Do Populations Evolve? (9.1)

Recall from Chapters 7 and 8:

- A population consists of all the members of a species that live in an area at a certain time. Each member has the genes that characterize the traits of the population, and these genes exist as pairs of alleles.

- All of the genes of the population's individuals make up the population's gene pool.

- Evolution occurs as a population's genes and their frequencies change over time.

- Natural selection favours some phenotypes over others, and causes populations and species to evolve over time. Individuals do not evolve.

The percentage of any specific allele in a gene pool is called the allele frequency. A population in which an allele frequency remains the same over generations is in a stable condition known as *genetic equilibrium*. A population that is in genetic equilibrium is not evolving in any way related to that gene. Any factor that affects the genes in the gene pool can change allele frequencies, disrupting a population's genetic equilibrium, and resulting in the process of microevolution.

Four agents, or causes, of evolutionary change are described below: mutations, gene flow, non-random mating, and genetic drift. A fifth agent, natural selection, is described on page SG-135.

Agents of Evolutionary Change	Illustration
Mutation • A mutation is a change that occurs in the DNA of an individual. • Mutations provide new alleles and therefore underlie all other mechanisms of evolution by producing variations, the raw material for evolutionary change. • Most mutations are harmful or even lethal to an individual and are quickly eliminated from the population's gene pool. • Occasionally a mutation results in a useful variation. Then the new gene becomes part of the population's gene pool. These heritable mutations have the potential to change the gene pool.	 30 black 25 black 5 grey
Gene Flow • **Gene flow** is the transfer of alleles from one population to another. • One or more individuals migrating into or out of a population may be responsible for a marked change in allele frequencies. • Individuals moving into a population may also add new alleles to the established gene pool of a population.	 20 grey 10 grey 10 black 20 black

Agents of Evolutionary Change	Illustration
Non-Random Mating • **Non-random mating** occurs when individuals select mates based on their phenotypes. • Inbreeding, or mating between relatives to a greater extent than by chance, is an example of non-random mating. • Inbreeding decreases the proportion of heterozygotes and increases the proportions of dominant and recessive homozygotes. • Inbreeding increases the frequency of inheriting recessive abnormalities.	
Genetic Drift – Founder Effect • **Genetic drift** refers to changes in the allele frequencies of a gene pool due to chance events. • The **founder effect** occurs when a few individuals found a colony. Because the founding group is so small, only a fraction of the total genetic diversity of the original population is represented. • The alleles carried by the founders are determined by chance alone.	20 grey 10 black → 1 grey 3 black
Genetic Drift – Bottleneck Effect • Sometimes a population becomes almost extinct because of a natural disaster or human interference. • The disaster acts a bottleneck, preventing the majority of genotypes from participating in the production of the next generation. • The alleles carried by the survivors are dictated by chance alone.	20 grey 10 black → 2 grey 3 black

Study Tip

Use **flash cards**. Write an agent of evolutionary change and its results on one side and draw a simple diagram on the other side to help remember details (**question 1**).

1. **K/U** Define or describe each term.

   a. gene pool _____

   _____

   b. allele frequency _____

   _____

   c. genetic equilibrium _____

   _____

   d. microevolution _____

   _____

2. **K/U a.** What role do mutations play in evolution?

   _____

   b. Describe what can happen to a mutation and the effects the mutation may have on a population.

   _____

   _____

   _____

3. **C** Draw a diagram to explain how genetic drift can shift a population's allele frequency in just a few generations.

4. **T/I** Compare and contrast the founder effect and the bottleneck effect.

   _____

   _____

   _____

5. **A** Many species of plants, such as the common pea plant, can self-pollinate.

   a. Which agent of evolution is likely to occur in plants that self-pollinate?

   _____

   b. Describe the impact self-fertilization can have on a population.

   _____

   _____

   _____

Evolution by Natural Selection (9.1)

In Chapters 7 and 8, you saw that the fittest members of a population survive to pass their traits on to offspring. Through this process of natural selection populations become adapted to their environment. Most traits on which natural selection acts are polygenic (controlled by more than one pair of alleles). In Chapter 6, you saw that polygenic traits, for example length of ears on corn plants, result in a range of phenotypes.

There are three types of natural selection.

Stabilizing Selection

- favours individuals near the middle of the range. Extreme phenotypes are selected against.
- results in a narrower phenotype range
- can improve adaptation to environmental factors that are constant

Directional Selection

- favours phenotypes at one end of the range
- results in a shifted range of phenotypes
- can occur as an adaptation to a changing environment

Disruptive Selection

- favours both extremes of the range. Tends to eliminate the intermediate phenotypes.
- can result in a split gene pool, and may result in the formation of new species

Sexual selection is not selection by the environment, but selection by mating partners. For example, males of some species compete for access to females. Females may prefer to mate with males with exaggerated phenotypic features, such as colourful feathers. Sexual selection is often powerful enough to produce features that are harmful to the individual's survival. For example, extravagant and colourful tail feathers or fins are likely to attract predators as well as interested members of the opposite sex.

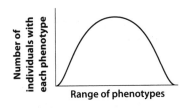

For polygenic traits, few individuals have extreme phenotypes. Most individuals have mid-range phenotypes.

Review the main points of the theory of evolution by natural selection on page SG-121 of this study guide.

Learning Check

1. **K/U** Identify whether each is an example of stabilizing, directional, or disruptive selection.

   a. a parrot population has only very large and very small tail feathers

   _____

   b. a population of ducks lays eggs of intermediate mass _____

   c. most individuals in a population of hummingbirds have long beaks

   _____

   d. a population includes only medium-sized spiders _____

   e. a population shifts from being mostly black moths to being mostly flecked

   moths _____

2. **T/I** Explain how sexual selection may affect the frequency of particular alleles in a population. Describe an example.

   _____

   _____

Study Tip

Draw simple **diagrams** (like the graph on this page) in your notes to help you remember a relationship.

Speciation (9.2)

A species is a group of interbreeding populations that share a gene pool and are isolated reproductively from other species. Populations of the same species exchange genes. Reproductive **isolating mechanisms** prevent different species from exchanging genes.

Pre-zygotic (pre-mating) Isolating Mechanisms	Example
Habitat isolation	Species in same area occupy different habitats.
Temporal isolation	Species reproduce at different seasons or different times of day, for example two similar species of crickets mate at different times of year.
Behavioural isolation	In animals, courtship behaviour differs, or they respond to different songs, calls, pheromones, or other signals.
Mechanical isolation	Genitalia are unsuitable for one another.
Gamete isolation	Sperm cannot reach or fertilize the egg.
Post-zygotic (post-mating) Isolating Mechanisms	**Example**
Hybrid inviability	Fertilization occurs but zygote does not survive, for example the offspring of a sheep and a goat.
Hybrid Sterility	Hybrid survives but is sterile and cannot reproduce, for example mules.
Hybrid Breakdown	First generation hybrid is fertile but the second generation hybrid has reduced fitness.

Whenever reproductive isolation develops, separate species have formed and speciation has occurred.

A new species can evolve when a population has been geographically isolated. This is called **allopatric speciation**.

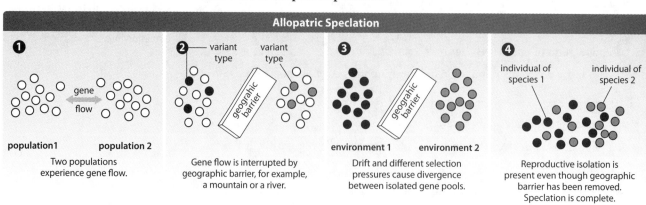

Allopatric Speciation

❶ population 1   population 2
Two populations experience gene flow.

❷ variant type   variant type
Gene flow is interrupted by geographic barrier, for example, a mountain or a river.

❸ environment 1   environment 2
Drift and different selection pressures cause divergence between isolated gene pools.

❹ individual of species 1   individual of species 2
Reproductive isolation is present even though geographic barrier has been removed. Speciation is complete.

In allopatric speciation, physical barriers develop and split the species into geographically separate populations.

In some cases a single population divides into two reproductively isolated groups without geographic isolation. This is known as **sympatric speciation**. It is more common in plants than it is in animals.

In one type of sympatric speciation, an error in meiosis results in polyploidy—having more than two sets of chromosomes. Polyploidy may result in immediate reproductive isolation as the number of chromosomes in the polyploid organism prevents it from successfully reproducing with others of its kind.

Speciation by Polyploidy: Example 2

If chromosomes do not separate properly during the first meiotic division in a plant, diploid (2*n*) gametes can be produced instead of normal haploid (*n*) gametes. ➡ If chromosomes do not separate properly during the first meiotic division in a plant, diploid (2*n*) gametes can be produced instead of normal haploid (*n*) gametes. ➡ Tetraploid plants may reproduce by self-pollination or by cross pollination with other tetraploid individuals.

Speciation by Polyploidy: Example 2

One plant is fertilized by pollen from a different species. ➡ The offspring is usually sterile because chromosomes are mismatched and cannot pair in meiosis. ➡ If there is a doubling of the chromosomes, meiosis is possible and fertility is restored. ➡ A new tetraploid (4*n*) species forms.

There are two theories about how quickly speciation occurs. Biologists generally agree that both the *gradualism* and *punctuated equilibrium* hypotheses can result in speciation depending on the circumstances.

1. The gradualism hypothesis states that evolution occurs at a slow, steady rate, with small, adaptive changes gradually accumulating over time in populations. Species originate through a gradual change of adaptations. Although much of the fossil record does not support this hypothesis, some fossil evidence does, such as the gradual evolution of sea lilies.

2. According to the punctuated equilibrium hypothesis, environmental changes lead to rapid changes in the gene pool of a small population that is reproductively isolated from the main population. Punctuated equilibrium is supported by fossil evidence.

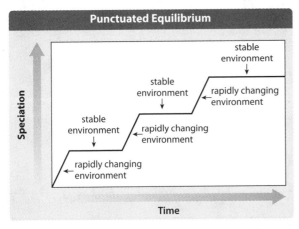

The *punctuated equilibrium* hypothesis states that speciation occurs relatively quickly, in rapid bursts separated by long periods of genetic equilibrium.

1. **K/U** For a species to remain distinct, it must remain reproductively isolated. Define the terms *pre-zygotic barrier* and *post-zygotic barrier* and give an example of each.

_____

_____

_____

2. **C** Draw a flow chart summarizing allopatric speciation.

3. **T/I a.** What is polyploidy?

_____

b. What causes polyploidy?

_____

c. Why is polyploidy much more common in plants than it is in animals?

_____

d. A tetraploid plant cannot produce viable seeds when crossed with a diploid plant from the original population. Why not?

_____

_____

Study Tip

Graphs are often used to show changes in science. Review **graph reading skills** on pages 638–641 of your textbook. Practise describing what a graph shows in your own words.

4. **C** Draw a graph to illustrate the gradualism hypothesis of evolution. Include a caption.

5. **C** Explain how this diagram can be used to illustrate the punctuated equilibrium hypothesis.

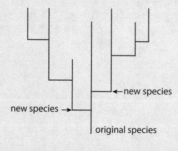

_____

_____

Adaptive Radiation (9.2)

Adaptive radiation is a form of allopatric speciation. It begins with a recent common ancestor and results in the formation of several new species. Each species exhibits different traits with which they can exploit an **ecological niche**. The cumulative effects of natural selection eventually make the populations in different environments so different from one another that interbreeding has become impossible.

Adaptive radiation occurs in a number of circumstances.

• When ancestral species colonize a new area, they can adapt to fill unexploited ecological niches. (Examples include Galapagos finches, Hawaiian *Drosophila*, Caribbean *Anolis* lizards, and cichlid fish).

• When one species becomes extinct, other species can adapt to fill their ecological niche. The new species may be favoured after an environmental change or because of a superior adaptation.

• The evolution of a new adaptation may allow a population to out-compete other groups or to exploit previously unexploited ecological niches.

Adaptive radiation is a type of **divergent evolution**, in which species that once were similar to an ancestral species become increasingly distinct, or diverge. Divergent evolution occurs when populations change as they adapt to different environmental conditions, eventually resulting in new species.

    Convergent evolution occurs when unrelated species occupy similar environments in different parts of the world. Since they share similar environmental pressures, they share similar pressures of natural selection and may evolve similar traits independently.

Turn to page 366 in your textbook to review how the finches of the Galapagos finches have adapted to gathering and eating different types of food.

Learning Check

1. **K/U** In Canada, there are about 25 species or subspecies of crossbills. Crossbills are birds that have twisted beaks allowing them to pry open closed conifer cones and eat the seeds. Different sized crossbills open different sized cones. Small-beaked crossbills feed primarily on softer larch cones; crossbills with a medium-sized bill feed on harder spruce cones; and heavy-beaked crossbills feed on tightly closed, and very hard pine cones.
   Use this example to explain divergent evolution.

   _____

   _____

   _____

   _____

Study Tip

Examples (question 1) can help you remember and understand why changes occur.

2. **A** Both bats and birds have wings and can fly, yet they have very different ancestors. Use this example to explain convergent evolution.

   _____

   _____

   _____

   _____

Human Activities and Speciation (9.2)

Extinction is a fact of life. Species are particularly vulnerable to extinction when they have small distributions, are declining in population size, lack genetic variability, or are harvested or hunted by humans.

The history of life on Earth includes many episodes of mass extinction in which many groups of organisms were wiped off the face of the planet. Normally, mass extinctions are followed by periods of adaptive radiation in which new species evolve to fill the empty niches.

In general, human activity does not affect rates of speciation. However, human alteration of the biosphere is currently causing a global mass extinction. Global diversity is dropping at an alarming rate.

Habitat loss is the single most important cause of species extinction. The reduction in habitat can occur in four different ways:
- a habitat can be completely removed or destroyed
- a habitat can become fragmented
- a habitat can be degraded or changed
- a habitat can become too frequently used by humans

Habitat destruction can create barriers to normal gene flow between split populations. The resulting small populations may become extinct if there is insufficient genetic diversity to permit adaptation to changing environmental conditions such as new diseases. Small populations with little genetic diversity are also subject to inbreeding, and the health problems associated with it.

Conservation and wildlife management programs must take into account the processes that affect gene pools to ensure that wild populations remain large enough and have sufficient genetic diversity to survive.

Study Tip

Make a note of **scientific terms** that you do not understand. Look them up in the **glossary** or in a previous section of your textbook or this study guide.

Learning Check

1. **C** Draw a flowchart showing one example of a human activity and the steps by which it leads (or led) to species loss. Use the giant panda, the grizzly bear, or a species of your choice. What could be changed at one or more points on the flowchart to change the outcome?

2. **T/I** What evidence is there to support the following statement: "Most biologists believe that Earth is currently faced with a mounting loss of species that threatens to rival the five great mass extinctions of the geological past. This new great mass extinction is primarily a human-caused event."

_____

_____

_____

_____

_____

Bringing It All Together

Complete this web diagram to summarize what you know about the mechanisms
and effects of speciation.

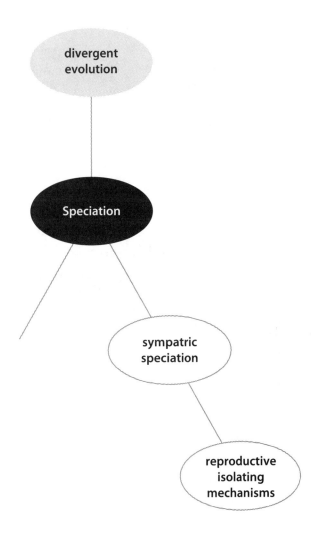

1. **K/U** Which phrase best describes genetic drift?
   A. individuals in a population selecting mates
   B. a change in allele frequencies due to two different interbreeding populations
   C. random change in genetic variation
   D. effects of the environment selecting certain individuals to survive
   E. introduction of new alleles into a population

2. **K/U** Which is a result of inbreeding?
   A. decrease in the frequency of homozygous genotypes
   B. decrease in the frequency of heterozygous genotypes
   C. increase in the frequency of homozygous genotypes
   D. increase in the frequency of heterozygous genotypes
   E. no change in the distribution of alleles

3. **K/U** Which favours the phenotypes at one extreme over the other?
   A. natural selection   B. directional selection
   C. disruptive selection   D. diversifying selection
   E. stablilizing selection

4. **K/U** Two species of North American garter snakes live in the same general region but in different habitats. What type of isolating mechanism is occurring in this case?
   A. gametic   B. mechanical
   C. behavioural   D. habitat
   E. temporal

5. **K/U** What is true about polyploid crop plants?
   A. They tend to be smaller.
   B. They have greater species diversity.
   C. They have only haploid gametes.
   D. They have fewer chromosomes.
   E. They can reproduce asexually.

6. **T/I** Which statement best describes Darwin's view of evolutionary change?
   A. a series of steps interrupted by periods of divergence
   B. a series of steps that lead to equilibrium
   C. slow and steady, before and after a divergence
   D. several rapidly changing steps, occurring after a divergence
   E. gradual change followed by a natural disaster

7. **K/U** Environmental influences create selective pressure, and result in
   A. positive and negative consequences.
   B. only positive consequences.
   C. only negative consequences.
   D. no changes to the population.
   E. mass extinctions every time.

8. **K/U** What is the most significant factor in the formation of a new species?
   _____

9. **K/U** List two examples of selective forces that can affect a population.
   _____
   _____

10. **K/U** What are the two types of reproductive isolating mechanisms that prevent gene flow between populations?
    _____

11. **T/I** **C** Identify the type of natural selection represented by each graph. Summarize what is occurring in each one.

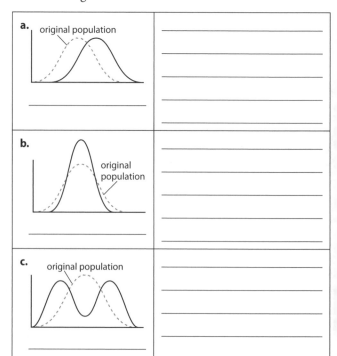

12. (C) Draw a series of diagrams to illustrate how a diploid parent cell could produce a tetraploid offspring.

13. (C) Compare divergent and convergent evolution.

_____

_____

_____

_____

_____

14. (T/I) What effects on speciation can occur when habitats are changed by human activities?

_____

_____

_____

_____

Self Study Guide

Question	If you answered this question incorrectly, see this Study Guide page for further review.	Question	If you answered this question incorrectly, see this Study Guide page for further review.
1	SG-133	8	SG-132
2	SG-133	9	SG-135
3	SG-135	10	SG-136, SG-137
4	SG-136	11	SG-135
5	SG-137	12	SG-137
6	SG-135	13	SG-139
7	SG-135	14	SG-140

Complete this concept map to summarize the factors that lead to evolution and the mechanisms by which they work.

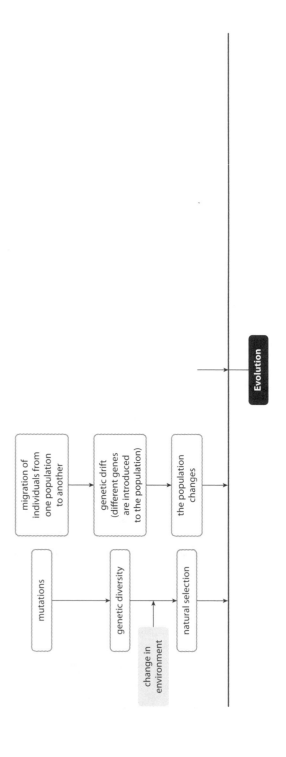

Unit 3 Practice Test

1. Which of the following is an example of a behavioural adaptation?
   - **A.** camouflage colouring of the stick insect
   - **B.** needle-sharp talons of an owl
   - **C.** compound eye of the honey bee
   - **D.** hibernation of ground squirrels
   - **E.** mimicry of other species by viceroy butterfly

2. Between 1848 and 1898, the population of black moths near Manchester England rose from two percent to ninety-five percent. What lead to this change in population?
   - **A.** behaviour of moths
   - **B.** introduction of predators
   - **C.** changing environmental conditions
   - **D.** behaviour, genetic make-up and introduction of predators
   - **E.** behaviour, genetic make-up and environmental factors

3. What must exist for natural selection to occur?
   - **A.** changing environmental conditions.
   - **B.** migration of new members into population.
   - **C.** diversity within a species.
   - **D.** increase in genetic mutations.
   - **E.** competition for resources.

4. An organism with many viable offspring has a
   - **A.** limited gene pool in the F_1 generation.
   - **B.** ability to quickly respond to environmental changes.
   - **C.** few predators in the environment.
   - **D.** high level of fitness.
   - **E.** high metabolic rate.

5. Natural selection is the mechanism that explains how
   - **A.** floods and volcanic eruptions lead to repopulating an area.
   - **B.** new species appear in the upper stratum of fossil sites.
   - **C.** parents pass on learned adaptations to the environment.
   - **D.** similar structural elements and origin can have a different function.
   - **E.** new species arise from ancestral species in response to the local environment.

6. In which period did mammals first appear?
   - **A.** Cambrian
   - **B.** Mesozoic
   - **C.** Triassic
   - **D.** Tertiary
   - **E.** Jurassic

7. What type of structures are the forearms of mammals?
   - **A.** vestigial
   - **B.** homologous
   - **C.** ohnologs
   - **D.** analogous
   - **E.** polygenetic

8. Which of the following is a vestigial structure found in humans?
   - **A.** vermiform appendix
   - **B.** pancreas
   - **C.** pelvic bone
   - **D.** gall bladder
   - **E.** calcaneus

9. What is the main effect of gene flow?
   - **A.** an increase in resistance to disease
   - **B.** a decrease in diversity
   - **C.** more homozygous individuals
   - **D.** a change in allele frequencies
   - **E.** an increased chance of extinction

10. Which phenotypes does directional selection favour?
    - **A.** both extremes
    - **B.** one extreme
    - **C.** intermediate
    - **D.** all
    - **E.** none

11. Which term describes the formation of a new species?
    - **A.** gradualism
    - **B.** genetic drift
    - **C.** founder effect
    - **D.** microevolution
    - **E.** macroevolution

12. Two populations live in the same geographic area and become reproductively isolated. What has occurred?
    - **A.** sympatic speciation
    - **B.** convergent evolution
    - **C.** punctuated equilibrium
    - **D.** allopatic speciation
    - **E.** directional selection

13. The speciation of Darwin's finches is an example of what phenomenon?
    - **A.** pre-zygotic isolating mechanism
    - **B.** non-random mating
    - **C.** adaptive radiation
    - **D.** sexual selection
    - **E.** convergent evolution

14. What is a mutagen?

_____

15. What theory suggests that geological processes operate at the same rates today as they did in the past?

_____
_____

16. What is gene flow?

_____

17. What type of natural selection is at work in each situation?

a. Trees in a windy area tend to remain the same size each year.

_____

b. The brain size of hominids steadily increases.

_____

c. The same species of moths tends to have blue stripes in opens areas and orange stripes in forested areas.

_____

18. Describe the main components of Darwin's theory of natural selection.

_____
_____
_____
_____

19. How does the study of biogeography support Darwin's and Wallace's observations. Give an example.

_____
_____
_____
_____

20. Many great thinkers supported Darwin's observations and lead to Darwin's formulation of the theory of evolution by natural selection. Complete the following chart.

Scientist	Theory/area of study	Summary
a.	Paleontology	
b. Lyell		
c. Lamarck		
c.	Natural selection	

21. Describe the impact of the founder effect on the gene pool of a population.

_____

_____

_____

22. Compare convergent and divergent evolution. Give examples.

_____

_____

_____

_____

23. Create a concept map to illustrate isolating mechanisms that can prevent gene flow between populations.

Self Study Guide

Question	If you answered this question incorrectly, see this Study Guide page for further review.	Question	If you answered this question incorrectly, see this Study Guide page for further review.
1	SG-106	13	SG-139
2	SG-108, SG-110	14	SG-108
3	SG-110	15	SG-120
4	SG-108	16	SG-132
5	SG-110	17	SG-135
6	SG-123	18	SG-110, SG-120
7	SG-123, SG-125	19	SG-123
8	SG-125	20	SG-120
9	SG-132	21	SG-132
10	SG-135	22	SG-136, SG-139
11	SG-136	23	SG-136, SG-140
12	SG-136		

Chapter 10 The Digestive System

Animals use energy released from carbohydrates, lipids, proteins, and nucleic acids—known as macromolecules—to perform metabolic functions. These macromolecules are broken down during the process of digestion. Water, vitamins, and minerals are also essential for metabolic functions.

The alimentary canal varies among animals. In general, herbivores have longer intestines than carnivores to accommodate their different diets.
As food moves through the human alimentary canal, it is processed in four stages.

1. Ingestion: takes place in the mouth.

2. Digestion: begins in the mouth and continues through the small intestine.

3. Absorption: takes place in the small and large intestines.

4. Elimination: takes place at the anus.

Physical digestion breaks food down into smaller pieces. In chemical digestion, enzymes and acids break macromolecules down into smaller molecules that can be absorbed through the cells that line the small intestine.

Several disorders such as peptic ulcers, hepatitis, and diabetes can affect the functioning of the digestive system. We have developed diagnoses and treatments for many of these diseases, and research is ongoing.

Chapter 11 The Respiratory System

Body cells need a constant supply of oxygen to carry out metabolic functions. The respiratory system is responsible for bringing oxygen into the body, delivering it to cells in all parts of the body, and carrying carbon dioxide away from the cells and out of the body.

Animals in different environments have a variety of types of respiratory systems. Fish obtain oxygen by passing water over gills, earthworms obtain oxygen through their skin, and insects have a network of branching tracheae that bring air close to all their body cells, where diffusion can occur.

In many animals, including humans, inhaling brings air into the lungs. Air travels through the nasal passages, pharynx, and larynx; into the bronchus; and through two bronchioles into two lungs protected by the ribs.

In the alveoli of the lungs, oxygen diffuses from the air into tiny capillaries. Oxygen-rich blood is then transported by the circulatory system to cells around the body. Carbon dioxide-rich blood is transported to the lungs, where the carbon dioxide diffuses from the capillaries into the air. The air is then released from the body by exhaling.

Some disorders of the respiratory system, such as pneumonia and bronchitis, can often be treated with antibiotics. For other disorders—including asthma, cystic fibrosis, and emphysema—treatments are used to relieve symptoms. Gene therapy is being explored as a cure for cystic fibrosis.

Chapter 12 The Circulatory System

In multi-celled animals, the circulatory system transports gases, nutrients, wastes, and other chemical substances from one part of the body to another. It also regulates body temperature and protects against blood loss and disease.

Vertebrates and other large complex animals have closed circulatory systems. A heart pumps blood into thick, elastic arteries, which carry the blood to small, thin capillaries. Materials diffuse from the capillaries into body cells and from body cells into the capillaries. Veins carry blood back to the heart.

Humans have a double circulatory system—the circulation of blood around the body (**systemic circulation**) is separate from the circulation of blood to the lungs (**cardiac circulation**). Separate chambers in the heart pump blood in each part of the system. To pump the blood, the SA node and the AV node (two areas of specialized tissue in the heart) emit electric signals that cause the cardiac muscle to contract and relax rhythmically. We experience this rhythmic pumping as a heartbeat. Valves in the heart and in the veins prevent blood from flowing backward.

Many factors can be measured to help monitor the health of the circulatory system, including electrical activity in the heart, blood pressure, stroke volume, and cardiac output.

Disorders of the circulatory system include arteriosclerosis, arrhythmias, congenital heart defects, stroke, hemophilia, and leukemia. Many common disorders can be prevented and controlled by lifestyle choices. Some, however, have other causes. Hemophilia is caused by a genetic sex-linked trait. Most causes of congenital heart defects are unknown.

Medical technology has brought some creative solutions to the treatment of circulatory system disorders, including angioplasty, bypass surgery, pacemakers, and xenotransplants.

CHAPTER 10

The Digestive System

Self Assessment

1. Which term refers to all of the chemical reactions that occur in an organism?

    A. essential nutrient   **B.** macromolecule   **C.** monosaccharide

    D. metabolism   **E.** enzyme

2. What is the main function of lipids?

    A. to provide quick energy for use by cells

    B. to store energy reserves for later use by cells

    C. to act as catalysts to speed up chemical reactions

    D. to direct an organism's growth

    E. to transport ions in cell membranes

3. What activity occurs during hydrolysis?

    A. Chemical bonds are formed, resulting in larger molecules.

    B. Catalysts increase the rate of the chemical reaction.

    C. Monomers separate into water and small molecules.

    D. Water is used to break macromolecules into smaller molecules.

    E. Water joins monomers into larger molecules.

4. What is the correct order of the four stages of food digestion?

    A. ingestion, digestion, absorption, elimination

    B. digestion, absorption, ingestion, elimination

    C. chemical digestion, absorption, elimination, ingestion

    D. absorption, ingestion, chemical digestion, elimination

    E. absorption, physical digestion, chemical digestion, ingestion

5. Which activity is an example of chemical digestion?

    A. muscular contractions of the intestinal wall

    B. churning and grinding of food by a gizzard

    C. glands releasing liquid and enzymes

    D. peristaltic contractions in the esophagus

    E. elimination of wastes through the anus

6. In humans, where does most chemical digestion occur?

    A. liver   **B.** stomach   **C.** mouth

    D. large intestine   **E.** small intestine

7. Which enzyme is produced in the stomach?

    A. pepsin   **B.** lactase   **C.** maltase

    D. chymotrypsin   **E.** amylase

8. What is the first region of the small intestine?

    A. alimentary canal   **B.** pancreas   **C.** jejunum

    D. ileum   **E.** duodenum

9. Tryspin functions best in an environment with which pH range?

    A. 2 to 4   **B.** 6 to 8   **C.** 8 to 10

    D. 10 to 12   **E.** 12 to 14

10. Which organ can supply the body with additional energy when needed?

    A. A. small intestine   **B.** liver   **C.** gall bladder

    D. pancreas   **E.** kidney

11. What is the primary cause of peptic ulcers?

    A. A. stress   **B.** lack of water   **C.** *E. coli* infections

    D. presence of *Helicobacter pylori*   **E.** loss of appetite

12. What is hepatitis?

    A. A sore in the lining of the duodenum.

    B. An accumulation of hard masses in gall bladder.

    C. The inability of pancreas to produce insulin.

    D. An inflammation of the intestines.

    E. An inflammation of the liver.

13. Which device helps surgeons examine the lining of the alimentary canal?

    A. stethoscope   **B.** nebulizer   **C.** endoscope

    D. sphygmomanometer   **E.** vascular stent

14. Type 1 diabetes occurs when

    A. the gall bladder is unable to produce bile.

    B. the liver produces more toxins than the body can cope with.

    C. a pregnant woman produces inadequate amounts of insulin.

    D. the body is unable to properly use the insulin it makes.

    E. the immune system destroys insulin-producing cells of the pancreas.

Self Study Guide

Question	If you answered this question incorrectly, see this Study Guide page for further review.	After completing your review, be sure to answer these questions in the Chapter 10 Practice Test.	Question	If you answered this question incorrectly, see this Study Guide page for further review.	After completing your review, be sure to answer these questions in the Chapter 10 Practice Test.
1	SG-152	1, 2, 3	8	SG-155	5
2	SG-152	3	9	SG-157	10
3	SG-152	3	10	SG-157	6
4	SG-154	5	11	SG-159	14
5	SG-157	8, 9, 10	12	SG-159	14
6	SG-157	13	13	SG-159	14
7	SG-157	6	14	SG-159	14

Key Terms

macromolecule

metabolism

essential nutrient

monosaccharide

disaccharide

polysaccharide

glycogen

lipid

amino acid

peptide bond

polypeptide

hydrolysis

enzyme

alimentary canal

mechanical digestion

chemical digestion

salivary glands

saliva

esophagus

peristalsis

gastric juice

chyme

pepsin

duodenum

villi

jejunum

ileum

bile

peptic ulcer

inflammatory bowel
disease

Crohn's disease

ulcerative colitis

hepatitis

cirrhosis

diabetes

Macromolecules and Essential Nutrients (10.1)

The human body uses complex organic molecules known as **macromolecules** (carbohydrates, lipids, proteins, and nucleic acids) to provide energy, to regulate cellular activities, and to build and repair tissues.

Carbohydrates provide short-term and long-term energy storage. **Monosaccharides** such as glucose and fructose, and **disaccharides** such as sucrose and lactose are small molecules and release energy quickly to the body. **Polysaccharides** are larger carbohydrates, and provide long-term energy storage.

Lipids (fats) are not soluble in water. They contain 2.25 times more energy per gram than other biological molecules. Some lipids store energy in our bodies and others protect cells from their environment.

Proteins are **polypeptides**—chains of linked **amino acids**. Proteins build and repair membranes and muscles, and serve as **enzymes** to help metabolic processes, and as antibodies to combat disease.

Before the body can use macromolecules, it breaks them down into molecules small enough to be absorbed by the cells. To do this it uses a process called hydrolysis, and digestive enzymes such as carbohydrase, lipase, and protease.

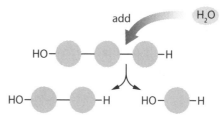

This simplified diagram shows how macromolecules are broken apart by hydrolysis. In this reaction, a molecule of water is added.

Specific digestive enzymes such as carbohydrase, lipase, and protease are also involved in hydrolysis reactions.

carbohydrates + carbohydrases + water → monosaccharide molecules

lipids + lipase + water → glycerol and fatty acids

proteins + protease + water → amino acid molecules

Minerals and vitamins are also essential nutrients. A few examples, with some of their functions, are listed below.

Vitamin or mineral	Function in the human body
Calcium	• forms bone, conducts nerve signals, contracts muscle, clots blood
Iron	• produces hemoglobin to transport oxygen in the blood
Magnesium	• supports enzyme function and is needed to produce protein
Vitamin A	• promotes good vision, and healthy skin and bones
Vitamin D	• helps absorb calcium and form bone
Vitamin E	• strengthens red blood cell membranes

Water makes up two-thirds of the mass of the human body. It is needed to:

transport nutrients

eliminate toxins and wastes

lubricate tissues and joints

regulate body temperature

perform many other functions

Learning Check

1. **K/U** List three macromolecule nutrients, a key function each one performs in the body, and a food that each one can be found in.

_____

_____

_____

2. **K/U** What two things are needed in the body to break macromolecules down using hydrolysis?

_____

_____

3. **K/U** Explain the role of three nutrients in the formation of healthy bones.

_____

_____

_____

4. **C** Use words or a diagram to show how two nutrients work together to perform a function in the body.

5. **A** Imagine you are training for a race.
   a. What nutrients would be important to consume in the weeks before the race? Why?

   _____

   b. What nutrients might you choose to consume just before the race or during the race? Why?

   _____

6. **A** Write one sentence to summarize the key information about nutrients in Section 10.1.

_____

_____

Obtaining and Processing Food (10.1)

Heterotrophs use a variety of mechanisms to obtain their food.

- Filter feeders, such as sponges, siphon water into their mouths and obtain small organisms to digest from this water.

- Substrate feeders, such as earthworms, live on their food and eat their way through it.

- Fluid feeders, such as spiders, suck or lick nutrient-rich liquids from plants or animals.

- Bulk feeders, such as humans, ingest large pieces of food and break it down inside their bodies.

Ingestion	Digestion	Absorption	Elimination
food is taken in	involves both physical breakdown of food, through motions such as chewing and chemical breakdown through hydrolysis	ifood is transported from the digestive system into the circulatory system which delivers the nutrients to the body cells	iundigested solid waste matter is removed from the body

Most animals digest their food in a long tube open at both ends, called the **alimentary canal**. As food moves along the tube, different parts of the digestive system process the food in different ways. The length of the digestive tract varies from animal to animal. Because the cellulose in plant cells is hard to digest, most herbivores have longer digestive tracts than carnivores, relative to their body size.

Learning Check

1. **K/U** Is each animal is a filter feeder, a substrate feeder, a fluid feeder, or a bulk feeder?

   a. dog

   _____

   b. snail

   _____

   c. clam

   _____

   d. honeybee

   _____

2. **K/U** Name the part(s) of the alimentary canal where each part of the digestive process occurs. Refer to page 408 in your textbook for help.

   a. ingestion

   _____

   b. digestion

   _____

   c. absorption

   _____

3. **A** Compare and contrast the digestive tract of a mouse (herbivore) and a cat (carnivore).

   _____

   _____

Study Tip

Look for **patterns** as you read, and predict how new information will fit into the patterns that you find. For example, there are patterns in the digestive systems of many animals. Thinking about how the human digestive system will fit into those patterns will help you understand and remember what you will learn in Section 10.2.

Organs in the Human Digestive System (10.2)

1. In the mouth, three pairs of **salivary glands** secrete **saliva** to begin the chemical digestion of food. The tongue and teeth work together to chew your food (physically digest it), and the tongue pushes it into the esophagus.

2. A series of wavelike muscular contractions in the esophagus, called **peristalsis**, transports the food into the stomach.

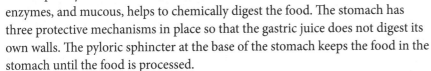
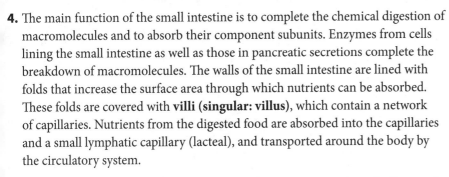

3. Three layers of muscle fibres in the stomach contract and relax to break down the food and mix it with gastric juice. The **gastric juice**, made up of hydrochloric acid, salts, enzymes, and mucous, helps to chemically digest the food. The stomach has three protective mechanisms in place so that the gastric juice does not digest its own walls. The pyloric sphincter at the base of the stomach keeps the food in the stomach until the food is processed.

To learn more about how the stomach protects itself from gastric juice, see page 413 of your textbook.

4. The main function of the small intestine is to complete the chemical digestion of macromolecules and to absorb their component subunits. Enzymes from cells lining the small intestine as well as those in pancreatic secretions complete the breakdown of macromolecules. The walls of the small intestine are lined with folds that increase the surface area through which nutrients can be absorbed. These folds are covered with **villi (singular: villus)**, which contain a network of capillaries. Nutrients from the digested food are absorbed into the capillaries and a small lymphatic capillary (lacteal), and transported around the body by the circulatory system.

5. Secretions from the liver and pancreas help digestion. Ducts from the liver and pancreas join to form one duct that enters the duodenum. The liver produces **bile** and bile salts, which are stored in the gall bladder. Bile emulsifies fat—emulsification physically breaks the fat into tiny droplets, increasing the surface area for chemical digestion. The pancreas produces enzymes and bicarbonate, which raises the pH level so the enzymes can function efficiently.

6. After the nutrients have been absorbed, the remaining material moves into the large intestine, where water is absorbed into the body, and the material is broken down further to form feces.

7. Feces are stored in the rectum and eliminated through the anus.

1. **K/U** Label the organs in the digestive system.

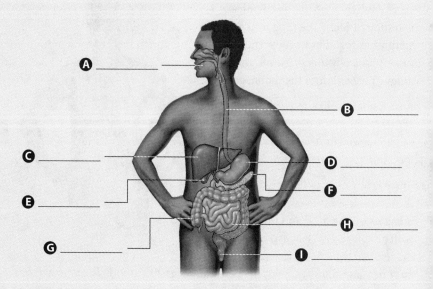

2. **K/U** Name two organs that help break up food physically. How do they help?

_____

3. **K/U** This structure appears in the small intestine. Add labels to the diagram.

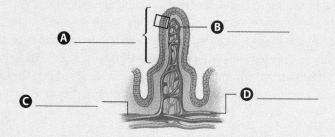

4. **A** In what ways might a person's digestion change if they had part of their liver removed? Why?

_____

_____

5. **T/I** **a.** Name two parts of the digestive system in which absorption occurs.

_____

b. What role does surface area play in this part of the digestive system?

_____

c. Describe something you are familiar with outside the human body where a large surface area helps absorption.

_____

_____

Chemical Digestion and Absorption (10.2)

The digestive secretions from the mouth, stomach, small intestine, liver, and pancreas contribute mucus, water, bile, and enzymes. Chemical digestion is carried out by protein molecules called enzymes. Enzymes specialize in breaking down one type of molecule. Different enzymes are effective at different pH levels and are active in different organs of the digestive system. In the equations below, the enzyme that breaks down each nutrient is shown above the arrow.

In the mouth (pH is about 7):

$$\text{starch, glycogen} \xrightarrow{\text{salivary amylase}} \text{maltose (a disaccharide)}$$

(NOTE: Both starch and glycogen are long chains of glucose molecules and can be digested by the same enzyme.)

In the stomach (pH is about 2):

$$\text{protein} \xrightarrow{\text{pepsin}} \text{peptides}$$

In the small intestine (pH is about 8):

$$\text{starch, glycogen} \xrightarrow{\text{pancreatic amylase}} \text{maltose}$$

$$\text{sucrose} \xrightarrow{\text{sucrase}} \text{glucose} + \text{fructose}$$

$$\text{maltose} \xrightarrow{\text{maltase}} \text{glucose}$$

$$\text{lactose} \xrightarrow{\text{lactase}} \text{glucose} + \text{galactose}$$

$$\text{lipids} \xrightarrow{\text{pancreatic lipase}} \text{fatty acids} + \text{glycerol}$$

$$\text{small polypeptides} \xrightarrow{\text{trypsin, chymotripsin}} \text{smaller peptides}$$

$$\text{peptides} \xrightarrow{\text{peptidases}} \text{smaller peptides} + \text{amino acids}$$

Absorption

Monosaccharides are absorbed into the circulatory system and transported to the liver, where they are converted to glucose. The glucose is transported to body cells, which use it for energy. The liver converts extra glucose to glycogen, and stores it temporarily.

Many amino acids are also transported by the circulatory system to the liver, where they are converted into sugars, which can be used for energy. Some amino acids are transported to body cells and used to build enzymes and other proteins, such as keratin. The liver converts waste amino acids to urea, which exits the body in urine.

Glycerol and fatty acids are absorbed into the cells of the small intestine, reassembled to form triglycerides, and coated with protein to make them water soluble. They then pass into the circulatory system, and are broken down again. The resulting glycerol and fatty acids are either used as energy or stored.

Examine **root words** and **suffixes** to draw connections between new terms. You will notice that sugar names often end with the same suffix, as do many enzyme names.

1. **K/U** Where do most of the enzyme reactions related to digestion occur?

_____

2. **K/U** Name an enzyme that helps break down each nutrient.
   a. sucrose _____
   b. lipid _____
   c. protein _____
   d. glycogen _____

3. **K/U** Why is it necessary to break down macromolecules before they are absorbed in the small intestine?

_____

4. **T/I** Why is protein broken down mostly in the stomach?

_____

5. **K/U** Chemical digestion partially breaks down macromolecules before they are absorbed in the small intestine. Give examples of how the resulting smaller molecules are further broken down after absorption.

_____

6. **A** What might be the consequences if a person has their pancreas removed? Why?

_____

7. **C** Complete this table to compare the chemical digestion of carbohydrates, proteins, and lipids.

	Carbohydrates	Proteins	Lipids
Organ(s) in which chemical digestion takes place			
Enzymes involved			
End products			
Function(s) in body			

Digestive System Disorders (10.3)

Digestive system disorders can occur when any part of the digestive system is not working properly.

For more information about endoscopes, see page 422 of your textbook.

Disorders of the Digestive Tract

	Description	Causes	Treatment
Peptic ulcer	• a sore in lining of stomach or duodenum • an endoscope inserted into the digestive tract will show the ulcer	• protective coating of the stomach is weakened, often because *Helicobacter pylori* attach to lining	• antibiotics • lifestyle changes such as losing weight, quitting smoking, and avoiding alcohol
Inflammatory Bowel Disease	• chronic inflammation that causes pain and prevents food from being absorbed adequately • **Crohn's Disease** can affect any part of the alimentary canal • children may not grow properly during adolescence • **ulcerative colitis** affects the colon and can cause loose, bloody stools, cramping, and abdominal pain.	• not completely understood • environmental, dietary, and genetic causes may be involved	• anti-inflammatory medication • it is sometimes necessary to remove part of the digestive tract
Constipation	• infrequent bowel movements and dry stools that are difficult to pass	• inadequate water intake • lack of good nerve or muscle function • unhealthy diet	• dietary changes including eating more fibre and drinking more liquids

Disorders of Accessory Organs

	Description	Causes	Treatment
Hepatitis	• inflammation of the liver, usually caused by a virus • can lead to cirrhosis	• drinking contaminated water (hepatitis A) • sexual contact with infected person (hepatitis B) • contact with infected blood (hepatitis C)	• there are vaccines for hepatitis A and B • hepatitis C may be treatable with medication
Cirrhosis	• scar tissue replaces healthy liver tissue and prevents the liver from functioning properly	• chronic alcoholism and hepatitis C are the most common causes	• in many cases the liver can heal itself • if liver failure occurs, a liver transplant is needed
Diabetes	• glucose is unable to enter body cells due to lack of insulin • in Type 1, the body cannot produce insulin • in Type 2, the body produces too little insulin or cannot use the insulin it makes	• Type 2 diabetes is associated with age, weight, family history, and is more common in some ethnic groups than others	• controlling blood sugar levels by controlling diet or by injecting insulin

Diabetes has become more common in Canada because of increasingly sedentary lifestyles and an ageing population. For more information about the variety of treatments available, see pages 423–425 of your textbook.

Learning Check

1. (K/U) Describe a disorder that affects each part of the digestive system.

a. small intestine _____

_____

_____

b. colon _____

_____

_____

c. liver _____

_____

_____

2. (T/I) List three advantages of using an endoscope instead of performing surgery to diagnose a problem in the digestive tract.

_____

_____

_____

3. (A) Why is it important to prevent hepatitis?

_____

4. (A) **a.** Why would removing part of the colon be a last resort in treating ulcerative colitis?

_____

_____

_____

b. How would removing part of the colon affect a person's digestion?

_____

_____

Study Tip

As you read, make links to other things you have read, and to things you have learned in other ways, as in **question 4**. The more knowledge you can link together, the more useful it will be to you.

Bringing It All Together

Complete this web to summarize what you know about the digestive system.

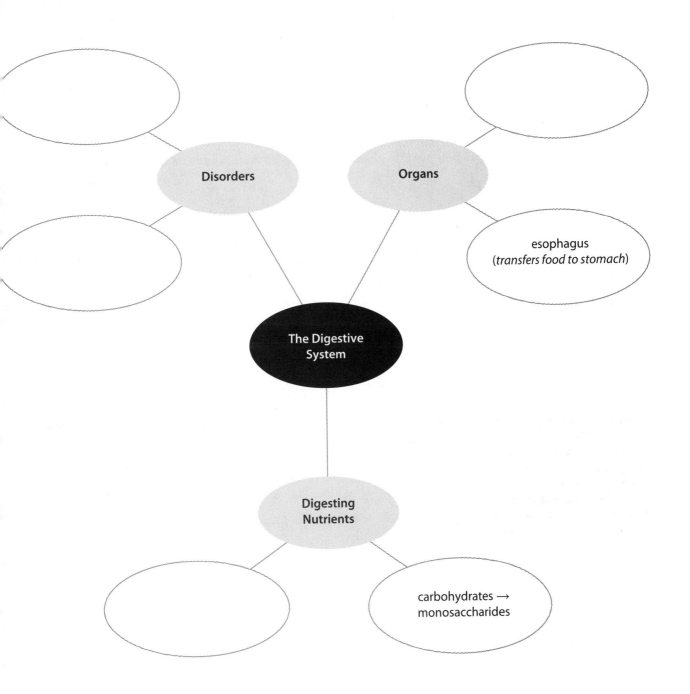

1. **(K/U)** Carbohydrates are composed of which elements?
   A. carbon, hydrogen, and sulfur
   B. carbon, hydrogen, and oxygen
   C. hydrogen, sulfur, and nitrogen
   D. carbon, oxygen, and nitrogen
   E. oxygen, sulfur, and nitrogen

2. **(K/U)** Which substance is an example of a disaccharide?
   A. lactose
   B. fructose
   C. glucose
   D. glycogen
   E. starch

3. **(K/U)** What are the end products of the hydrolysis of a lipid?
   A. simple sugars
   B. glycerol and fatty acids
   C. amino acids
   D. nucleotides
   E. monosaccharides

4. **(K/U)** What method do baleen whales use to obtain their food?
   A. substrate feeding
   B. bulk feeding
   C. fluid feeding
   D. filter feeding
   E. parasitic relationships

5. **(K/U)** The pyloric sphincter is located between
   A. the pharynx and the esophagus.
   B. the esophagus and the duodenum.
   C. the esophagus and the stomach.
   D. the stomach and the duodenum.
   E. the stomach and the jejunum.

6. **(K/U)** Which organ produces bile?
   A. kidney
   B. pancreas
   C. gall bladder
   D. liver
   E. salivary glands

7. **(K/U)** Insulin regulates the
   A. physical breakdown of lipids.
   B. production of gastric juice.
   C. absorption of glucose.
   D. release of hydrolytic enzymes.
   E. chemical breakdown of carbohydrates.

8. **(K/U)** Where is nuclease produced?
   _____

9. **(K/U)** Name an enzyme that can break down each macronutrient.
   a. protein _____
   b. a lipid _____
   c. a monosaccharide _____
   d. sucrose _____
   e. starch _____

10. **(K/U)** List two factors that can affect enzyme action.
    _____
    _____

11. **(K/U)** Why are the pancreas and the gall bladder considered to be accessory glands of digestion?
    _____
    _____
    _____

12. **(T/I) (A)** Explain how water is important to athletes.
    _____
    _____
    _____
    _____

3. T/I A Describe how starch is digested and absorbed by the body.

_____

_____

_____

4. T/I A Describe how recent advancements in genetic engineering have helped treat patients with diabetes. What are the advantages of this method?

_____

_____

_____

_____

_____

_____

Self Study Guide

Question	If you answered this question incorrectly, see this Study Guide page for further review.
1	SG-152
2	SG-152
3	SG-152
4	SG-154
5	SG-155
6	SG-154
7	SG-154
8	SG-157
9	SG-157
10	SG-157
11	SG-155, SG-157
12	SG-157, SG-158
13	SG-152, SG-157
14	SG-159

CHAPTER 11

The Respiratory System

Self Assessment

1. What is the process by which air enters and leaves the lungs?

   A. external respiration   **B.** internal respiration   **C.** gas exchange

   D. breathing   **E.** cellular respiration

2. What is the movement of air or water over a respiratory surface?

   A. cellular respiration   **B.** ventilation   **C.** gas exchange

   D. internal respiration   **E.** breathing

3. What structure allows oxygen to enter an insect's body?

   A. gills   **B.** windpipe   **C.** tracheae

   D. skin   **E.** spiracles

4. How does the ribcage move during inhalation?

   A. up and out as the diaphragm moves down

   B. down and in as the diaphragm moves down

   C. down and in as the diaphragm moves upward

   D. up and out as the diaphragm moves upward

   E. up and in as the diaphragm moves upward

5. What is the maximum volume of air that can be moved into and out of the lungs during a single breath?

   A. inspiratory reserve volume

   B. expiratory reserve volume

   C. tidal volume

   D. vital capacity

   E. residual volume

6. Which structure is the entrance to the windpipe?

   A. glottis   **B.** larynx   **C.** pharynx

   D. epiglottis   **E.** bronchiole

7. In which structure does gas exchange occur?

   A. intercostals   **B.** alveoli   **C.** bronchi

   D. bronchioles   **E.** diaphragm

8. What is external respiration?

   A. The action of drawing oxygen-rich air into the lungs.

   B. The action of releasing waste air from the lungs.

   C. A series of energy-releasing chemical reactions that take place within the cells.

   D. The exchange of oxygen and carbon dioxide between the inhaled air and the blood.

   E. The exchange of oxygen and carbon dioxide between the blood and the body's tissue cells.

9. What component of blood plasma is used to transport most of the oxygen used during respiration?

A. bicarbonate ion   **B.** hydrogen ion   **C.** fibrinogen

D. hemoglobin   **E.** water

10. In what form is most carbon dioxide transported in the blood?

A. bicarbonate ions   **B.** hemoglobin   **C.** carbonic acid

D. carbaminohemoglobin   **E.** hydrogen ions

11. What common throat ailment causes inflammation of the voice box?

A. tonsillitis   **B.** laryngitis   **C.** bronchitis

D. asthma   **E.** emphysema

12. Which disease can be treated with antibiotics?

A. viral pneumonia   **B.** asthma   **C.** acute bronchitis

D. chronic bronchitis   **E.** emphysema

13. What is the most common cause of emphysema?

A. bacterial infection   **B.** viral infection   **C.** allergic reaction

D. yeasts   **E.** smoking

14. What is the name for cancer cells that spread from their original site?

A. carcinomas   **B.** lymphatic cells   **C.** epithelial cells

D. abscesses   **E.** metastatic cells

15. Which technology has been used to vaporize tumors and seal small holes in airways and blood vessels?

A. TPM (two-photon microscopy)

B. YAG (yttrium aluminum garnet) laser

C. chemotherapy

D. radiation therapy

E. high-resolution CT scan

Self Study Guide

Question	If you answered this question incorrectly, see this Study Guide page for further review.	After completing your review, be sure to answer these questions in the Chapter 11 Practice Test.	Question	If you answered this question incorrectly, see this Study Guide page for further review.	After completing your review, be sure to answer these questions in the Chapter 11 Practice Test.
1	SG-167	13	9	SG-170	10
2	SG-166	2, 8	10	SG-170	10, 13
3	SG-167	8	11	SG-171	14
4	SG-168	1	12	SG-171	14
5	SG-168	3	13	SG-171	14
6	SG-168	6	14	SG-171	14
7	SG-168	6, 7	15	SG-171	14
8	SG-167	1, 2, 13			

Key Terms

respiratory system

respiration

inspiration

expiration

gas exchange

ventilation

diffusion gradient

diaphragm

spirograph

tidal volume

inspiratory reserve volume

expiratory reserve volume

vital capacity

residual volume

pharynx

trachea

glottis

larynx

bronchus

pleural membrane

bronchiole

alveolus

hemoglobin

tonsillitis

laryngitis

pneumonia

bronchitis

asthma

emphysema

cystic fibrosis

carcinoma

computed axial tomography (CAT or CT)

two-photon microscopy

bronchoscopy

Study Tip

As you study different respiratory systems, look for **patterns** such as common purpose, and different ways animals have adapted to their environment.

Respiratory Systems of Animals in Aquatic or Moist Environments (11.1)

The main function of a **respiratory system** is to bring oxygen into the body and make it available to the cells that need it. As well, this system must ensure that carbon dioxide can leave each cell and be removed from the body. Almost all animals need oxygen to carry out cellular **respiration**. All respiratory systems include a large, moist area for the exchange of oxygen and carbon dioxide, and a method of moving oxygen (dissolved in water or air) over that area.

- Some animals, like earthworms, use their entire outer surface for **gas exchange**. Oxygen diffuses into capillaries, and carbon dioxide diffuses out. These animals must live in damp or aquatic environments to keep their entire surface moist enough for this gas exchange to occur.

- Many aquatic organisms take in oxygen through gills, specialized folds in the body surface. Most fish take in water through their mouths and pump it over their gills. Clams use cilia to move water over their gills.

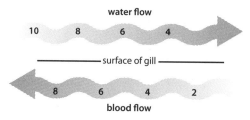

As water flows over gills in one direction, blood flows within the gills in the opposite direction. At every point along the surface of the gill the oxygen concentration is higher in the water than it is in the blood, so oxygen flows into the blood. (Oxygen concentrations on the diagram are in mg/L.)

Learning Check

1. What is the main purpose of the respiratory system in any animal?

_____

2. The diagram above shows oxygen diffusion in fish gills. Draw a diagram to show the concentrations of carbon dioxide as it diffuses from blood to water.

3. Give two reasons why humans are unable to perform all of our gas exchange through our skin.

_____

_____

Respiratory Systems of Land Animals (11.1)

Land animals have different types of respiratory systems.

Insects have a system of branching respiratory tubes (spiracles and tracheae) that connect body cells directly with the environment. Oxygen enters the body through spiracles and diffuses into tracheae. Gas exchange occurs throughout the body, close to all body cells. Carbon dioxide exits the body in the opposite direction.

Large active land animals, such as mammals and birds, require more oxygen than could be delivered by tracheal systems. They use muscles to draw air into lungs, where gas exchange takes place across a large moist surface.

A muscular **diaphragm** and the rib muscles work together to expand the lungs, which draws air in through the trachea. As the rib muscles and diaphragm relax, the lungs get smaller and expel air through the trachea. This breathing process is controlled by the brain.

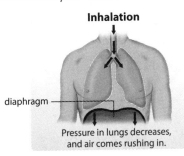

Inhalation

diaphragm

Pressure in lungs decreases, and air comes rushing in.

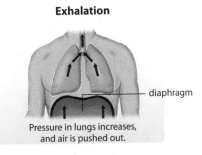

Exhalation

diaphragm

Pressure in lungs increases, and air is pushed out.

In inhalation, the diaphragm moves down, and the rib cage moves up and out increasing the volume in the chest cavity. This decreases air pressure in the chest cavity, the lungs expand and air moves in. In exhalation, the diaphragm and rib cage move back to their original positions decreasing the volume in the chest cavity. This increases the air pressure inside the lungs, and air moves from the lungs to the lower-pressure environment outside of the body

A **spirograph** can be used to measure how much air a person can inhale and exhale.

For more information about using spirographs see page 448 of your textbook.

Learning Check

1. **C** Construct a Venn diagram to compare the respiratory system of an insect and of a mammal.

Study Tip

Some information is stated in the written text. Using **inference**, or putting clues together, (**question 3**) will help you learn even more.

2. **K/U a.** What is the advantage of using muscles to draw air in and out of the lungs?

_____

   b. Why would this be important to a large land animal?

_____

3. **T/I** A spirograph can measure the volume of air the lungs can take in beyond what is inhaled in a normal breath (**inspiratory reserve volume**). What might a low inspiratory reserve volume tell you about a person's health?

_____

The Human Respiratory System (11.2)

Humans have developed a respiratory tract that transports warm, moist, clean air to our lungs deep within our bodies.

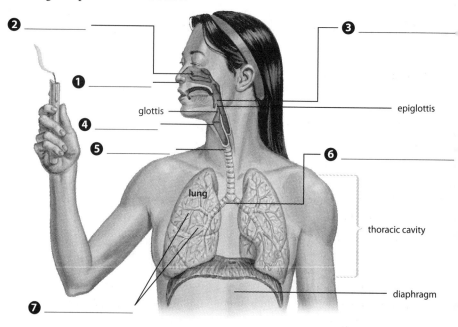

1. Air enters the respiratory system through the nostrils or the mouth.

2. Inside the nasal passages air is warmed and moistened. Cilia cleanse it of dust.

3. The warm, moist air passes through the **pharynx** into the **glottis** and the larynx. The epiglottis closes when you swallow to keep food from entering the glottis.

4. Air passing through the **larynx** produces sound—your voice.

5. The flexible **trachea** is strengthened and held open with rings of cartilage.

6. Two **bronchi** carry air from the trachea to the lungs.

7. Air travels through microscopic **bronchioles** to 50 million tiny sacs called **alveoli** in the lungs, where gas exchange occurs. Each alveolus is surrounded by a network of capillaries. The walls of the alveolus and of the capillaries are only one cell thick, and gases can diffuse easily between them.

Learning Check

1. **K/U** Add the missing labels to the diagram above.
2. **A** This tissue is found inside the lung.

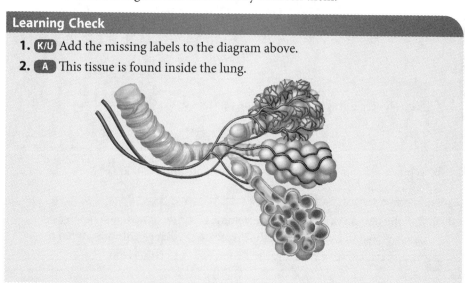

a. What are the clusters of sacs in the diagram on the previous page called?

_____

b. What microscopic tubes carry air into and out of the sacs?

_____

c. What are the net-like structures around the sacs?

_____

d. Why are there so many small sacs in our lungs?

_____

_____

3. **T/I** The nasal passages contain a dense network of capillaries, but gas exchange does not take place there. What function might this network serve?

_____

_____

4. **K/U** Some components of the human digestive system play a role in the respiratory system as well. What are the components, and what additional roles does each one serve?

_____

_____

_____

5. **C** Draw a flowchart tracing the structures that air travels through as you exhale. Start your flowchart with the alveoli.

Study Tip

A **flowchart** (**question 5**) is a clear, concise way to show steps in a process. It is also a useful visual reference when studying for a test.

Gas Exchange and Transport in Humans (11.2)

Cross-section of lung tissue

During external respiration, oxygen and carbon dioxide diffuse between the air in the alveoli and the blood in the capillaries that surround the alveoli.

The blood entering the lungs has carried its oxygen to other parts of the body, and now has little oxygen dissolved in it. It has picked up carbon dioxide from body cells and has a high concentration of carbon dioxide. In the alveoli, oxygen diffuses from the air (where the concentration is high) into the blood. Carbon dioxide diffuses from the blood into the air.

In blood, almost all the oxygen is carried attached to molecules of **hemoglobin**.

When the oxygenated blood reaches body cells, internal respiration occurs. Cells have been using oxygen to generate energy, and now have a low concentration of oxygen. They have a high concentration of carbon dioxide.

In blood, most of the carbon dioxide is carried as dissolved bicarbonate ions (HCO_3^-).

$$CO_2 \quad + \quad H_2O \quad \rightarrow \quad H_2CO_3 \quad \rightarrow \quad H^+ \quad + \quad HCO_3^-$$

Carbon dioxide   Water   Carbonic acid   Hydrogen ions   Bicarbonate

Learning Check

1. **K/U**

   a. This diagram shows internal respiration—gas exchange between capillaries and body cells. Draw arrows on the diagram to show the direction(s) in which oxygen and carbon dioxide travel.

Cross-section of muscle tissue

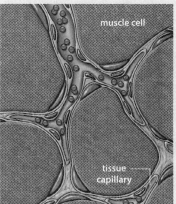

muscle cell

tissue capillary

   b. Why is internal respiration necessary?

   _____

   _____

2. **A** Imagine a person enters an environment where the concentration of oxygen is very low. How might that affect their respiratory process?

   _____

   _____

3. **A** Think back to Chapter 10. What essential nutrient can help ensure that our cells get the oxygen they need? How does this nutrient help?

   _____

   _____

   _____

Study Tip

Details are easier to remember if you can keep the big picture in mind. **Question 3** points out one connection between the respiratory system and the digestive system. When you learn something new, try to **connect** it to something you already know.

Respiratory System Disorders (11.3)

Many disorders of the respiratory system can be caused by changes in the external environment as well as lifestyle choices.

Disorder	Description	Cause	Treatment
Pneumonia	• alveoli fill with thick fluid, making gas exchange difficult • can affect one or both lungs	• bacterial infection (including *Streptococcus pneumoniae*) • viral infection	• antibiotics or anti-viral medications. • a vaccine is available for bacterial pneumonia
Bronchitis	• bronchi become red and inflamed • coughing brings up mucus • in chronic bronchitis, cilia lining the bronchi may be destroyed, which limits the lungs' ability to clear mucus • chronic bronchitis is a chronic obstructive lung disease (COPD)	• bacterial infection • prolonged exposure to dust, chemicals, or cigarette smoke can cause chronic bronchitis	• antibiotics (short-term bronchitis) • chronic bronchitis cannot be cured, but can be treated by quitting smoking, taking medications, and exercising
Asthma	• airways become inflamed and bronchioles constrict, making it difficult for air to pass • wheezing, coughing, and shortness of breath occur	• inhaled irritants, such as pollen, dust, and smoke can cause an asthma attack in some people	• can be managed by using an inhaler to inhale medication in mist or powder form. • the medication relaxes the muscles around the airways
Emphysema	• alveoli lose elasticity, burst and fuse into enlarged spaces, reducing surface area for gas exchange, and making it difficult to get enough oxygen • a chronic obstructive lung disease (COPD)	• smoking is the main cause	• no known cure • symptoms can be relieved by using an inhaler to open airways and a slow-flow oxygen tank to boost the supply of oxygen to the body
Cyctic fibrosis	• thick mucus in the lungs results in inflammation, infection due to trapped bacteria, and damage to lung tissues	• a gene mutation causes cells lining the airways to release thick mucus • also causes ducts in the pancreas to be blocked	• gene therapy is being explored • symptoms can be treated with medicine that thins the mucus and with antibiotics
Lung cancer	• uncontrolled cell growth and division causes cells to form a carcinoma • cancerous cells can break away and spread cancer to other organs	• smoking is the main cause • other causes include pollutants, radon gas, and asbestos	• radiation and chemotherapy to destroy the cancerous cells • surgery or laser surgery to remove tumours

For more details about the treatment of the disorders in this table, see pages 455–459 of your textbook.

Diagnosing respiratory system disorders can be difficult, since the respiratory system is located deep within the body.

- In **computed axial tomography** (CT scan), an X-ray device rotates around the body while it records images to produce a three-dimensional picture of the body's interior.

- In **two-photon microscopy**, special microscopes emit photons that penetrate body tissue, and images of the interior of tissue can be made. A fluorescent marker can be added to the tissue to target a particular point in the sample.

- In **bronchoscopy**, a special type of endoscope is used to examine the trachea and lungs. Doctors can also use bronchoscopy to take samples of mucus and tissue.

1. **K/U** Create a table to describe symptoms, causes, and treatment for laryngitis and tonsillitis. Refer to the information on page 455 in your textbook.

2. **K/U** List two technologies a doctor might use to diagnose each disorder.
   a. asthma

   _____

   b. cystic fibrosis

   _____

   c. lung cancer

   _____

3. **T/I** **C** Draw a cause-and-effect map to show one cause of emphysema and several of its effects.

Study Tip

Cause-and-effect maps (**question 3**) are good ways to show what causes something to happen. Like flowcharts, they are also useful visual references when you study for a test.

Bringing It All Together

Add to this web diagram to summarize what you have learned about the respiratory system.

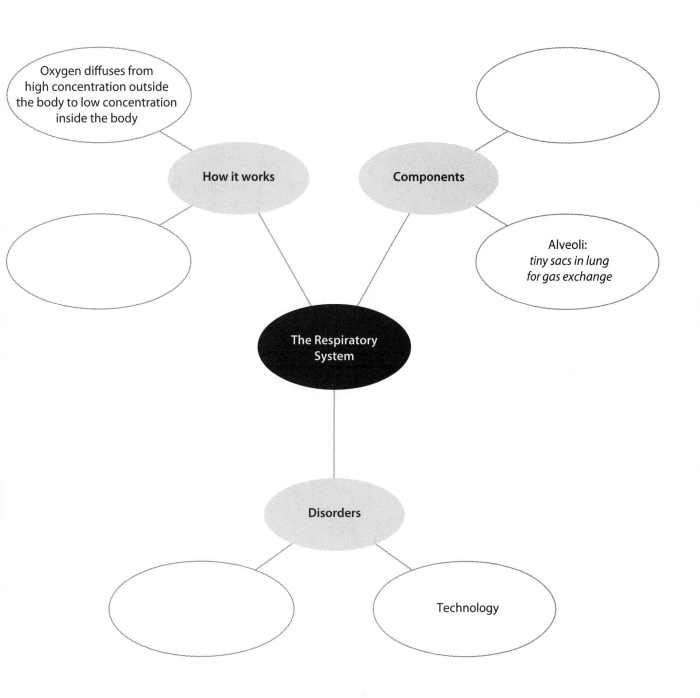

Oxygen diffuses from high concentration outside the body to low concentration inside the body

How it works

Components

Alveoli:
tiny sacs in lung for gas exchange

The Respiratory System

Disorders

Technology

1. **K/U** How is the process of inhalation accomplished?
   A. relaxation of intercostal muscles
   B. relaxation of diaphragm
   C. inward movement of rib cage
   D. increase in pressure of the thoracic cavity
   E. decrease in pressure of the thoracic cavity

2. **K/U** Diffusion of carbon dioxide between the blood and the body's tissue cells is part of what process?
   A. internal respiration
   B. external respiration
   C. breathing
   D. cellular respiration
   E. expiration

3. **T/I** What is the additional volume of air that can be forced out of the lungs beyond a tidal exhalation?
   A. inspiratory reserve volume
   B. expiratory reserve volume
   C. residual volume
   D. total lung volume
   E. vital capacity

4. **T/I** What could happen if the cilia lining the respiratory tract were damaged?
   A. lung temperature increases
   B. breathing rate decreases
   C. more foreign particles in the airways
   D. less mucus is produced
   E. tidal volume decreases

5. **K/U** What path does an oxygen molecule follow as it passes from the nasal cavity to the alveolus?
   A. left bronchus, larynx, bronchioles, trachea
   B. larynx, trachea, left bronchus, bronchioles
   C. larynx, right bronchus, trachea, bronchioles
   D. trachea, larynx, bronchioles, right bronchus
   E. pharynx, trachea, bronchioles, left bronchus

6. **K/U** What structure is responsible for preventing food from entering into the lungs?
   A. pharynx   B. glottis
   C. trachea   D. epiglottis
   E. larynx

7. **K/U** What is true about the capillary network surrounding each alveolus?
   A. It helps increase surface area for the exchange of gases.
   B. It reduces the air temperature so diffusion occurs faster.
   C. It produces mucus to protect the lungs.
   D. It supports the structure of the alveoli.
   E. It prevents harmful gases from entering the respiratory system.

8. **K/U** What two main conditions are necessary for respiratory surfaces to be efficient?
   _____

9. **K/U** What are the two structures that control the air pressure inside the lungs?
   _____

10. **K/U** How is carbon dioxide transported in the blood?
    _____

11. **T/I** What structural characteristics of alveoli help with the process of gas exchange?
    _____

12. **T/I** **A** How have air breathing vertebrates adapted their respiratory systems to cope with life on land?
    _____

13. (C) (A) **a.** Explain the process of external respiration in detail.

_____

_____

_____

_____

_____

_____

b. Write the chemical equation that represents how carbon dioxide is transported to the site where external respiration occurs.

_____

14. (K/U) (T/I) Describe three situations that could increase your exposure to carcinogens, which could eventually lead to the development of lung cancer.

_____

_____

_____

_____

Self Study Guide

Question	If you answered this question incorrectly, see this Study Guide page for further review.
1	SG-168
2	SG-170
3	SG-167
4	SG-168
5	SG-168
6	SG-168
7	SG-170
8	SG-168
9	SG-168
10	SG-170
11	SG-170
12	SG-167
13	SG-168, SG-170
14	SG-171

The Circulatory System

Self Assessment

1. Which animal has a closed circulatory system?

    A. dragonfly   **B.** centipede   **C.** grasshopper

    D. ant   **E.** squid

2. The walls of the heart are composed of what type(s) of muscle?

    A. cardiac muscle   **B.** skeletal muscle

    C. smooth muscle   **D.** cardiac and smooth muscle

    E. skeletal and smooth muscle

3. Which blood vessel carries oxygen-rich blood from the lungs to the left atrium?

    A. pulmonary artery   **B.** inferior vena cava

    C. superior vena cava   **D.** pulmonary vein

    E. aorta

4. Which statement is true?

    A. Veins have highly elastic walls and lack valves.

    B. Veins have highly elastic walls and valves.

    C. Veins have thin walls and valves.

    D. Veins have thin walls and lack valves.

    E. Veins have fixed walls and lack valves.

5. Which blood component plays a key role in the process of clotting?

    A. erthrocytes   **B.** leukocytes   **C.** lymphocytes

    D. thrombocytes   **E.** monocytes

6. Which statement best describes the function of red blood cells?

    A. To carry oxygen to and from cells.

    B. To carry oxygen and carbon dioxide to and from cells.

    C. To engulf foreign particles.

    D. To play a role in the formation of antibodies.

    E. To transport nutrients to cells.

7. The pacemaker is the bundle of specialized muscle tissue called the

    A. sinoatrial node.   **B.** atrioventricular node.

    C. bundle of His.   **D.** Purkinje fibres.

    E. chorde tendinae.

8. What causes the "lub" sound in a normal heartbeat?

    A. The movement of blood into the ventricles.

    B. The movement of blood into the atria.

    C. The opening of the atrioventricular valves.

    D. The closing of the semilunar valves.

    E. The opening and closing of the heart valves.

9. When does systolic pressure occur?

    A. During ventricular relaxation.

    B. During ventricular contraction.

    C. During arterial relaxation.

    D. During arterial contraction.

    E. During arterial and ventricular contraction.

10. What is a normal blood pressure measurement for a healthy teenager?

    A. 120/80   **B.** 85/125   **C.** 160/110

    D. 40/80   **E.** 105/70

11. What does cardiac output indicate?

    A. The level of oxygen delivered to the body.

    B. The amount of carbon dioxide produced by the body.

    C. The number of heartbeats per minute.

    D. The amount of blood forced out the heart with each heartbeat.

    E. The amount of pressure placed on arterial walls.

12. What is the condition where plaque builds up inside the arterial walls?

    A. arrhythmia   **B.** arteriosclerosis   **C.** atherosclerosis

    D. aneurysm   **E.** angioplasty

13. What causes a stroke?

    A. Pulmonary arteries are blocked.

    B. Systemic arteries are blocked.

    C. Coronary arteries and veins are blocked.

    D. Arteries supplying blood to the brain are damaged.

    E. Arteries supplying blood to the heart are damaged.

14. Which blood disorder can occur when blood is lacking erythrocytes?

    A. arteriosclerosis   **B.** arrhythmia   **C.** ischemic stroke

    D. hemophilia   **E.** anemia

Self Study Guide

Question	If you answered this question incorrectly, see this Study Guide page for further review.	After completing your review, be sure to answer these questions in the Chapter 12 Practice Test.	Question	If you answered this question incorrectly, see this Study Guide page for further review.	After completing your review, be sure to answer these questions in the Chapter 12 Practice Test.
1	SG-179	1, 2	8	SG-179	2
2	SG-179	2	9	SG-181	5, 11
3	SG-181	1, 2	10	SG-181	5, 11
4	SG-181	1	11	SG-181	6
5	SG-183	3	12	SG-185	11
6	SG-183	3, 9, 10	13	SG-185	5, 11
7	SG-179	4	14	SG-185	3, 9, 10

Key Terms

circulatory system

heart

blood, blood vessel

open circulatory system

closed circulatory system

pulmonary artery, and vein

aorta

atrioventricular valve

semilunar valve

pulmonary circulation

systemic circulation

cardiac circulation

vasodilation, vasoconstriction

sinoatrial (SA) node

atrioventricular (AV) node

electrocardiogram (ECG)

blood pressure

systolic pressure

diastolic pressure

sphygmomanometer

cardiac output

stroke volume

arteriosclerosis

angioplasty

coronary bypass

aneurysm

arrhythmia

pacemaker

congenital heart defect

ischemic stroke

hemorrhagic stroke

hemophilia

leukemia

nanotechnology

xenotransplant

Study Tip

Think about what you have already learned about the circulatory system from studying the digestive and the respiratory systems.

The Circulatory System Supports other Systems (12.1)

Some animals, such as insects, have **open circulatory systems**. The heart pumps fluid through vessels into body cavities. The fluid reenters the vessels through pores.

Larger, more complex animals, including all vertebrates, have **closed circulatory systems**. The heart pumps blood through vessels. From these vessels, blood diffuses into body cells. It returns to the heart through the vessels. In a healthy person, blood is never pumped out into a cavity in a closed circulatory system.

Each type of **circulatory system** has three main functions:

1. It supports the respiratory system by transporting oxygen to cells and carbon dioxide away from cells, and supports the digestive system by transporting nutrients to cells and waste materials away for elimination.

2. It keeps all systems healthy by transporting vital chemical substances and by regulating the body's temperature.

3. It protects against blood loss and infection.

Learning Check

1. **K/U a.** Where does oxygen enter the human circulatory system? _____

   b. Describe oxygen's path in the circulatory system.

   _____

   _____

   c. Where does carbon dioxide exit the circulatory system? _____

2. **K/U a.** Where do nutrients enter the human circulatory system? _____

   b. Describe the path of nutrients in the circulatory system.

   _____

3. **T/I** Page 450 of your textbook describes a dense network of capillaries in your nasal passages to warm the air before it enters your lungs.

   a. How does this help to regulate the body's temperature?

   _____

   _____

   b. How does it support the respiratory system?

   _____

   _____

4. **T/I a.** What happens to a cut after it bleeds for a while?

   _____

   b. This is an example of which main function of the circulatory system?

   _____

The Human Heart (12.1, 12.2)

Humans and other mammals have a double circulatory system. Half of the heart circulates blood to and from the lungs (**pulmonary circulation**). The other half of the heart circulates blood to and from the rest of the body (**systemic circulation**) including supplying blood to the heart muscle itself (cardiac circulation).

A four-chambered **heart** pumps blood around the human circulatory system following a specific path.

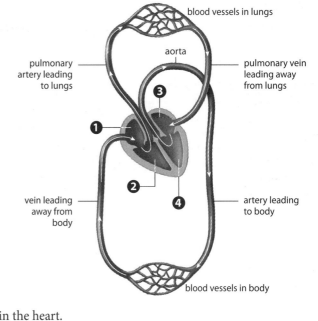

1. Blood coming from the body (with a high concentration of carbon dioxide and a low concentration of oxygen) is carried by veins called the *vena cavae* into the right atrium of the heart. (Notice the right atrium appears on the left side, when we look at the front of the heart.)

2. From the right atrium, blood flows into the right ventricle and is then pumped to the lungs in the **pulmonary arteries**.

3. Oxygenated blood returns from the lungs through the **pulmonary veins** into the left atrium of the heart.

4. The oxygenated blood flows into the left ventricle and is pumped into the **aorta** to travel around the body.

Valves between each atrium and ventricle (**atrioventricular valves**) and at the entrance to the pulmonary artery and the aorta (**semilunar valves**) keep blood from flowing backward in the heart.

The walls of the heart are made of cardiac muscle. A bundle of specialized tissue in the heart, the **sinoatrial (SA) node** or pacemaker, sends out a signal that stimulates the cardiac muscle in the atria to contract and relax rhythmically. When the signal reaches the **atrioventricular (AV) node,** it sends a signal through fast-conducting *Purkinje fibres* that stimulates the ventricles to contract.

When the heart beats, the familiar "lub-dub" sound occurs. The "lub" is caused by vibrations resulting from the atrioventricular valves closing due to ventricular contraction. The "dub" is heard when the semilunar valves close due to back pressure of blood in the aorta and pulmonary arteries. Doctors can use a stethoscope to pick up and amplify the sound of heartbeats. An irregular heartbeat can be a sign of a valve becoming narrow or not closing completely. An **electrocardiogram** can detect irregularities in the electric pulses that cause the heart to beat, and can help detect problems that a doctor cannot find with a stethoscope.

For more information about how an electrocardiogram works, including diagrams, see page 490 of your textbook.

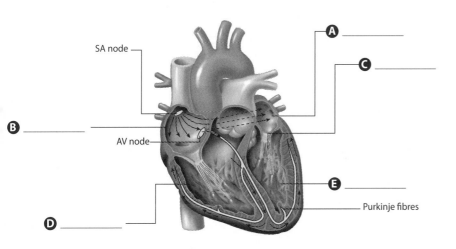

Learning Check

1. **K/U** Label the diagram of the human heart on the previous page.
2. **a. K/U** What type of valve controls the flow of blood from the atria to the ventricles?

   _____

   b. A Why is it important to keep blood moving forward in the heart?

   _____

   _____

3. **K/U** Name the four main blood vessels that connect to the heart.
   a. the main artery leading to the body _____
   b. the main artery leading to the lungs _____
   c. the main veins coming from the body _____
   d. the main vein coming from the lungs _____
4. **K/U** How does the SA node cause the heart to beat?

   _____

   _____

5. **K/U** What technologies can a doctor use to monitor the beating of a heart?

   _____

   _____

6. **C** Draw a flowchart to show the path of blood through the heart. Start with the *venae cavae*.

7. **T/I** List three characteristics of our heart and describe how each one helps the circulatory system transport gases and nutrients efficiently.

   _____

   _____

   _____

Study Tip

Use what you know about **root words** and **prefixes** to help you remember the names of the main veins and arteries in the circulatory system (**question 3**).

The Blood Vessels (12.1, 12.2)

There are three main types of blood vessels in the human circulatory system.

A. Arteries carry blood away from the heart. Artery walls have thick muscles to help move the blood.

B. Veins carry blood to the heart. Veins have less muscle in their walls than arteries do. They have valves to prevent blood from flowing backward. Skeletal muscles surrounding the veins also help to keep blood moving forward.

C. Capillaries are spread throughout the body and are only one cell thick. Nutrients, gases, and wastes in the capillaries diffuse between the circulatory system and body cells.

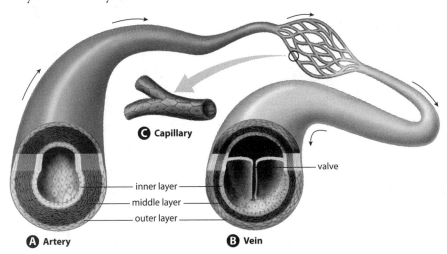

C Capillary

valve

inner layer
middle layer
outer layer

A Artery

B Vein

As blood is pumped out of the heart, it exerts pressure on the walls of the pulmonary artery and the aorta. When the ventricle contract, the **blood pressure** increases. This phase is called **systolic pressure**. When the ventricles relax, the pressure decreases. This is called **diastolic pressure**.

Blood pressure can be measured using a **sphygmomanometer**, or blood pressure cuff. The average blood pressure of a healthy young person is less than 120 mmHg/80 mmHg (systolic/diastolic). Higher than normal blood pressure may indicate disorders of the circulatory system. Continued high blood pressure causes the heart to work harder to pump blood, and can lead to artery damage, heart attacks, strokes, and kidney failure.

Several measurements can help monitor cardiovascular fitness. For example,

cardiac output	=	**heart rate**	×	**stroke volume**
(the amount of blood		(beats per minute)		(the amount of blood
delivered to the body)				pumped in each heartbeat)

The average person has a cardiac output of 4900 mL/min when at rest. Someone with a high stroke volume can achieve this output with a lower heart rate than someone with a low stroke volume can.

Cardiovascular exercise strengthens the circulatory system and increases the stroke volume.

1. **K/U** What is each type of blood vessel called?

   a. vessels that carry blood to the heart _____

   b. thin vessels throughout the body where diffusion occurs _____

   c. vessels that carry blood from the heart _____

2. **K/U** **a.** What causes blood to move through arteries?

   _____

   b. What keeps blood moving through veins?

   _____

3. **K/U** **a.** What is systolic blood pressure?

   _____

   b. What is diastolic blood pressure?

   _____

4. **A** Use a flowchart to show why blood pressure increases when a person is exercising.

Study Tip

You can use a **cause-and-effect diagram** or a **flowchart** to organize your thoughts about why things happen (**question 4**).

5. **A** When the average person is running, will their cardiac output be higher or lower than 4900 mL/min? Why?

   _____

   _____

6. **A** **K/I** **a.** A person has a resting cardiac output of 4900 mL/min and a heart rate of 90 beats per minute. What is the person's stroke volume?

   _____

   _____

   b. An athlete has a normal cardiac output, but a very low heart rate. Why might this be?

   _____

   _____

Blood and its Components (12.1)

Blood is made up of four main components: plasma (55%), white blood cells and platelets (1%), and red blood cells (44%).

Plasma is a clear yellowish fluid made up mostly of water and dissolved proteins. Plasma also carries other substances, including nutrients, gases, and wastes.

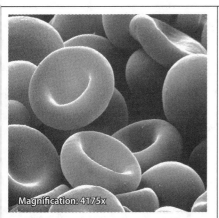

Magnification: 4175x

Red blood cells, or erythrocytes, have no nucleus. Each contains approximately 280 million molecules of hemoglobin, which transports oxygen in the blood.

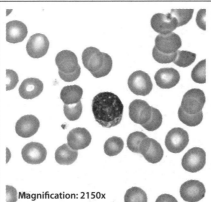

Magnification: 2150x

White blood cells, or leukocytes, help fight infection by destroying pathogens.

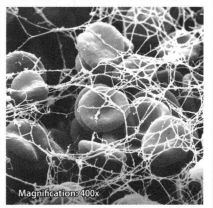

Magnification: 400x

Platelets, or thrombocytes, are fragments of cells that play a key role in blood clotting.

The components of blood are essential in helping the circulatory system carry out its main functions.

Transportation of gases, nutrients, wastes, and other chemical substances

Many substances are transported by being dissolved in the plasma. For example, nutrients are absorbed into blood in the capillaries in the walls of the small intestine, transported by blood to the liver, converted into other substances, and transported by blood to other parts of the body. Blood carries waste products from cells to the kidneys for excretion and carbon dioxide to the lungs for gas exchange.

The transportation of large quantities of oxygen relies on hemoglobin, a molecule found in red blood cells. Oxygen is absorbed by blood in the lungs, binds chemically to the hemoglobin, and is released in the presence of body cells that require it.

Protection Against Disease

The different types of white blood cells work together to destroy pathogens. The most numerous types are phagocytes. They engulf and destroy viruses, bacteria, and other pathogens in a process known as phagocytosis. Different types of white blood cells engage in phagocytosis in different parts of the body. White blood cells known as basophils secrete substances that attract phagocytes to a pathogen.

Preventing Blood Loss

When the body is injured, platelets release chemicals that lead to the formation of a blood clot, preventing the loss of large amounts of blood.

Step 1	Step 2	Step 3	Step 4	Step 5
An injured blood vessel releases a chemical that attracts platelets.	The platelets release chemicals that combine with plasma chemicals to produce thromboplastin.	Thromboplastin reacts with prothrombin to produce thrombin.	Thrombin reacts with fibrinogen in the plasma to produce fibrin.	Strands of fibrin form a mesh over the damaged area, as in the image on the previous page. This prevents blood cells from escaping. Eventually a clot forms.

Blood also helps to regulate body temperature. When the body becomes too warm, **vasodilation** (widening of the vessels) occurs in capillaries near the skin to allow more blood to flow through them. Heat is given off to the surroundings. When the body becomes too cool, **vasoconstriction** (narrowing of the vessels) occurs in the capillaries near the skin, so that heat is conserved for the body core. Shivering and sweating are other ways the body regulates its temperature.

Learning Check

1. **K/U** Which component of blood is primarily responsible for each event?

   a. initiating blood clots _____

   b. transporting wastes _____

   c. transporting glucose _____

   d. killing bacteria _____

2. **K/U** Which components of blood are whole cells?

   _____

3. **K/U** How do different types of white blood cells work together?

   _____

   _____

4. **A** How does the amount of hemoglobin in the blood relate to the blood's ability to transport oxygen?

   _____

   _____

5. **T/I** Vasodilation also occurs during physical activity even if the body temperature does not rise. What function might this serve?

   _____

6. **T/I** **C** A boy falls and scrapes his knee on the sidewalk. Bacteria from the sidewalk enter the cut. Draw one or more cause-and-effect maps to show how the components of the boy's blood become involved to help repair tissues and prevent further damage.

Circulatory System Disorders (12.3)

Many circulatory system disorders can be prevented by maintaining a healthy weight, exercising, and not smoking. Advanced treatments such as transplants, artificial organ parts, and targeted drug delivery have been developed to treat many of these disorders.

For more information about these disorders and their treatments see pages 494 to 501 of your textbook.

Disorder	Description	Cause	Treatment
Arteriosclerosis	• artery walls thicken and lose elasticity • blood pressure increases • can lead to chest pain, stroke, blood clots, heart attack, and heart failure	• fatty deposits (plaque) on inside of artery walls	• medication can reduce clot formation • angioplasty, inflating a tiny balloon inside an artery, can open the artery and a stent can keep it open • can transplant another artery to bypass the blockage (coronary bypass) • lifestyle changes can help reduce blood pressure
Aneurysm	• a bulge in the artery wall, usually the aorta, that can burst and lead to death	• weakening of the artery wall	• surgery to replace damaged portion of artery
Heart valve diseases	• valve does not close properly and allows backward blood flow (*regurgitation*)(heart murmur) • thickening of valve prevents adequate blood flow (*stenosis*)	• aging, infections, damage from previous heart attacks, connective tissue disorders	• surgery to repair valves or replace them with human, animal, or synthetic valves
Arrhythmia	• abnormal speed or rhythm of the heartbeat • some are harmless but some lead to insufficient blood flow	• abnormal functioning of the SA node or the AV node	• medication or implantation of a **pacemaker** to send regular electric signals to heart muscle, initiating heartbeats
Congenital heart defects	• a variety of symptoms caused by defects in the heart that have been present since birth	• mostly unknown	• surgery to repair defects
Stroke	• damage to arteries supplying blood to the brain cuts off the brain's supply of oxygen and nutrients	• a clot in a blood vessel **(ischemic stroke)** • a burst blood vessel **(hemorrhagic stroke)**	• clot-busting medication and other medications, surgery • treatment must be started within hours of the stroke
Hemophilia	• uncontrolled bleeding because clots do not form • internal bleeding can cause death	• genetic sex-linked trait causes insufficient clotting proteins in the blood	• injections of blood clotting protein factor VIII helps some hemophiliacs
Leukemia	• abnormally high numbers of immature white blood cells cannot fight disease, and crowd out red blood cells, causing fatigue, and possibly death	• cancer	• chemotherapy, blood transfusions, transplant of healthy bone marrow to generate healthy white blood cells

1. **K/U** Which disorders primarily affect each part of the circulatory system?

   a. the heart

   _____

   b. the blood vessels

   _____

   c. the blood

   _____

2. **K/U** List two disorders that cannot be prevented by lifestyle choices. Explain what causes each one.

   _____

   _____

3. **K/U** One circulatory system disorder puts a person at risk of developing several other disorders. Which one is it? How can it lead to the other disorders?

   _____

   _____

4. **T/I** Technology allows surgeons to use data from a CT scan or cardio MRI to create a model of a person's heart. They can then plan and practise surgery on the model. What advantages could this provide?

   _____

   _____

5. **C** Create a table to compare the treatments on pages 500 and 501 of your textbook (xenotransplants, artificial hearts, and targeted drug delivery). Include a description of each treatment, advantages, and potential problems or issues.

Study Tip

A **table** (**question 5**) can help you organize information. Choosing what information you can fit in the cells of a table helps you to identify the most important facts about a topic. Those facts are then easily accessible when you study for a test.

Bringing It All Together

Add to this web diagram to summarize what you have learned about the circulatory system.

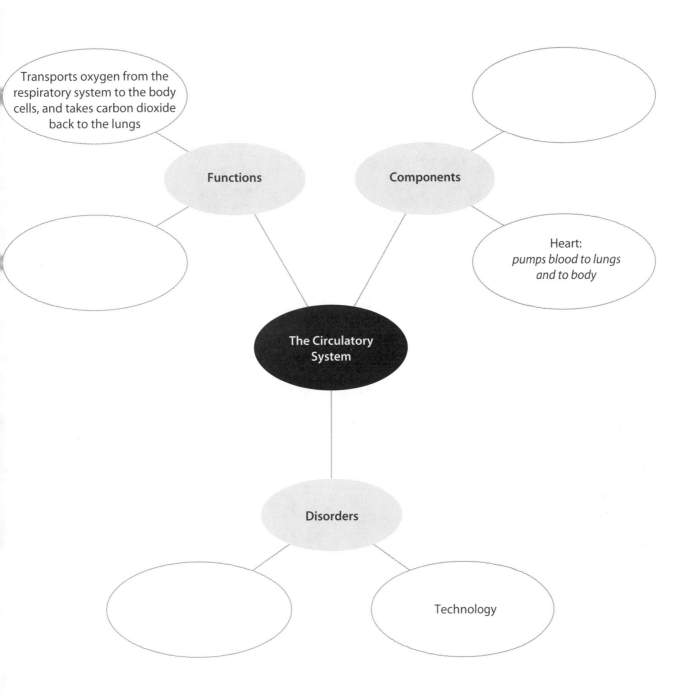

Transports oxygen from the respiratory system to the body cells, and takes carbon dioxide back to the lungs

Functions

Components

Heart:
pumps blood to lungs and to body

The Circulatory System

Disorders

Technology

CHAPTER 12   Practice Test

1. **K/U** Which type of blood vessel has highly elastic walls?

   A. arterioles

   B. arteries

   C. capillaries

   D. venuoles

   E. veins

2. **K/U** Which chamber of the heart pumps deoxygenated blood towards the lungs?

   A. right atrium

   B. left atrium

   C. aortic branch

   D. right ventricle

   E. left ventricle

3. **K/U** Which white blood cells secrete substances that attract phagocytes to destroy pathogens?

   A. basophils

   B. eosinophils

   C. leukocytes

   D. monocytes

   E. neutrophils

4. **T/I** The Purkinje fibres initiate the contraction of the

   A. SA node.

   B. AV node.

   C. chordae tendinae.

   D. ventricles.

   E. atria.

5. **K/U** Which statement is true?

   A. Blood pressure is generally measured at a vein.

   B. Blood pressure is the same in arteries and veins.

   C. Blood pressure is highest in the aorta.

   D. Blood pressure is measured by an ECG.

   E. Blood pressure is always at a constant level.

6. **K/U** What is a good indicator of cardiovascular fitness?

   A. The maximum stroke volume achieved during exercise.

   B. The ratio of cardiac output compared to stroke volume.

   C. The measurement of calories consumed during exercise.

   D. The difference between efficiencies found in the lungs and heart.

   E. The length of time it takes the heart to recover to its resting heart rate.

7. **K/U** A vascular stent is used during which procedure?

   A. coronary angiography

   B. angioplasty

   C. coronary bypass

   D. mitral valve replacement

   E. treatment of a stroke

8. **K/U** What valve is found between the right atrium and the right ventricle.

_____

9. **K/U** Name three types of proteins that are found in plasma.

_____

10. **T/I** Which ion must be present for the production of thrombin?

_____

11. **K/U** List three factors that can affect blood pressure.

_____

_____

2. T/I C List two structural characteristics of each type of blood vessel. Describe how each characteristic relates to the function of the blood vessel.

Blood Vessel	Structural Characteristic	Function
Artery	a.	
	b.	
Capillary	c.	
	d.	
Vein	e.	
	f.	

3. T/I What is the significance of each wave in the electrocardiogram?

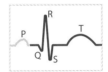

a. P wave _____

b. QRS wave _____

c. T wave _____

4. C A Describe three societal issues related to xenotransplant procedures.

_____

_____

_____

Self Study Guide

Question	If you answered this question incorrectly, see this Study Guide page for further review.	Question	If you answered this question incorrectly, see this Study Guide page for further review.
1	SG-181	8	SG-179
2	SG-179	9	SG-183
3	SG-183	10	SG-183
4	SG-179	11	SG-185
5	SG-181	12	SG-181
6	SG-181	13	SG-179
7	SG-185	14	SG-185

Add information to the web diagram to summarize the main functions, components, and disorders of the digestive, respiratory, and circulatory systems. Show as many links between the systems as you can.

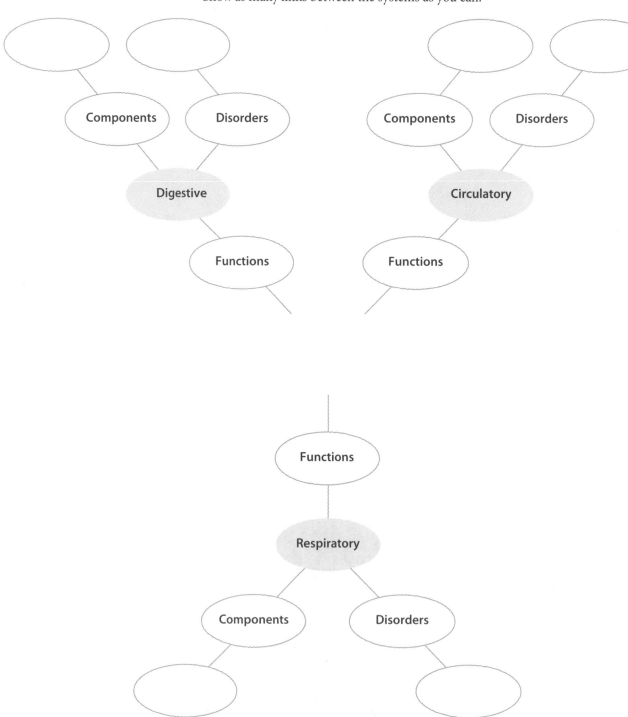

Unit 4 Practice Test

1. **(K/U)** Which molecule is a monosaccharide?
   A. cellulose   **B.** maltose   **C.** sucrose
   D. lactose   **E.** fructose

2. **(K/U)** What products are formed when a lipid is hydrolized?
   A. amino acids   **B.** glycerol and fatty acids **C.** simple sugars
   D. polysaccharides   **E.** nucleotides

3. **(K/U)** Where does the chemical digestion of protein start?
   A. mouth   **B.** pharynx   **C.** stomach
   D. duodenum   **E.** large intestine

4. **(K/U)** Food passing through the small intestine receives secretions from which organs?
   A. liver and pancreas   **B.** pancreas and gall bladder
   C. gall bladder and liver **D.** kidneys and liver
   E. adrenal glands and kidneys

5. **(K/U)** The liver converts excess glucose into which substance?
   A. glycogen   **B.** glycerol   **C.** triglycerides
   D. polysaccharides   **E.** glucagon

6. **(K/U)** What is external respiration?
   A. breathing   **B.** exchange of gases in the tissues
   C. cellular respiration **D.** release of air from lungs
   E. exchange of gases in the lungs

7. **(K/U)** What is the amount of air that enters or leaves the lungs during a normal respiratory cycle?
   A. respiratory volume **B.** tidal volume   **C.** residual volume
   D. vital capacity   **E.** inspiratory volume

8. **(K/U)** Carbon dioxide enters the blood through which process?
   A. diffusion   **B.** active transport
   C. facilitated transport **D.** air pressure
   E. blood pressure

9. **(K/U)** Asthma is caused by the inflammation of which part of the respiratory system?
   A. pharynx   **B.** bronchi   **C.** bronchioles
   D. trachea   **E.** larynx

10. **(K/U)** Which statement is true about the vena cavae?
    A. They join with the aorta.
    B. They carry blood away from the right atrium.
    C. They carry blood to the right atrium.
    D. They supply nutrients to coronary arteries.
    E. They have high blood pressure readings.

11. **T/I** Which blood component lacks a nucleus?
   A. erythrocytes   **B.** thrombocytes   **C.** basophil
   D. neutrophil   **E.** lymphocyte

12. **K/U** What is the optimal pH range for most human enzymes?

_____

13. **K/U** What are the two basic processes involved in breathing?

_____

14. **K/U** What are two physical adaptations that enable organisms to carry out gas exchange in aquatic environments?

_____

15. **T/I** Why is blood considered a connective tissue?

_____

_____

16. **K/U** Which part of the heart is referred to as the pacemaker?

_____

17. **K/U** What is hypertension?

_____

18. **K/U** **T/T** Describe the functions of each substance.
   a. gastric juice _____

_____

   b. bile _____

_____

   c. pancreatic fluid _____

_____

19. **T/I** Explain why the process of exhalation is considered to be passive.

_____

_____

20. **T/I** What internal mechanisms are used by the human body to cope with excessive heat when exercising?

_____

_____

21. **K/U** How are nanotechnology techniques being used in the treatment of cancer?

_____

_____

22. (T/I) Describe the chemical digestion of a complex carbohydrate in detail. Give the location and a summary of each chemical reaction involved.

_____

_____

23. (C) (A) Use a graphic organizer to compare external and internal respiration.

24. (A) Explain how the digestive system and the cardiovascular system help each other.

_____

_____

_____

_____

Self Study Guide

Question	If you answered this question incorrectly, see this Study Guide page for further review.	Question	If you answered this question incorrectly, see this Study Guide page for further review.
1	SG-152	13	SG-168
2	SG-152	14	SG-166
3	SG-157	15	SG-183
4	SG-155	16	SG-179
5	SG-155	17	SG-185
6	SG-167	18	SG-157
7	SG-168	19	SG-168
8	SG-170	20	SG-183
9	SG-171	21	SG-171
10	SG-181	22	SG-157
11	SG-183	23	SG-157
12	SG-157	24	SG-162

Unit 5 Plants: Anatomy, Growth, and Function

Chapter 13 Plants: Uses, Form, and Function

Plants provide many essential ecosystem services. From producing oxygen and food, to providing timber, textiles, and medicines, plants and plant products affect every aspect of your life.

Plants have always been used by humans but some of the ways we use them are changing. For example, to achieve food and energy security, many people are turning toward sustainable agriculture and biofuels—fuels made from renewable plant sources.

The plant body, like the human body, is made up of different types of cells, organized into tissues, organs, and organ systems.

- Meristematic tissue is the tissue from which all other plant tissues develop.

- Dermal tissue forms a protective outer covering for the plant.

- Ground tissue makes up most of the plant's body and carries out many life functions.

- Vascular tissue transports water and other molecules from one part of the plant to another.

A plant's basic organs—roots, stems, and leaves—allow the plant to obtain water and other nutrients from the soil, produce glucose and oxygen in the leaves, move substances around as necessary, and remain anchored and supported.

The transportation of water and other substances in a plant depends on diffusion, active transport, and fluid pressure and tension in the xylem and phloem tissue.

Chapter 14 Plants: Reproduction, Growth, and Sustainability

In the plant kingdom, both sexual and asexual reproduction occur.

In Chapter 3 you saw that plants reproduce sexually by sporic reproduction, that is, with an alternation of generations. While all plants produce diploid ($2n$) sporophytes and haploid (n) gametophytes, these take different forms in different groups of plants.

- In non-vascular plants, the gametophyte is the dominant generation, while in vascular plants the sporophyte is the dominant generation.

- In seedless plants, fertilization requires a moist or wet environment. In seed plants, pollen is carried by wind or by animals. Some plants are self-pollinating, and some are cross-pollinating.

- In angiosperms, most of the reproductive cycle takes place in the flower.

Plants also reproduce asexually, producing clones. Humans have developed methods of artificially propagating plants such as:

  division
  grafting
  taking leaf, stem, or root cuttings
  layering
  air layering
  cell culturing

Artificial propagation can result in new plants more quickly, as well as new plants with known characteristics.

Plants produce several hormones to control their growth and development. They also respond to environmental stimuli such as light and gravity, the presence of nutrients, and the acidity of the soil.

These characteristics enable plants to carry out their roles in ecosystems as ecosystem pioneers, and as agents of succession. Plant biodiversity is a major contributor to ecosystem resilience.

Self Assessment

1. What happens to most of the oxygen generated by plants during photosynthesis?
   A. It is released into the atmosphere.
   B. It is used by the plant during cellular respiration.
   C. It is combined with carbon dioxide to form glucose.
   D. It is absorbed into the soil surrounding the plant root system.
   E. It is converted into light energy.

2. What crop is most commonly grown in Canada?
   A. corn   B. oats   C. canola
   D. flaxseed   E. wheat

3. What term describes a group of specialized cells that work together to perform a function?
   A. organ   B. organ system   C. cytoplasm
   D. organelle   E. tissue

4. Where is lignin found?
   A. parenchyma cells   B. sclerenchyma cells
   C. collenchyma cells   D. vascular tissue
   E. meristematic tissue

5. The hard covering of seed coats is due to the presence of what material?
   A. stone cells   B. fibres   C. xylem
   D. stoma   E. phloem

6. What is vascular cambium necessary for in a plant?
   A. transport of water   B. transport of nutrients   C. primary growth
   D. secondary growth   E. gas exchange

7. In gymnosperms, xylem consists of what type of cells?
   A. companion cells   B. periderm   C. tracheids
   D. sieve tube elements   E. vessel elements

8. What type of cell is found in a root cap?
   A. guard cell   B. collenchyma   C. scherenchyma
   D. parenchyma   E. aerenchyma

9. In monocots, xylem cells form a ring around a central core of what material?
   A. bark   B. phloem   C. pith
   D. endodermis   E. Casparian strip

10. What type of stems are found in potato plants?
    A. tuber   B. bulb   C. corms
    D. stolon   E. rhizome

11. Which part of a leaf contains chloroplasts?

  A. cuticle   **B.** mesophyll cells   **C.** petiole

  D. veins   **E.** aerenchyma

12. Dicots have which characteristics?

  A. palmate veins, flowers in thee parts, and presence of wood

  B. parallel veins, flowers in four or five parts, and presence of wood

  C. parallel veins, fibrous roots, and vascular tissue in a ring formation

  D. pinnate veins, fibrous roots, and vascular tissue in a star shape

  E. palmate veins, taproots, and vascular tissue in a star shape

13. How are sugars transported across the cell membrane?

  A. passive transport   **B.** active transport   **C.** diffusion

  D. osmosis   **E.** exocytosis

14. What role does adhesion serve in plants?

  A. It evaporates water from the stems.

  B. It causes attraction between water molecules found in leaves.

  C. It causes water molecules to stick to xylem walls.

  D. It produces negative pressure to cause water to leave the plant.

  E. It helps dissolved minerals move out of the phloem of the plant.

15. What type of carbohydrate is used for transport in the phloem?

  A. glycogen   **B.** glucose   **C.** fructose

  D. sucrose   **E.** maltose

Self Study Guide

Question	If you answered this question incorrectly, see this Study Guide page for further review.	After completing your review, be sure to answer these questions in the Chapter 13 Practice Test.	Question	If you answered this question incorrectly, see this Study Guide page for further review.	After completing your review, be sure to answer these questions in the Chapter 13 Practice Test.
1	SG-198	8	9	SG-203	10, 13
2	SG-198	8, 9	10	SG-203	13
3	SG-200	3, 10	11	SG-203	6, 12
4	SG-198	2, 8	12	SG-203	13
5	SG-198	2, 8	13	SG-205	10, 14
6	SG-200	3, 4, 10	14	SG-205	10, 14
7	SG-201	3, 4, 10, 14	15	SG-205	7, 14
8	SG-203	2, 3			

CHAPTER 12

Summary

Key Terms

photosynthesis

cellulose

agriculture

food security

sustainable agriculture

textile

timber

biofuel

shoot system

root system

meristematic tissue

dermal tissue

epidermis

guard cell

stoma

root hairs

ground tissue

xylem

phloem

root cap

cortex

endodermis

taproot

fibrous root

aerenchyma

cuticle

mesophyll

palisade mesophyll

spongy mesophyll

venation

transpiration

root pressure

cohesion-tension model

translocation

pressure-flow model

To learn more about medicines derived from plants and about agriculture in Canada, see page 540 and page 537 of your textbook.

Plants Are Valuable Bioresources (13.1)

Plants are essential to the health and functioning of the biosphere. They provide many important ecosystem services. Nearly everything that you do each day depends on plants.

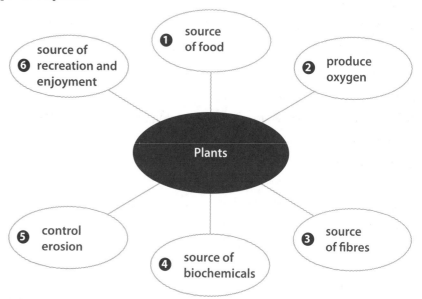

1. In **photosynthesis**, plants use light energy to convert water and carbon dioxide into glucose, which is used as energy by the plants themselves and by other organisms in the food chain. Plants are a source of food for all heterotrophs. Humans grow about 150 plant species commercially for food.

2. Another product of photosynthesis is oxygen, which is necessary for cellular respiration by all living things, including humans.

$$\text{carbon dioxide} + \text{water} \xrightarrow{\text{(in the presence of light)}} \text{glucose} + \text{oxygen}$$

3. The main component of cell walls in plants is **cellulose**, a complex carbohydrate. Humans use plant fibres as building and clothing materials. Products such as **timber**, rope, paper, and **textiles** are all made from plant fibres.

4. People have extracted chemicals from plants for hundreds of years. For example, Aboriginal peoples in North America use a tea made from blackberry plants to treat stomach ailments and a tea made from evergreen bark and needles to prevent scurvy. Approximately 25% of all current prescription medicines contain plant products. Chemicals in plants are also used as fuel. Wood and coal are examples. **Biofuels** are produced from renewable plant sources, such as crops and crop residues.

5. Plants slow down the movement of water on soil and prevent erosion and flooding.

6. Many people enjoy recreation and tourism activities in areas with a variety of plant life.

Many of these uses provide several types of benefits to humans. Agriculture, for example, provides food and economic benefits. Some of the most common crops grown in Canada are wheat, canola, barley, and corn. As the human population on Earth grows, we are faced with making decisions about agricultural practices that will ensure **food security** for the future. Many scientists and farmers are turning toward **sustainable agriculture** to balance current and future needs of society and the environment.

Learning Check

1. **K/U** Write the ecosystem service (from the previous page) that each situation represents.

   a. Corn, beans, and squash are common crops in many North American Aboriginal societies. _____

   b. Jeans fabric is woven from cotton. _____

   c. Wood pulp is used to make paper. _____

   d. Two compounds from rosy periwinkle are used to treat leukemia and Hodgkin's disease. _____

   e. Dust storms can occur in areas where plants have been removed.

   _____

2. **C** Create a web diagram to show how you have used plants in your activities today. Think of the categories described on the previous page.

3. **K/U** Ecosystem resources are important to species other than humans. Describe three examples of how other species use the resources plants supply.

   _____

   _____

   _____

4. **A** Draw a food web to show how all consumer organisms rely on the food energy plants create in photosynthesis.

5. **T/I** A friend argues that you can obtain a higher yield from crops by spraying pesticides and using lots of fertilizer every year. Explain why that may not be beneficial in the long term.

   _____

   _____

Study Tip

Web diagrams, like the one on the previous page, can help you **organize** information and find it quickly when you are studying.

Types of Plant Cells (13.2)

Plants are made up of cells, tissues, organs, and systems—just as you are.

Plant cells have:

• a cell wall to provide support.

• a large central vacuole, for storage of food, enzymes, and other materials.

• chloroplasts, where photosynthesis takes place.

There are three main types of plant cells.

Type of Cell	Example	Functions
Parenchyma • flexible, thin-walled • very common	Magnification: 350×	• storage • photosynthesis • gas exchange • protection • tissue repair and replacement
Collenchyma • elongated, unevenly thickened walls • flexible	Magnification: 100×	• support and flexibility • tissue repair and replacement
Sclerenchyma • very thick, tough cell walls • most die once they have completed development, losing their cytoplasm, but retaining their walls	Magnification: unavailable	• support mature plant

Learning Check

1. **K/U** Label the key features of this plant cell.

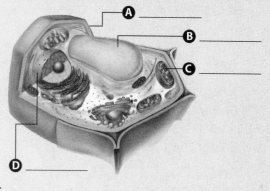

A _____
B _____
C _____
D _____

2. **A** Which type of plant cell would probably be found in each plant part? How do you know?

a. the chloroplasts in a leaf _____

b. the bark on a tree _____

3. **T/I** **a.** Why do plants need some cells with very thick, tough cell walls?

_____

b. In humans, what body part provides a similar function to the cell wall?

_____

Types of Plant Tissues (13.2)

Plant cells are organized into four main types of tissue.

Type of Tissue	Location and Function
Meristematic Tissue • undifferentiated, embryonic tissue	• found in areas of rapidly dividing cells – *apical meristems* at tips of roots and stems – *intercalary meristems* along stems and base of leaf blades – *lateral meristems* allow stems, trunks, and bark to become thicker as plant grows taller
Dermal Tissue • Made up of epidermal cells and pairs of **guard cells** that surround a stoma, or small opening for gas exchange	• outer covering of a plant • guard cells control opening size of stoma • Trichomes are tiny hairs on some epidermal cells that reduce evaporation and keep surfaces cool. Some also secrete toxic substances. • **Root hairs** on root epidermal cells increase surface area for absorption of water and nutrients.
Ground Tissue • includes all three types of cells	• forms most of a plant's internal and external material • involved with photosynthesis, storage, and support
Vascular Tissue • internal systems of tubes **Xylem** • Tracheids and vessel elements begin as living cells growing end to end. When they mature, their contents die, leaving the cell walls in place. **Phloem** • Sieve tube elements are alive at maturity, and have no nucleus. Nutrients pass through these cells. Companion cells do have nuclei, and perform life functions for the sieve tube elements.	• Runs lengthwise through the stem of the plant to connect the roots and the leaves. • In non-woody flowering plants it is arranged in vascular bundles. In woody plants it is arranged in concentric rings. • Xylem transports water from the roots to the leaves. • Phloem transports nutrients from the leaves to the rest of the plant.

There are diagrams of each type of tissue on pages 547 to 550 of your textbook.

Learning Check

1. **K/U** Name the type of tissue that performs each function.

   a. protects a plant from the outside environment

   _____

   b. transports nutrients from the leaves

   _____

   c. allows a plant to grow

   _____

   d. makes up most of a plant

   _____

2. (K/U) What type of cell makes up xylem tissue? How do you know?

_____

3. (C) Sketch and label the components of phloem tissue. Use Figure 13.13 on page 550 of your textbook as a reference.

4. (K/U) This micrograph shows epidermis on the underside of a leaf.

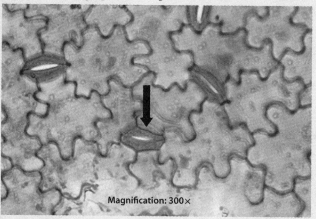

Magnification: 300×

a. What type of cell is the arrow pointing to? _____

b. What is that cell's function? _____

5. (A) What gas diffuses into a plant through the stomata

a. during the day? _____

b. at night? _____

6. (T/I) The word *vascular* is used to describe a human body system as well as a type of plant tissue. What is similar about the meaning of vascular in both cases?

_____

_____

7. (A) A leaf is cut off an African violet plant and placed on moist potting soil. Roots and shoots develop from the base of the leaf. What type of plant tissue accounts for this?

_____

Plant Organs and their Functions (13.3)

Plants have three basic organs that enable them to perform life functions: roots, stems, and leaves.

Roots

Roots take in water and dissolved minerals. They anchor and support the plant. They also store carbohydrates, water, and other nutrients.

Some plants have a **taproot**—a thick root with smaller lateral branching roots. The taproot can store food, or extend far into the soil to reach water. Other plants have **fibrous roots** made up of many, similarly sized, branching roots. Some aquatic plants have spongy tissue called **aerenchyma** through which oxygen can move in their roots.

Root tips contain meristematic cells. These cells are covered and protected by the **root cap**, which also secretes a slimy substance to reduce friction as the root grows through soil and rock.

This cross section of a root shows how water moves through the epidermis, cortex, and endodermis to reach the vascular tissue that will transport it to the rest of the plant.

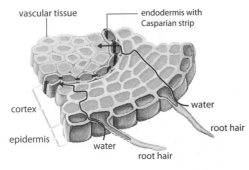

Stems

Stems provide support for a plant's leaves and reproductive structures. Stems of annual plants are often short, flexible, and green. Stems of perennials are often sturdier, woody, and in some cases covered with bark.

The stems of some plants are specialized to perform specific functions.
- Potato plants form underground stems called tubers (the potatoes we eat).
- Onions and tulips form buds, which are shortened, compressed stems.
- Strawberry plants form stolons, or runners.

Leaves

The main function of all leaves is to convert light energy from the Sun into chemical energy (food) by photosynthesis.
- Light passes through the transparent upper layers of a leaf (the upper epidermis and the **cuticle**).
- Light passes into the parenchyma cells in the **mesophyll**. **Palisade mesophyll** cells are tightly packed and contain many chloroplasts. **Spongy mesophyll** cells contain some chloroplasts and are more loosely packed to allow oxygen, carbon dioxide, and water vapour to move around the cells.
- Gases enter and exit the leaf through the stomata in the lower epidermis.

Differences in the size, shape, and texture of leaves can help identify plant species.
- Leaves can be simple or compound.
- **Venation**, the pattern of veins on the leaf, can be palmate, pinnate, or parallel.
- Leaves can be arranged opposite one another, alternate to one another, or whorled around a stem.

Table 13.6 on page 558 of your textbook summarizes many of the structural differences between monocots and dicots.

Learning Check

1. **K/U** What type of root does each plant have?

a. carrot _____

b. grass _____

c. dandelion _____

2. **K/U** As root tips push through hard soil, why are the meristematic cells not damaged?

_____

_____

3. **C** Use the information on the previous page to label the parts of the leaf.

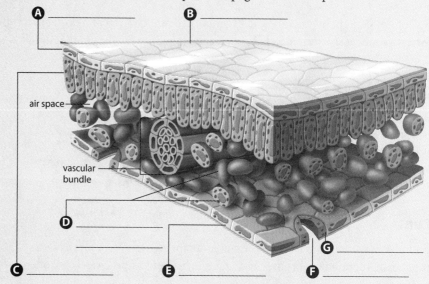

4. **T/I** Why do gases need to move around inside a leaf?

_____

_____

5. **C** Draw the typical venation pattern of each type of plant. Use pages 557 and 558 of your textbook as a reference.

a. a monocot   **b.** a dicot

6. **C** Describe one difference between monocots and dicots other than venation type.

_____

7. **A** Draw a flowchart to show the path water takes from the soil into a plant's root and up to its leaves.

Transport in Plants (13.4)
Moving Water

Water moves from soil into plant roots by osmosis. It also moves out of the ends of the veins in plant leaf cells by osmosis. Approximately 90% of the water that reaches the leaves, however, is lost through **transpiration**. Transpiration increases on dry days and decreases on humid days, when drops of water may appear on plant leaves. How does water get from the roots at the bottom of the plant to the leaves near the top?

It is *pushed* from the bottom following these steps.

1. A plant moves minerals from the soil into its roots by active transport.
2. The increased concentration of minerals in the xylem causes water to move in by osmosis.
3. This additional water increases the pressure in the xylem and *pushes* water up into the rest of the plant (**root pressure**).

It is also *pulled* from the top.

Water molecules show cohesion (stickiness to one another) and adhesion (stickiness to the xylem walls). As water is lost through transpiration in the leaves, the column of water in the xylem is *pulled* up to replace it, in what is described as the **cohesion-tension model**. As the column of water is pulled up in the xylem, more water enters the roots to replace it.

Moving Sucrose

Sucrose and other organic molecules move to many parts of a plant in a process known as **translocation**.

• Glucose created in photosynthesis in the leaves is converted to sucrose and moves to the roots for storage.

• Stored glucose moves from the roots to developing flowers, fruits, or leaves.

The molecules are pushed through phloem from *source* to *sink* using the **pressure-flow model**.

1. Sucrose is added to phloem at a source.
2. The increased concentration causes water to flow in, causing an increase in pressure, which pushes the sucrose and water through the sieve tube of phloem toward a sink.
3. At the sink, the sucrose is removed, and water flows out of the sieve tube.

The destination for the sucrose changes depending on the plant's needs, but the flow is always from source to sink.

1. **K/U** List four words or phrases that help describe how each substance moves in a plant.

a. water

_____

b. sucrose

_____

2. **C** What is osmosis? Use words or a diagram to explain.

3. **C** Add notes to this diagram to describe the pressure flow model of sucrose movement in a plant.

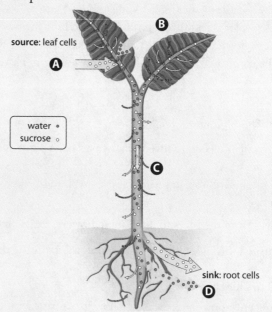

4. **C** Draw and label a diagram to explain the cohesion-tension model of water movement in a plant.

5. **T/I** Why does a plant move minerals from the soil into its roots by active transport instead of letting them move by diffusion?

_____

_____

Bringing It All Together

Add information to this table to summarize what you have learned about the uses, form, and function of plants.

Part of Plant	Uses	Form	Function
Leaves			• photosynthesis to produce glucose • guard cells surround stomata (for gas exchange)
Stem	• fibres used for paper, timber, and textiles		
Roots		• taproot (typically dicots) or fibrous root (typically monocots)	
Entire plant	• recreation opportunities such as hiking, camping, photography		

1. **K/U** Which plant has been successfully used to treat patients with Hodgkin's disease?

   A. hemlock tree   **B.** pine tree

   C. rosy periwinkle   **D.** ginseng

   E. goldenseal

2. **K/U** What type of cells allow plants to bend without breaking?

   A. parenchyma cells   **B.** collenchyma cells

   C. sclerenchyma cells   **D.** guard cells

   E. epidermal cells

3. **K/U** Which statement about ground tissue is true?

   A. It is where new cells are produced.

   B. It transports water, minerals, and other substances throughout the plant.

   C. It makes up most of the inside of a plant.

   D. It forms the outer covering of the plant.

   E. It includes xylem and phloem.

4. **K/U** What is the name for the dermal tissue formed in older woody plants?

   A. lateral meristems   **B.** vascular cambium

   C. cork cambium   **D.** periderm

   E. trichomes

5. **K/U** Where is the Casparian strip located in a plant?

   A. between the epidermis and cortex

   B. between the cortex and the vascular tissue

   C. on the outside of the epidermis

   D. embedded in the vascular tissue

   E. lining the inner surfaces of the root hairs

6. **K/U** Where does most of the photosynthesis take place in plants?

   A. palisade mesophyll   **B.** spongy mesophyll

   C. upper epidermis   **D.** vascular bundles

   E. stoma

7. **K/U** In what direction does positive pressure drive the flow of water in phloem?

   A. only upwards   **B.** only downwards

   C. between sources   **D.** from source to sink

   E. from sink to source

8. **K/U** What are the two main ecosystem services provided by plants?

   _____

9. **K/U** Name "the three sisters" crops that some North American Aboriginal societies traditionally depended on.

   _____

10. **K/U** What are the main functions of vascular tissue?

    _____

    _____

11. **K/U** What is the name of the process in which water evaporates from the inside of a leaf to the outside through the stomata?

    _____

12. **C** Draw a diagram of the internal structure of a leaf. Label the cuticle, guard cell, palisade mesophyll, spongy mesophyll, stoma, and upper and lower epidermis.

13. **T/I** List two distinguishing characteristics that could be used to classify this flowering plant.

   _____

   _____

14. (T/I) Describe the two mechanisms that allow water and sap to flow through tracheid and vessel elements, even though these parts are dead by maturity and no longer have living contents.

_____

_____

_____

15. (T/I) (A) Do plants have organs like animals do? Give examples to support your answer.

_____

_____

_____

_____

_____

16. (A) Why is the evolution of xylem such an important adaptation for the success of plants on land?

_____

_____

_____

Self Study Guide

Question	If you answered this question incorrectly, see this Study Guide page for further review.	Question	If you answered this question incorrectly, see this Study Guide page for further review.
1	SG-198	9	SG-198
2	SG-200	10	SG-201, SG-205
3	SG-201	11	SG-203, SG-205
4	SG-201	12	SG-205
5	SG-203	13	SG-203
6	SG-203	14	SG-205
7	SG-205	15	SG-205
8	SG-198	16	SG-201, SG-205

Self Assessment

1. What is the dominant generation in ferns?
  A. zygote   **B.** Female gamete   **C.** male gamete
  D. sporophyte   **E.** gametophyte

2. Angiosperms are known for what reproductive strategy?
  A. swimming sperm   **B.** single fertilization
  C. double fertilization   **D.** dominant gametophyte plant
  E. unprotected zygote and embryo

3. What is the name for the sticky "lip" of the pistil that captures pollen grains in a flower?
  A. stigma   **B.** fliament stalk   **C.** anther
  D. ovule   **E.** sepal

4. What is the name for a flower that contains either pistil or stamen but not both?
  A. complete   **B.** incomplete   **C.** compound
  D. imperfect   **E.** perfect

5. What is the name for the first part of the embryo to appear outside a seed?
  A. hypocotyl   **B.** radicle   **C.** filament stalk
  D. pistil   **E.** stamen

6. How do auxins affect plants?
  A. They prevent the ageing of leaves.
  B. They stimulate cell division and elongation in stems and roots.
  C. They induce and maintain seed dormancy.
  D. They close the stomata.
  E. They inhibit shoot growth.

7. Which plant hormone can be used to promote the ripening of fruit?
  A. abscisic acid   **B.** bicarbonate   **C.** gibberellins
  D. cytokinins   **E.** ethylene

8. A vine that twists around a fence is responding to which environmental stimulus?
  A. chemotropism   **B.** phototropism   **C.** gravitropism
  D. thigmotrophism   **E.** hydrotropism

9. What macronutrient could be used to enhance the cell walls and membranes of plants?
  A. calcium   **B.** manganese   **C.** molybdenum
  D. potassium   **E.** sulfur

10. Most plants grow well in soils with which pH range?
  A. pH 1 to 3   **B.** pH 4 to 5   **C.** pH 6 to 7
  D. pH 7 to 9   **E.** pH 10 to 12

11. Which plant is an example of a pioneer species?

    A. moss   **B.** lichen   **C.** deciduous tree

    D. coniferous tree   **E.** angiosperm

12. What does this diagram represent?

0 Years   300 Years

    A. convergent radiation   **B.** adaptive radiation   **C.** climax community

    D. natural succession   **E.** ecological succession

13. When does secondary succession occur?

    A. There is no soil for plants to grow in.

    B. The ecosystem has been damaged but the soil remains intact.

    C. Bacteria colonize an ecological niche.

    D. Liverworts attach themselves to hardened beds of lava.

    E. Mosses inhabit bare rocks left by retreating glaciers.

14. What is true about highly diverse ecosystems?

    A. They are easily destroyed by disease.

    B. They are badly affected by competition from invasive species.

    C. They are not stable and cannot easily survive an extreme weather event.

    D. They are very stable and can withstand ecological disruptions.

    E. They are unable to cope with change and have little resilience.

Self Study Guide

Question	If you answered this question incorrectly, see this Study Guide page for further review.	After completing your review, be sure to answer these questions in the Chapter 14 Practice Test.	Question	If you answered this question incorrectly, see this Study Guide page for further review.	After completing your review, be sure to answer these questions in the Chapter 14 Practice Test.
1	SG-212	9	8	SG-217	5, 11
2	SG-213	8, 12	9	SG-217	6
3	SG-213, SG-214	3	10	SG-217	6
4	SG-213	3	11	SG-219	7, 14
5	SG-214	2, 13	12	SG-219	7, 15
6	SG-217	4, 10	13	SG-219	7, 15
7	SG-217	4, 10	14	SG-219	15

Key Terms

pollination

sepal

petal

stamen

pistil

seed coat

germination

radicle

hypocotyl

artificial propagation

hormone

apical dominance

nastic response

tropism

phototropism

gravitropism

thigmotropism

ecological succession

primary succession

pioneer species

climax community

secondary succession

Reproduction in Seedless Plants (14.1)

As you saw in Chapter 3, all plants reproduce sexually by sporic reproduction.

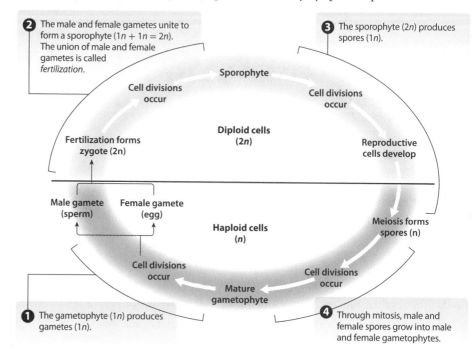

In seedless plants, such as mosses and ferns the gametophyte is a free-living, independent plant. The sperm must swim from the male gametophyte to the egg. Therefore, fertilization must take place in a moist environment, and the sperm have flagella.

In non-vascular mosses, the gametophyte is larger and longer-lived than the sporophyte. The smaller sporophyte depends on the gametophyte for food and support.

In vascular ferns, the sporophyte is larger and longer-lived.

Learning Check

1. **K/U** Fill in the blanks to complete each statement.

   a. The dominant form of mosses is _____ (n, 2n).

   b. The dominant form of ferns is _____ (n, 2n).

   c. The male and female gametes are _____ (n, 2n).

   d. In _____ (mosses, ferns), the sporophyte depends on the gametophyte to live.

   e. In seedless plants, sexual reproduction requires

   _____.

   f. Spores are formed through the process of _____ (meiosis, mitosis).

Flowers and Sexual Reproduction (14.1)

Seed-producing plants include the flowering angiosperms and the non-flowering gymnosperms. Seed plants also follow the reproductive cycle shown on the previous page.

In all seed plants:
- the gametophytes are not free-living plants.
- the male gametophytes develop into pollen grains that produce sperm cells.
- the female gametophytes produce egg cells.
- the entire male gametophyte (the pollen grain) travels to the female gametophyte (**pollination**).

In *gymnosperms*, including coniferous trees, pollination relies on wind. Seeds develop unprotected on the parent plant.

The reproductive organs of *angiosperms* are contained in the plant's flower.
- **Sepals** protect the flower bud.
- **Petals** attract pollinators.
- The *anthers* in **stamens** form pollen grains, containing sperm.
- Female gametophytes develop in the *ovary* of each **pistil**. Fertilization takes place on the *stigma* of each pistil.

Complete flowers have sepals, petals, stamens, and one or more pistils. *Incomplete flowers* do not have one or more of these parts.

   Perfect flowers have both pistils and stamens. *Imperfect flowers* have pistils or stamens, but not both. Some plants with imperfect flowers have both male and female flowers on one plant. Others do not.

   Dicots usually have petals, sepals, and stamens in multiples of four or five. Monocots usually have petals, sepals, and stamens in multiples of three.

Learning Check

1. **K/U** Label the key parts of this flower.

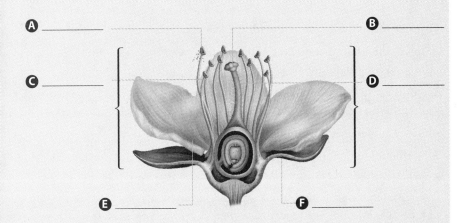

A _____   **B** _____

C _____   **D** _____

E _____   **F** _____

> **Study Tip**
>
> A quick, **labelled sketch** in your notes can help you remember features and characteristics of different flowers.

2. **A** A squash plant has five flowers on it. Two have stamens and three have pistils. Classify these flowers as complete, incomplete, perfect, or imperfect.

_____

_____

The Life Cycle of Flowering Plants (14.1)

This diagram shows the stages of the life cycle of flowering plants. Read about each stage as you examine the diagram.

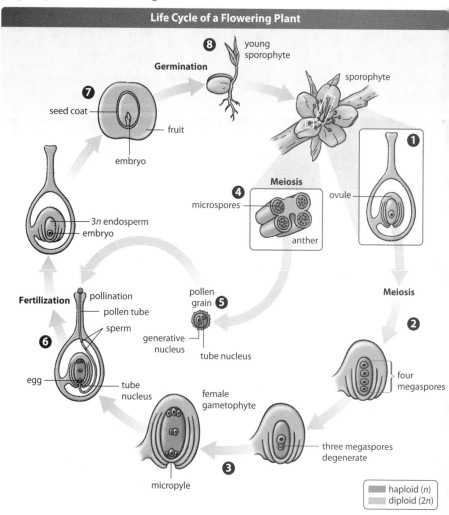

Life Cycle of a Flowering Plant

1. Inside the flower's ovary, an ovule containing an embryo sac begins to grow.

2. Inside the ovule, meiosis results in four haploid megaspores. Three disintegrate, leaving one female gametophyte.

3. Mitosis results in eight haploid nuclei divided into seven cells. (The two nuclei that share a cell are called *polar nuclei*.)

4. In the anther, meiosis produces microspores.

5. Each microspore undergoes mitosis to form a tube cell and a generative cell.

6. When the pollen grain lands on a stigma, a pollen tube forms. Two sperm cells form from the generative cell, and travel through the pollen tube to the ovule. One fuses with the egg to form a zygote. The other fuses with the polar nuclei to form a triploid (3n) cell that will become the nutrient-rich endosperm.

7. After fertilization, the embryo develops into the seed, the ovule develops into the protective seed coat, and the ovary develops into the fruit. In some plants, other organs also become part of the fruit.

8. When a seed absorbs water, it begins to **germinate**. The **radicle** emerges into the soil and becomes the plant's roots. The **hypocotyl** emerges above the soil.

Variations exist in this life cycle.

• Some plants are *self-pollinating*. They can pollinate themselves or another flower on the same plant. Most angiosperms are *cross-pollinating*.

• Some plants are pollinated by animals. They have strong scents, bright colours, or produce sweet nectar. Others are pollinated by wind, and produce great quantities of light pollen grains.

• Nutrient-rich endosperm nourishes the embryo as it grows. In some monocots, the endosperm makes up most of the mass of the seed. In dicots, the cotyledons absorb most of the endosperm as the seed matures.

Learning Check

1. **K/U** In what part of a flowering plant does each process occur?

   a. development of pollen grain _____

   b. pollination _____

   c. development of fruit _____

   d. germination _____

2. **a.** **C** Create a flowchart to show the stages in the development of the female gametophyte in a flowering plant.

   b. Create a flowchart to show the stages in the development of the male gametophyte in a flowering plant.

3. **K/U** What function do the polar nuclei have in the female gametophyte?

   _____

4. **T/I** Why is angiosperm fertilization called double fertilization?

   _____

5. **T/I** Infer what cross-pollinating means.

   _____

   _____

6. **T/I** Describe similarities and differences between sexual reproduction in seed plants and sexual reproduction in non-seed plants. Use a T-chart or a Venn diagram.

Study Tip

A **Venn diagram (question 6)** can help you compare and contrast two ideas. Venn diagrams in your notes make it easy to find key ideas when you review for a test.

Asexual Reproduction in Flowering Plants (14.1)

In asexual reproduction, a parent plant produces offspring that are genetically identical to it. Asexual reproduction does not introduce genetic variation, but does produce quick, reliable reproduction when environmental conditions are stable. Humans use the ability of plants to reproduce asexually to artificially propagate agricultural plants.

Table 14.1 on pages 590 and 591 of your textbook describes eight types of artificial propagation.

Table 14.1 on pages 590 and 591 of your textbook describes eight types of artificial propagation.

Study Tip

Simple **diagrams** can help you remember information. After you have read Table 14.1 on pages 590 and 591 in your textbook, examine each diagram and describe to yourself how each type of propagation works.

Learning Check

1. **K/U** For each example, name the type of propagation and one purpose or advantage.
   a. Part of a stem is placed in a growth medium. Roots and shoots develop, becoming a new plant.

   _____

   b. A section of low-hanging branch is bent to touch the ground, cut, and buried, while still attached to the parent plant. After roots and shoots develop, it is cut away from the parent.

   _____

2. **K/U** Name and describe a type of propagation that has each purpose or advantage.
   a. Can be used with plants that do not easily form roots from stem or leaf cuttings.

   _____

   b. Can shorten the time until a tree bears fruit.

   _____

3. **A** Suppose you own a nursery. You have several lilac bushes and want to produce several more for sale next spring.
   a. What type of propagation would you choose?

   _____

   b. Why

   _____

   _____

4. **A** Suppose you own an orchard with two types of apple trees. You want to produce apples with characteristics of both types. Varieties of apples cannot be reliably grown from seed.
   a. What type of vegetative propagation would you chose?

   _____

   b. Why

   _____

   _____

5. **T/I** Think back to Chapter 13. What type of plant cell results in new growth in each form of propagation?

   _____

Plant Growth and Development (14.2)

Once a seed germinates, the development of the plant is guided by plant hormones, environmental stimuli, as well as the presence of light, water, nutrients, and acidity.

Plant **hormones** work in different combinations to stimulate or inhibit growth in different areas of the plant. For example:

Auxins stimulate cell division and elongation in stems and roots. They also influence a plant's response to light and gravity. Auxins produced by the apical meristem cause **apical dominance**, in which plant growth is mostly upward.

Cytokinins promote cell division and prevent aging of leaves and fruit.

Gibberellins stimulate cell elongation in shoots and seed germination in seeds. They can promote early flowering and are often used commercially to increase fruit size.

Ethylene promotes ripening of fruit. Fruits such as bananas are often picked and shipped unripe. At their destination, ethylene is introduced.

Abscisic acid keeps seeds dormant, inhibits shoot and leaf growth, and closes stomata.

Plants respond in many ways to environmental stimuli.

• Plants grow toward a light source. This is caused by an unequal distribution of auxin, and is called **phototropism**. 	• **Gravitropism** describes a response to gravity. Roots generally exhibit positive gravitropism. Stems exhibit negative gravitropism. 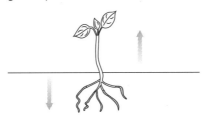
• Some plants respond to mechanical stimuli, known as **thigmotropism**. An example is a vine that will twist around a fence or tree. 	• A flower that closes its petals at night and opens them during the day is exhibiting a **nastic response**—a reversible response to a stimulus that is not associated with the direction of the stimulus. 

Plants require nutrients to carry out growth, reproduction, and other cellular processes, and will respond to their presence or absence in various ways. For example, plants require nitrogen, magnesium, and iron to manufacture chlorophyll.

Most plants grow best in a narrow range of slightly acidic soil, ranging from pH 6 to 7. (pH 7 is neutral.) Fewer plant species tolerate slightly basic soil, ranging from pH 7 to 8. Plants that tolerate slightly basic soil include geraniums, beans, lettuce, pears, and plums.

Learning Check

1. (K/U) A plant placed in a window develops new growth on one side only. What type of response is this?

_____

2. (K/U) A plant sends out runners that develop roots wherever they touch the ground. What type of response is this?

_____

3. (K/U) An unripe pear in a bowl with ripe apples will ripen earlier than if it were alone. What hormone causes this?

_____

4. (A) If a houseplant is getting too tall, you can cut off the top of the plant. This will encourage new side branches to grow. How does this work?

_____

5. (T/I) Why is gravitropism advantageous for a plant?

_____

6. (C) The minerals in Table 14.3 on page 597 of your textbook are arranged by the amount present in a plant. List the minerals that are involved with each type of cell function in the table below. Some minerals may belong in more than one group.

Photosynthesis	Growth, maintenance, and repair	Reproduction

7. (T/I) Describe a situation where two plant hormones work together.

_____

_____

8. (A) **a.** What plant hormone controls a plant's response to gravity?

_____

b. Describe how the hormone controls this response.

_____

_____

9. (A) Predict how a plant might react to an absence of nitrogen, magnesium, and iron.

_____

_____

Study Tip

Organizing information in new ways (**question 6**) can help you see and remember relationships.

Succession and Sustainability (14.3)

As you learned in Chapter 13, plants provide many ecosystem services, including providing food, habitat, and oxygen; trapping carbon dioxide; filtering water; reducing erosion; and cycling nutrients such as nitrogen and phosphorus.

Ecosystems undergo frequent change. Small and large ecological disturbances occur frequently. These can include natural disturbances such as forest fires, floods, and disease outbreaks, and disturbances caused by humans, such as road building, clear cutting of forests, and pesticide spraying. Plants play a key role in **ecological succession**—establishing and developing communities. In fact, some plants rely on ecological disturbances to survive.

An ecological disturbance can make an area appear barren, with no vegetation or topsoil. Before long, new species appear. This process is known as **primary succession**. The first species that appear in primary succession are called **pioneer species**, and are often small plants such as liverworts. As these organisms die, soil begins to form, and larger plants such as mosses can take root. Grasses and shrubs often follow.

As plants grow, they compete for light and living space. Some species are better able to survive in the new conditions. These form a **climax community**—a relatively stable population, and the final stage of ecological succession.

If soil remains intact after an ecological disturbance, colonization can begin more quickly. Often seeds and roots remain buried in the soil, and plants such as grasses can find enough nutrients in the soil to survive. In fact, the seeds of jack pine trees will only germinate after a fire. Recolonization of an area when soil remains intact is called **secondary succession**.

| Annual plants | Shrubs | Grasses/ herbs | Pines | Young oak/ hickory | Pines die, oak/hickory mature | Mature oak/hickory forest |

| 0 | 1–2 years | 3–4 years | 4–15 years | 5–15 years | 10–30 years | 50–75 years |

Topics in biology have many **connections** to one another. As you read about succession, list other ideas you have learned about in this course that relate to succession and sustainability.

1. **K/U** Number these events in the order they would occur. Add any steps you think are missing in the space provided.

   a. _____ Shrubs and low trees grow.

   b. _____ Small plants cling to the rocks and grow.

   c. _____ Larger plants grow in the soil.

   d. _____ The ecosystem becomes relatively stable.

   e. _____ More soil is created.

   f. _____ Tall trees grow.

   g. _____ Trees that need a lot of sunlight die.

   h. _____ A flood washes away all vegetation and topsoil on a hillside.

   i. _____ _____

   j. _____ _____

2. **K/U** Describe a small or large ecological disturbance that has occurred in your neighbourhood.

   _____

   _____

3. **T/I a.** Describe an example of an ecosystem near you that is changing.

   _____

   b. How are plants involved in the change?

   _____

4. **A** How would species diversity in an ecosystem affect the way the ecosystem responds to a disruption? Use an example if it helps you explain.

   _____

   _____

5. **A** The illustration on the previous page shows secondary succession in a terrestrial forest. What roles do you think plants would play in ecological succession in an aquatic environment?

   _____

   _____

6. **T/I** Skim Chapters 3, 7, and 13 of your textbook. Describe two ideas that appear in each chapter that could help someone understand ecological succession.

   _____

   _____

   _____

   _____

   _____

   _____

Bringing It All Together

Add information and connections to this web to summarize what you know about plant reproduction and growth.

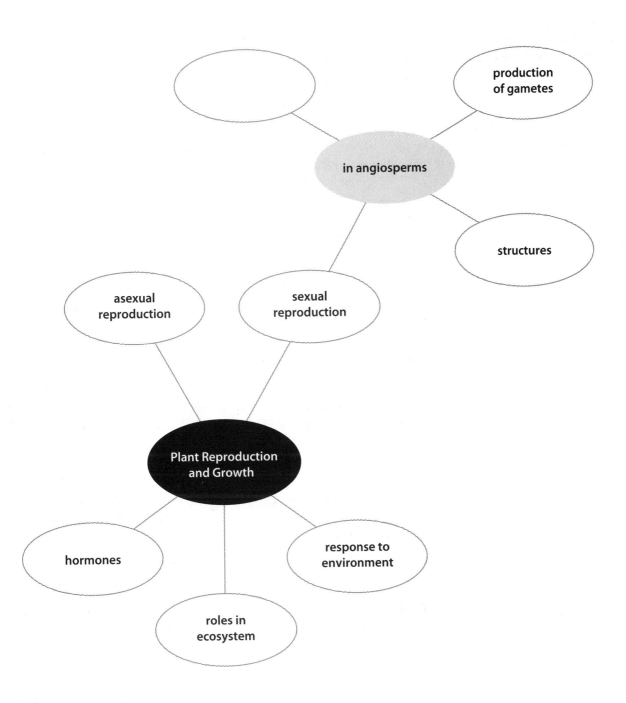

1. (K/U) Sporic reproduction involves
   A. a haploid gametophyte and a haploid sporophyte.
   B. a diploid gametophyte and a diploid zygote.
   C. a haploid gametophyte and a diploid sporophyte.
   D. a diploid gametophyte and a haploid sporophyte.
   E. a diploid gametophyte and a haploid zygote.

2. (K/U) What is true about gymosperm reproduction?
   A. Sperm is transferred to the egg by swimming in water.
   B. Sperm is transferred to the egg by a pollen tube.
   C. Protected seeds develop within the ovary wall.
   D. The female reproductive structure is the pistil.
   E. Double fertilization occurs.

3. (K/U) Which plant is dioecious?
   A. corn
   B. birch tree
   C. pine tree
   D. ginkgo tree
   E. fig tree

4. (T/I) What happens when the apical meristem is removed from a plant?
   A. The plant grows side branches.
   B. The plant grows rapidly.
   C. The cell walls are weakened.
   D. Bud growth is inhibited.
   E. Leaf stomata stop working.

5. (K/U) Which activity is **not** a growth response?
   A. expansion of roots into soil
   B. vines twisting around a tree
   C. opening and closing of flower petals
   D. plant bending towards light coming in a window
   E. extension of pollen tube towards the ovule

6. (K/U) Which micronutrient assists plants with the process of photosynthesis?
   A. copper
   B. manganese
   C. iron
   D. chlorine
   E. zinc

7. (T/I) What is the correct order for the stages of primary succession from earliest to latest?
   I A mature community develops.
   II The decay of pioneer species creates soil.
   III Lichens being breaking down rocks and forming soil.
   IV Micro-organisms and insects begin to occupy the area.
   V Sun-tolerant trees begin to grow.
   A. II, III, V, IV, I
   B. II, IV, III, V, I
   C. III, II, V, I, IV
   D. IV, II, III, I, V
   E. III, II, IV, V, I

8. (K/U) What is sexual reproduction?
   _____

9. (K/U) What is the dominant generation in non-vascular plants?
   _____

10. (K/U) What plant hormone can grocers use to speed up the ripening process of fruit?
    _____

11. (K/U) What type of trophism has occurred when a plant responds by growing away from the stimulus?
    _____

12. (T/I) What adaptations allow gymnosperms to reproduce in a dry environment?
    _____
    _____
    _____
    _____

13. (T/I) Describe the process of double fertilization.
    _____
    _____
    _____
    _____
    _____

4. (T/I) Describe the series of events that will occur after each situation.

a. A glacier retreats over a landmass.

_____

_____

_____

b. Lightning causes a forest fire.

_____

_____

_____

15. (A) (C) What observations can you make about the forest succession illustrated in the graph below? Describe what an observer might see in the area at each time A, B and C.

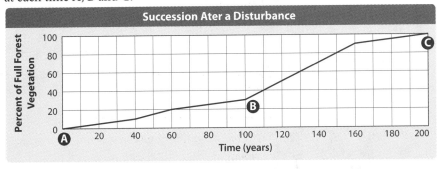

_____

_____

_____

Self Study Guide

Question	If you answered this question incorrectly, see this Study Guide page for further review.	Question	If you answered this question incorrectly, see this Study Guide page for further review.
1	SG-212	9	SG-212
2	SG-213	10	SG-217
3	SG-213	11	SG-217
4	SG-217	12	SG-213
5	SG-217	13	SG-214
6	SG-217	14	SG-219
7	SG-219	15	SG-219
8	SG-212, SG-213, SG-214		

Add information and connections to this web diagram to summarize what you know about plant anatomy, growth, and function. Include information from other units that is relevant.

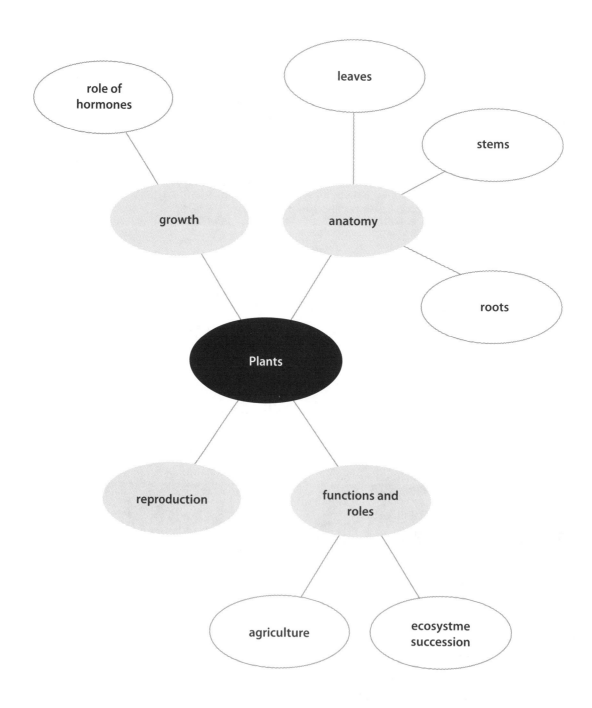

Unit 5 Practice Test

1. **T/I** Which fuel is a first generation biofuel?
   - **A.** coal
   - **B.** liquid petroleum
   - **C.** natural gas
   - **D.** corn
   - **E.** peat

2. **K/U** Which describes the structure of parenchyma cells?
   - **A.** flexible, with thin walls
   - **B.** elongated, occur in long strands
   - **C.** thick walls, lack cytoplasm
   - **D.** needle-shaped, with thick walls
   - **E.** short and irregular shaped

3. **K/U** Which tissue contain parenchyma, collenchyma, and sclerenchyma cells?
   - **A.** apical meristem
   - **B.** intercalary meristem
   - **C.** ground tissue
   - **D.** dermal tissue
   - **E.** vascular tissue

4. **K/U** What type of specialized epidermal cell controls the gas exchange in plants?
   - **A.** root hairs
   - **B.** stomata
   - **C.** trichomes
   - **D.** guard cells
   - **E.** tracheids

5. **K/U** All materials that enter a root must pass through which structure?
   - **A.** root cap
   - **B.** cortex
   - **C.** pith
   - **D.** aerenchyma
   - **E.** cuticle

6. **K/U** The age of a tree is calculated by counting the annual rings in which tissue?
   - **A.** dermal tissue
   - **B.** apical meristem
   - **C.** phloem
   - **D.** bark
   - **E.** xylem

7. **K/U** What is a whorled leaf arrangement?
   - **A.** Two leaves attached to the stem directly opposite each other.
   - **B.** Leaves arranged in a step-like pattern on either side of the stem.
   - **C.** Three or more leaves evenly spaced around a stem.
   - **D.** Veins that branch off from a common point.
   - **E.** Veins that branch off along the central vein.

8. **K/U** What is true about pressure in the phloem?
   - **A.** Negative pressure drives the flow from source to sink.
   - **B.** Positive pressure drives the flow from source to sink.
   - **C.** Positive pressure drives the flow from sink to source.
   - **D.** Negative pressure drives the flow from sink to source.
   - **E.** Pressure changes can occur in only direction.

9. **K/U** What is the name for the female gametophytes in seed plants?
   - **A.** ovules
   - **B.** pistils
   - **C.** stamens
   - **D.** microspores
   - **E.** macrospores

10. **K/U** Angiosperms always produce
    - **A.** one sperm cell in each pollen grain.
    - **B.** two sperm cells in each pollen grain.
    - **C.** two haploid megaspores from the ovule.
    - **D.** three haploid megaspores from the ovule
    - **E.** polar nuclei from the process of meiosis.

11. **K/U** The $3n$ cell formed as the result of double fertilization develops into which structure?
    - **A.** endosperm
    - **B.** seed coat
    - **C.** cotyledon
    - **D.** dicotyledon
    - **E.** embryo

12. **K/U** Which hormone is classified as an inhibitory hormone?
    - **A.** molybdenum
    - **B.** gibberellins
    - **C.** auxins
    - **D.** cytokinins
    - **E.** abscisic acid

13. **K/U** Where is the process of secondary succession most likely to occur?
    - **A.** on a rocky shore line
    - **B.** on a volcanic island after an eruption
    - **C.** in the landscape left from a retreating glacier
    - **D.** in an empty field where crops were once grown
    - **E.** in the rocky landscape of the Artic

14. (K/U) What is a concentration gradient?

_____

15. (K/U) What two processes facilitate long distance transport through xylem?

_____

_____

16. (K/U) How does sucrose enter into phloem?

_____

17. (T/I) What characteristic of angiosperms has allowed them to become the most diverse and widespread type of plant on Earth?

_____

18. (T/I) An example of companion planting involves three different plants called "the three sisters." Explain the principles behind this type of agricultural practice.

_____

_____

_____

19. (K/U) What are two functions of roots?

_____

_____

20. (C) Create a series of diagrams to illustrate the processes of phototropism, negative gravitropism, and thigmotropism.

21. (K/U) Complete the table to compare monocots and dicots.

	Dicot	Monocot
Number of embryonic seed leaves		
Venation		
Number of flower parts		
Root system		

22. (T/I) One of the goals of agricultural scientists is to find genetic combinations that maximize the yield in crop plants. What are some of the consequences of this research?

_____

_____

_____

_____

23. (T/I) Describe how dandelions, cacti, and aquatic plants have developed different root systems in response to their specific environmental conditions.

_____

_____

_____

24. (T/I) What are the main functions of the cotyledon found in dicot plant seeds.

_____

25. (T/I) What is one advantage and one disadvantage of asexual reproduction in plants compared to sexual reproduction?

_____

_____

26. (T/I) What types of adaptations have been made by plants that are dependent on the presence of wind for pollination?

_____

_____

27. (A) Describe some of the adverse effects of deforestation. How is it affecting the biosphere?

_____

_____

_____

Self Study Guide

Question	If you answered this question incorrectly, see this Study Guide page for further review.	Question	If you answered this question incorrectly, see this Study Guide page for further review.
1	SG-198	15	SG-205
2	SG-200	16	SG-205
3	SG-201	17	SG-213
4	SG-200	18	SG-198
5	SG-203	19	SG-203
6	SG-201	20	SG-217
7	SG-203	21	SG-203, SG-213, SG-215
8	SG-205	22	SG-198, SG-199
9	SG-213	23	SG-203
10	SG-214	24	SG-215
11	SG-214	25	SG-213, SG-214
12	SG-217	26	SG-213, SG-214
13	SG-219	27	SG-219
14	SG-205		

Answers

Chapter 1 Self Assessment, page SG-4

1. D	**2.** E	**3.** C	**4.** A
5. B	**6.** B	**7.** E	**8.** A
9. E	**10.** B	**11.** B	**12.** C
13. A	**14.** D		

Defining a Species, page SG-6

1. All three are useful for defining species. Morphological and biological are based on observations; phylogenetic is based on relationships. Morphological and phylogenetic can be used with separated or extinct species; biological cannot. Morphological is difficult when there is significant variation within a species.

2. a. Morphological: A chicken and a duck have different shaped bills and the duck has webbed feet.
b. Biological: Fertile offspring are not produced.
c. Phylogenetic: Can be used with extinct species, such as the lizards' ancestor.

Using Hierarchical Categories to Identify and Name Organisms, page SG-7

1. B

2. Domain, Class, Family, Genus

3. Both include and organize information into more and more specific categories.

4. a. *Branta canadensis* **b.** Domain, kingdom, and phylum **c.** *Branta sandvicensis*; same genus (*Branta*)

Determining Relationships Among Species, page SG-9

1. A

2. a. Artiodactyla **b.** *Aepyceros melampus* and *Oryx gazella* **c.** *Aepyceros melampus*; same family (Bovidae)

3. The tree should show a common stem with dogs, wolves and seals on one branch and cats and hyenas on another branch.

4. The goosberry, tomato, and potato all share a common ancestor, but the tomato and potato are more closely related to each other than they are to the gooseberry.

5. a. We are closely related to chimpanzees.
b. phylogenetic

6. It might indicate if a disease could be passed from one species to the other or help predict how the disease might affect one species based on its effects on the other.

7. a. Mostly anatomical evidence, such as structure of legs and hoofs, shape of teeth and head, and size of animal. **b.** It can help them predict how horses may react to diseases and other environmental factors, and understand what traits they may be able to breed in their horses.

What are Kingdoms and Domains?, page SG-10

1. B

2. There are too many diverse organisms to classify them into specific groups alone. General groups help us understand relationships among the organisms.

3. a. Eukaryota; members of Prokaryota are all unicellular. **b.** Prokaryota; this is a Bacteria.
c. Prokaryota; this is an Archaea.

Using a Dichotomous Key, page SG-11

1. E

2. In choice 1, it was determined that the organism was prokaryotic. Bacteria are eukaryotic.

3. Knowing if an organism is a heterotroph is only helpful once Bacteria, Archaea, and Protista have been ruled out, since these kingdoms include heterotrophs as well as autotrophs.

4. a. Smell the twigs. **b.** Whether the leaves are light or dark, and shiny or hairy. This will tell you if the tree is *Betula occidentalis* or *Betula kenaica*.

What Types of Biodiversity Are There?, page SG-12

1. a. species **b.** ecosystem **c.** genetic

2. Species diversity; there are many types of species living in this ecosystem. Ecosystem diversity; the ecosystem changes as the water gets deeper.

3. Genetic diversity is a subset of species diversity, which is a subset of ecosystem diversity.

4. Answers may vary. For example: **a.** the plants and animals in a ravine **b.** the front or backyard of a house

Why Is Biodiversity Important?, page SG-13

1. Some individuals may be able to survive colder temperatures and reproduce.

2. A diverse ocean ecosystem has many plants, (that provide oxygen) and animals (that provide food). If some species populations decline, the whales can still get what they need from the remaining species.

3. Advantages: uniform size and maturity makes harvesting easier and more efficient. Disadvantages: disease resistance is reduced, genetic information is lost for future generations.

4. If the population of an endangered species becomes very small, there is little genetic diversity. Living zoos could increase the organisms' genetic diversity, with benefits such as improving disease resistance.

5. Some individuals in a species may be more able to withstand higher temperatures, and pass on this trait to future generations.

Human Impact on Biodiversity, page SG-14

1. Answers may vary. For example: building homes and roads, and damming rivers decreased diversity; restoring wetlands, installing bird feeders and birdhouses, and reducing pesticide use increased diversity.

2. **a.** The new plant species might out-compete existing species, decreasing biodiversity. **b.** The dam would destroy the river ecosystem, decreasing biodiversity. **c.** Animals crossing the road might be hit by cars, decreasing biodiversity. **d.** The plants could provide food and shelter for animals, increasing biodiversity.

3. Answers may vary. For example: building new roads → snakes and frogs are killed crossing the road → weasels and birds that prey on them starve → larger predators also decrease in number

Chapter 1 Practice Test, page SG-16

1. E   2. D   3. B   4. D
5. D   6. A   7. D

8. Study of cell types and genes.

9. **a.** Clockwise from top right: cell membrane, chromosomes, ribosomes, nucleus **b.** Eukaryotic **c.** It has a membrane-bound nucleus.

10. **Morphology:** Advantage: simplicity. Disadvantage: having to decide how much difference between individuals is too much variation. **Phylogeny:** Advantage: can be applied to extinct species, considers DNA analysis. Disadvantage: evolutionary histories are not known for all species.

11. **i.** first word is the genus name **ii.** second word is the species name **iii.** genus is capitalized **iv.** species is lower case **v.** both are italicized (underlined when written by hand)

12. Eukarya; Animalia; eukaryotic; heterotrophs; No cell wall. Eukarya; Protista; eukaryotic; autotrophs, heterotrophs; Cellulose in some, occasionally no cell wall. Archaea; Archaea; prokaryotic; autotrophs, heterotrophs; Not peptidoglycan; occasionally no cell wall. Eukarya; Plantae; eukaryotic; autotrophs; Cellulose

Chapter 2 Self Assessment, page SG-18

1. B   2. C   3. B   4. D
5. C   6. E   7. D   8. A
9. E   10. A   11. D   12. B
13. A   14. A   15. C

Viruses and Prions Cause Diseases in Plants and Animals, page SG-20

1. **a.** Viruses have either DNA or RNA and can replicate. **b.** Viruses lack the metabolic machinery to carry out most of the processes associated with living organisms.

2. No cell plan. A prion is not a living cell.

3. Diagrams should show key features of Figure 2.3 on page 55 of the student textbook.

Comparing Two Domains: Archaea and Bacteria, page SG-22

1. C   2. D

3. **a.** binary fission. **b.** cell with single chromosome → chromosome duplicates → cell elongates, the two chromosomes separate → cell wall forms → original cell splits into two smaller, genetically identical cells

4. Diagrams may vary. Prokaryotic cells have a single, circular chromosome and plasmids composed of non-chromosomal DNA. They have no membrane bound organelles.

5. This trait can be passed to other cells in the colony when plasmids are transferred in the process of conjugation.

6. **Archaea:** do not cause disease, some fix atmospheric carbon dioxide, some release methane gas, can be used as antibiotics and to clean up heavy metal contamination. **Bacteria:** cause diseases in plant and animals, some fix nitrogen or decompose organic matter, can be used as antibiotics and to produce fermented food

Evolution of the Eukaryotic Cell, page SG-24

1. E

2. Mitochondria, chloroplasts, and prokaryotic cells have similar membranes and ribosomes, all reproduce by binary fission, and each contains a circular chromosome with similar gene sequences.

3. *Endo* means "within," and symbiosis describes two or more organisms living in close association. In endosymbiosis, eukaryotic cells were formed by prokaryotic cells living symbiotically inside the host cell.

4. Tree diagrams should have two branches: Prokaryotes and Eukaryotes. Eukaryotes branch should split into three: animals, fungi, and plants. Since all eukaryotes have mitochondria, mitochondria arose in eukaryotes before the split between animals, fungi, and plants. Since only plants have chloroplasts, chloroplasts arose on the plants branch, after animals and fungi had branched off.

Eukaryotes: Life Cycles and Reproduction, page SG-26

1. **a.** Both describe sets of chromosomes in cells; haploid cells have one set, diploid cells have two sets. **b.** A gamete is a haploid sex cell; a zygote is a diploid cell

formed when two haploid gametes fuse (fertilization). **c.** Both are a type of cell division; meiosis produces haploid gametes, mitosis produces identical diploid copies of the parent cell.

2. **a.** Clockwise: meiosis, haploid (*n*), gametes, zygote, mitosis, diploid (*2n*) **b.** One generation in the life cycle is haploid and one is diploid. The diploid organism produces haploid spores through meiosis. The gametes join through fertilization to form a diploid zygote, which grows into a new corn plant though mitosis.

3. Drawing should show key features of gametic life cycle in Figure 2.17 on page 70 of the student textbook.

4. **Similar:** both have a reproductive stage that produces a new organism. **Different:** bacteria reproduce asexually through binary fission, and only use mitosis; fish reproduce sexually through gametes, and use meiosis and mitosis.

Kingdom Protista, page SG-28

1. **a.** Scientists have placed organisms into this kingdom that do not fit into other kingdoms. **b.** Organisms are classified in other kingdoms because they have specific characteristics.

2. digesting food, getting rid of excess water

3. **b. Phylum:** Pyrophyta; two flagella, cause red tides; *Gonyaulax catenella*. **Group:** Euglenoids; one flagella, autotrophic or heterotrophic; *Euglena*. **Group:** Diatoms; silica cell wall, unique double shells, reproduce asexually by mitosis; phytoplankton. **c. Phylum:** Ciliophora; fixed shape, many cilia used for locomotion and feeding; *Paramecia*. **Phylum:** Zoomastigina; one or more flagella, can be parasitic, free-living, or mutualistic; protist living in gut of termites. **d. Phylum:** Sporozoa; all parasitic, life cycle alternates between sexual and asexual reproduction, cause malaria; *Plasmodium*. **e. Phylum:** Myxomycota; stream along as a multinucleated mass of cytoplasm; plasmodial slime moulds. **Phylum:** Acrasiomycota; individual amoeboid cells in colonies; cellular slime moulds. **Phylum:** Oomycota; filamentous organisms, free-living or parasitic, create fungus-like threads; water moulds.

Chapter 2 Practice Test, page SG-30

1. E   **2.** D   **3.** A   **4.** E

5. C   **6.** D   **7.** B

8. It would have a thick protein layer.

9. chloroplasts, mitochondria

10. Both are complete cells; haploid cells have one set of chromosomes, diploid cells have two sets.

11. a. plant-like protists; they use photosynthesis to obtain nutrition **b.** fungus-like protists; they absorb nutrients from other organisms living or dead **c.** animal-like protists or protozoans; they consume other organisms for food

12. Genetic engineers can insert a gene into the genetic material of a virus. The virus then enters a host cell and directs the cell to make multiple copies of the virus. Each copy contains the added gene to redirect cell activity.

13. Diagrams should show key features of the attachment, entry, provirus formation, and cell division steps in Figure 2.3 on page 55 of the textbook.

14. a. Mitochondria, chloroplasts, and prokaryotic cells have similar membranes and ribosomes, all reproduce by binary fission, and each contains a circular chromosome with similar gene sequences. **b.** Evolution of mitochondria; all eukaryotic cells have mitochondria but only plant cells have chloroplasts.

Chapter 3 Self Assessment, page SG-32

1. D   **2.** B   **3.** A   **4.** B

5. A   **6.** C   **7.** D   **8.** E

9. C   **10.** B   **11.** D   **12.** E

13. A   **14.** C   **15.** D

Algae – The Evolutionary Link between Protists and the Plant Kingdom, page SG-35

1. Algae: lack true roots, stems, leaves; live in aquatic or moist environments; zygotes and embryos unprotected. **Plants:** most have true roots, stems, and leaves; live in terrestrial or aquatic environments; zygotes and embryos are protected. **Both:** autotrophic by photosynthesis, have chlorophyll, store food energy as starch, have similar DNA sequences.

2. Three of the following: Cellulose and xylem tissue (in vascular plants) help support the plant against the force of gravity. Cellulose cell wall keeps plant cells from drying out. Embryo enclosed to protect it and keep it from drying out. Sporic life cycle gives embryos a better chance of survival on land. Spores or seeds dispersed by wind so the new plants do not compete with the parent plant. Vascular plants have special tissues (xylem and phloem) that transport materials through the plant.

Kingdom Plantae, page SG-37

1. a. non-vascular plants, seedless vascular plants, seed producing vascular plants
b. Non-vascular plants: no vascular tissue, gametophyte dominant, spores. Seedless vascular plants: xylem and phloem, sporophyte dominant, spores. Seed producing vascular plants: xylem and phloem, sporophyte dominant, seeds.

2. A seed contains a fertilized embryo and a food supply. A spore is a reproductive cell with a very small food supply; it is fertilized after leaving the plant.

3. a. spores **b.** female or male gamete **c.** male or female gamete **d.** fertilization **e.** mitosis

4. Vascular plants have internal systems that collect and transport materials, so can store water. Non-vascular plants depend on osmosis and diffusion to collect and move materials.

5. Monocots: one cotyledon, vascular bundles in leaves are usually parallel, vascular bundles in stem are scattered, multiples of three flower parts. **Dicots:** two cotyledons, vascular bundles in leaves are usually netlike, vascular bundles in stem are arranged in a ring, multiples of four and five flower parts

Kingdom Fungi, page SG-39

1. multicellular (except for yeast), eukaryotic, heterotrophic by absorption, lack chloroplasts, cell walls made of chitin

2. They consume decomposing animal and plant material.

3. Lichens are formed by a symbiotic (or parasitic) relationship between a fungus and a cyanobacterium or a green alga.

4. Chytrids: Sexual reproduction: spores have flagella. Asexual reproduction: cytoplasm cleaves in a sporangium, producing motile zoospores.
Sac Fungi: Sexual reproduction: ascospores within asci, usually within a fruiting body. Asexual reproduction (most common): spores. Yeasts reproduce asexually by mitosis or budding.
Zygospore Fungi: Sexual reproduction: nuclei of haploid hyphae fuse to produce diploid zygospores. With moisture, zygospores undergo meiosis. Asexual reproduction: spores. **Club Fungi:** Sexual reproduction (most common): Hyphae from two mating types fuse, producing mycelium with two nuclei which form fruiting bodies that release spores

Kingdom Animalia, page SG-43

1. Cnidarians: tissue, two body layers, sac plan, radial symmetry, no coelom. **Flatworms:** organs, three body layers, bilateral symmetry, acoelomate. **Roundworms:** organs, three body layers, bilateral symmetry, Pseudocoelomate.

2.

1a. deuterostome with no segmentation echinoderm	**1b.** protostome with no segmentation (go to 2)
2a. radial symmetry two germ layers Cnidaria	**2b.** bilateral symmetry three germ layers (go to 3)
3a. no body cavity Platyhelminthes	**3b.** body cavity (go to 4)
4a. pseudocoelomate Nematoda	**4b.** coelmate (go to 5)
5a. segmentation and protostome Arthropoda	**5b.** segmentation and deuterostome Echinodermata

3. a. Invertebrates include all of the animals that do not have a backbone composed of bone or cartilage.
b. Sponges: asymmetrical, aquatic, sessile, loosely organized cells, no well-defined tissues, two layers of cells, sac body plan, reproduce asexually and sexually, filter-feeders. **Cnidarians:** radial symmetry, aquatic, two body forms, well-defined tissues, no organs, two layers of cells, sac body plan, sting their prey. **Worms:** bilateral symmetry, segmented, motile, acoelomates, defined organs, defined head end, three cell layers, sac body plan. **Molluscs:** bilateral symmetry, segmented, motile, coelomates, defined organs, defined head end, three cell layers, tube-within-a-tube body plan, second most diverse animal phylum. **Echinoderms:** radial symmetry, aquatic, motile, coelomates, defined organs, exoskeleton, tube feet, water vascular system, carnivorous, herbivorous, and filter feeders. **Arthropods:** bilateral symmetry, segmented, motile, coelomates, defined organs and head end, three cell layers, tube-within-a tube body plan, exoskeleton, largest animal phylum.

4. a. Vertebrates have movement muscles attached to a nonochord that extends through the length of the body. They have a nerve chord (brain and spinal chord) that extends along the back and is protected by the skull and the spine.
b. Fish: aquatic, breath through gills; lampreys have cartilage skeleton, no jaws, no paired fins; sharks and rays have cartilage skeleton, jaws, paired fins; bony fish have bony skeleton, jaws, paired fins, most have swim bladders. **Amphibians:** breath through lungs and moist skin; have limbs; external fertilization; dependence on water puts many populations at risk due to climate change, pollution, habitat destruction. **Reptiles:** breathe through lungs; ectothermic; have limbs, three-chambered heart; internal fertilization; scales and eggs with shells prevent dehydration; incubation temperature often determines sex of offspring; a few give birth to live offspring. **Birds:** breathe through lungs; endothermic; have limbs, four-chambered heart, feathers, hollow bones, toothless skulls, compact bodies, high body temperature, unique respiratory system; most can fly; internal fertilization, shelled eggs. **Mammals:** breathe through lungs; endothermic; have limbs, hair, four-chambered heart, well developed

brains; internal fertilization, most have live offspring, a few lay eggs (montremes) or partially developed offspring in a pouch (marsupials), females secrete milk to feed young.

The Biodiversity Crisis, page SG-44

1. a. The variety of groups in an ecosystem. **b.** The variety of genes in a population (gene pool). **c.** The reduction in genetic, species, and ecosystem diversity that could be the beginning of a mass extinction.

2. The rapid death of a large percent of all organisms within an area.

3. Food Sources: climate change affects growth of plants that animals depend on for food; decreases animal population and genetic diversity. **Habitat:** higher temperatures on mountains reduce habitat for cold-weather plants; decreases genetic diversity. **Reproduction:** warmer or cooler temperatures change gender balance in reptile populations; could lead to species extinction. **Pollination:** climate change mismatches the life cycles of plants and pollinators; decreases population and genetic diversity of both organisms. **Aquatic Ecosystems:** increased water temperature reduces insect populations and can change gender imbalance; reduces animal populations that eat insects; decreases fish growth; reduces ecosystem diversity.

Chapter 3 Practice Test, page SG-46

1. C	**2.** B	**3.** B	**4.** D
5. A	**6.** E	**7.** C	

8. Examples could include the production of embryos, and the development of vascular tissue, seeds, and flowers.

9. Gymnosperms are cone bearing (non-enclosed seeds) while angiosperms have seeds in fruit (enclosed in protective tissue).

10. Answers could include: eukaryotic, multicellular organisms that cells lack cell walls; hetertrophic; usually mobile at one stage in life; reproduce sexually, produce an embryo that undergoes stages of development.

11. Diagram should show key features of Figure 3.8 on page 94 of the student textbook.

12. For example, species diversity on mountains decreases when temperatures increase, flowering plants that rely on insect pollination may reproduce less successfully if increasing temperatures cause them to flower before their insect pollinator is in adult form.

13. a. Across each row:
Seedless, vascular; plantae; ferns, club mosses, horsetails, whisk ferns.
Link between protests and plants; protista; green algae.
Animal lacking backbone; animalia; sponges, cnidarians, worms, molluscs, echinoderms, arthropods.
Lack vascular tissue, flowers, seeds; plantae; bryophytes (mosses, liverworts, hornworts).
Heterotrophic; Fungi; Fungi imperfecti, chytrids, sygospore, club fungi.
Cone producing; Plantae; Gymnosperms (conifers).
Animal with backbone; animalia; fish, amphibians, reptiles, birds, mammals.
Flowering plants; Plantae; Angiosperm (flowering plants).
b. Tree diagram should have two branches: non-vascular plants and vascular plants. Vascular plants splits into seedless and seed-producing, then seed-producing splits into monocots and dicots.

Unit 1 Practice Test, page SG-49

1. B	**2.** C	**3.** B	**4.** E
5. D	**6.** A	**7.** A	**8.** C
9. E	**10.** B	**11.** A	**12.** B

13. Prokaryotic cells lack a true nucleus while eukaryotic cells have a membrane-bound nucleus.

14. methanogenesis

15. endosymbiosis

16. Chlorophyta

17. modern amphibians, reptiles, birds, and mammals

18. domain, kingdom, phylum, class, order, family, genus, species

19. They would examine anatomical characteristics like body size, shape, and physical features, and look at physical and chemical functions including internal processes and DNA evidence.

20. Viruses are not cellular and cannot carry out life functions on their own.

21. **Bacteria (binary fission):** cell grows, copies its original single chromosome, and elongates, the two chromosomes separate, the cell partitions then splits into two, smaller genetically identical cells. **Viruses (replication):** virus attaches to and enters host cell, uses host to replicate and assemble more viruses which break out of the host (lytic cycle); some make a provirus by adding their DNA to the host's chromosome and replicating the DNA (lysogenic cycle), then continue the lytic cycle.

22. Diagram should show key features of Figure 3.9 on page 97 of the student textbook.

23. Scientists develop new techniques such as DNA testing to more accurately classify organisms. Recent examples include classifying green algae as protists not plants, and reorganising the evolutionary tree to show birds have descended from dinosaurs.

24. Organisms may vary. **Protista:** eukaryote, unicellular and multicellular; cellulose cell walls, some have no cell walls; autrophic and heterotrophic; asexual and sexual reproduction. **Plantae:** eukaryote, multicellular, cellulose cell walls, autrotrophic, sexual reproduction. **Fungi:** eukaryote, mostly multicellular, chitin cell walls, heterotrophic, sexual and asexual reproduction. **Animalia:** eukaryote, multicellular, no cell wall, heterotrophic, sexual reproduction.

25. Answers may vary. For example: **a.** Climate change, pollution, habitat destruction, competition from invasive species, illegal trade. **b.** There is less fruit on the trees because they bloomed before the pollinating insects could fertilize them.

Chapter 4 Self Assessment, page SG-54

1. D	**2.** B	**3.** A	**4.** B
5. D	**6.** C	**7.** E	**8.** D
9. B	**10.** A	**11.** D	**12.** D
13. A	**14.** B	**15.** B	

DNA, Genes, and Chromosomes, page SG-57

1. **a.** Diagrams should show key features of DNA nucleotide diagram on page SG-56 of the study guide.

   b. Diagram should show key features of DNA strand diagram on page SG-56 of the study guide, except nucleotides should be in this order: CCTGA. G and A should have double rings.

2. GGACT

3. **A.** sugar-phosphate "handrails" **B.** double hydrogen bonds between A and T **C.** triple hydrogen bonds between G and C **D.** deoxyribose (sugar)

4. length, centromere location, banding pattern

5. double helix unwinds → each DNA strand is used as a template for a new strand → each new DNA molecule has one original DNA strand and one new strand

Human Karyotypes, page SG-58

1. The sex chromosomes; in males, they are not homologous chromosomes so they are not numbered.

2. Male; the sex chromosomes are XY.

3. **a.** It would have three number 21 chromosomes. **b.** It would have 22 single chromosomes and either an X or a Y chromosome.

The Cell Cycle, page SG-59

1. **a.** Cell carries out normal functions, grows, and copies genetic material. **b.** Cell grows rapidly. **c.** DNA is replicated. **d.** Cell makes more molecules to prepare for cell division. **e.** Copied DNA separates and cell prepares to divide. **f.** Cytoplasm and the organelles divide into two identical daughter cells.

2. a. To replace dead skin cells and repair damaged skin cells.

b. Actively dividing cells mover through the phases of the cell cycle. Cells that are no longer dividing remain in the G1 phase.

Mitosis and Cytokinesis, page SG-60

1. Growth, maintenance, and regeneration of cells.

2. So it can carry out its normal functions and survive.

3. Interphase: cell carries out its normal functions, grows, copies genetic material. **Prophase**: chromatin condenses into chromosomes, nuclear membrane breaks down, nucleolus disappears, centrosomes move apart, spindle apparatus forms. **Metaphase**: chromosomes line up at equator of cell, spindle fibres attach to centomere of each chromosome. **Anaphase**: centromeres split apart, sister chromatids separate, spindle fibres pull sister chromatids to opposite poles, one complete diploid set of chromosomes at each pole. **Telophase**: chromatids unwind into strands of chromatin, spindle fibres break down, nuclear membrane forms around each new set of chromosomes, two diploid cells are formed.

Meiosis, page SG-62

1. Diagrams should show key feature of Figure 4.13 on page 171 of the student textbook.
Interphase: germ cell grows, copies genetic material. **Prophase I**: pairs of homologous chromosomes align side by side, segments of chromosomes can be exchanged, centrosomes move apart, spindle apparatus forms. **Metaphase I**: chromosomes line up at equator of cell, spindle fibres attach to centromere of each chromosome. **Anaphase I**: homologous chromosomes separate and move to opposite poles, centromeres do not split, sister chromatids still held together; half the number of chromosomes. **Telophase I**: homologous chromosomes uncoil, spindle fibres disappear; cytokinesis takes place, nuclear membrane forms around each group of homologous chromosomes; each new cell is haploid. **Prophase II**: spindle apparatus forms in each new cell, spindle fibres attach to the chromosomes. **Metaphase II**: sister chromatids line up at equator of cell. **Anaphase II**: centromeres split,

sister chromatids separate and move to opposite poles. **Telophase II**: nuclear membrane forms around each set of chromosomes, spindle fibres disappear; cytokinesis takes place; four haploid cells are formed.

2. Meiosis produces genetically unique haploid gametes; mitosis produces genetically identical diploid somatic (body) cells.

3. Crossing over involves homologous non-sister chromatids exchanging pieces of chromosome, so individual chromosomes may contain maternal and paternal genes. Independent assortment involves combinations of maternal and paternal chromosomes that can occur in a gamete.

4. Both begin with a diploid germ cell, result in haploid gametes, and involve meiosis I and meiosis II. Oogenesis occurs in females before puberty; has two arrested states (prophase I and metaphase II); meiosis II not completed until fertilization; uneven division during meiosis produces two polar bodies and one gamete. Spermatogenesis occurs in males after puberty; no arrested states; meiosis II occurs before sperm leave testes; even division during meiosis produces four gametes.

5. Meiosis produces genetically unique gametes, which increases the genetic variation. Since the gametes are haploid, the offspring produced by combining two gametes with be diploid like the parents.

Reproduction, Technology, and Society, page SG-64

1. a. In vitro fertilization involves removing immature eggs from the ovaries, fertilizing them, and implanting the embryo in the uterus. This process bypasses the blocked oviduct. **b.** In artificial insemination, sperm are collected and concentrated before being placed in the woman's vagina. This process increases the possibility of fertilization.

2. a. It is normally used when a couple has a history of genetic disorders in their family. **b.** Issues could include the ethics of screening for non-medical traits such as gender or intelligence, respecting the rights of people with genetic disorders, access to screening, and how it is funded.

3. Diagrams should show these steps: isolate human insulin gene on chromosome → choose a vector bacteria to clone the gene → cut insulin gene and insert it into vector DNA → recombinant DNA produced → insert recombinant DNA into production bacteria → bacteria uses human insulin gene to produce insulin → insulin harvested for human use

4. Yes. They are genetically identical so they are a natural type of clone.

5. Gene Cloning: used to produce copies of a gene or a gene product; products used in laboratory study, added to other organisms, or used as medicine; the cloned organism has different DNA than the parent organism. **Therapeutic Cloning:** used to produce human stem cells, which can grow into different types of cells; produces genetically identical cells; the cells are used to treat medical disorders. **Reproductive Cloning:** used to produce an animal that has the same nuclear DNA as another animal; produces genetically identical cells; the egg is allowed to grow into a new organism

Chapter 4 Practice Test, page SG-66

1. C   **2.** E   **3.** C   **4.** A

5. B   **6.** D   **7.** E

8. genetic reduction and genetic recombination

9. deletion, duplication, inversion, and translocation

10. Mitosis has one cell division, which produces two identical, diploid daughter cells. Meiosis has two cell divisions, which produce four non-identical, haploid daughter cells.

11. The cell theory states that all new cells are the product of existing cells. Traits must be passed from the parent cell to the offspring cell.

12. Diagrams should show key features of Figure 4.15 on page 173 of the student textbook.

13. Fraternal twins are formed when two eggs are fertilized by two sperm cells. Identical twins are formed when a single zygote divides into two zygotes during the first few days of development.

14. Answers may vary. Benefits could include disease resistance in plants and increased milk and meat production in animals. Risks could include modified DNA spreading to unmodified organisms or modified organisms outcompeting unmodified organisms of the same species.

Chapter 5 Self Assessment, page SG-68

1. D   **2.** D   **3.** C   **4.** A

5. E   **6.** C   **7.** E   **8.** E

9. B   **10.** D   **11.** A   **12.** E

13. B

Mendel's Crosses and the Law of Segregation, page SG-71

1. Wrinkled seeds is a recessive phenotype and can only be expressed when the genotype is homozygous recessive.

2. a. A. P generation **B.** F_1 generation **C.** F_2 generation **D.** dark (or homozygous dominant) **E.** white (or homozygous recessive) **F.** dark (heterozygous) **G.** 3 dark: 1 light

   b. All individuals have two copies of each factor. These copies separate randomly during meiosis, and each gamete receives one copy of every factor.

3. a. The F stands for filial, which refers to a child's relationship to a parent, and the 2 indicates it is the second generation.

   b. Genotype described the alleles for **gen**etic traits. **Ph**enotype describes **ph**ysical traits.

One-Trait (Monohybrid) Crosses and Test Crosses, page SG-73

1. P cross: round seeds × wrinkled seeds; $RR \times rr$. Punnett square should show R and R on one side and r and r on the other. F_1 genotypes: Rr, Rr, Rr, Rr. F_1 phenotypes: round.
   F_1 cross: $Rr \times Rr$. F_2 genotypes: RR, Rr, Rr, rr. F_2 phenotypes: 3 round: 1 wrinkled.

2. Use a test cross. P: *B?* (unknown genotype) × *bb* (recessive genotype). Answer should include Punnett squares for the two possibilities: *Bb* × *bb* and *BB* × *bb*. As the Punnett squares will show, if all F_1 have black fur, then the unknown genotype of P is homozygous dominant. If any of F_1 have white fur, then the unknown genotype is heterozygous (*Bb*).

3. The phenotype is represented by all the genotypes that make it up, so you can add them. Similarly, to find the number of vehicles in a parking lot you can add the number of cars, the number of trucks, and the number of motorcycles.

The Law of Independent Assortment, page SG-75

1. **a.** tall plant; white flowers; *PPTT*; *pptt*; purple; tall
   b. purple flowers tall; tall plants; *PpTt*; *PT, Pt, pT, pt*
   c. purple tall; 3; white short

2. All offspring have normal starch, so the parent plant must be homozygous dominant (*WW*). Some offspring have colourless seeds, so the parent plant must be heterozygous (*Aa*). The parent's genotype is *AaWW*.

Using Pedigrees to Track Autosomal Recessive Disorders, page SG-77

1. three; aa; recessive; homozygous; recessive; recessive; heterozygous; Punnett

2. *AA* × *Aa* = *AA, AA, Aa, Aa*. Heterozygotes (*Aa*) have a normal phenotype so the children will not be affected by this trait.

3. Two affected parents will always have affected children. *aa* × *aa* = *aa, aa, aa, aa*. So the children have a 0% chance of having the dominant phenotype.

Autosomal Dominant Genetic Disorders, page SG-78

1. **a.** I-1 is not affected, I-2 is affected. **b.** I-1 is *aa* and I-2 must be *Aa*, since he is affected but not all their children have the disorder.

2. aa, not affected: II-1, II-3, II-5, III-1, III-3, III-4, III-5; Aa, affected: II-2, II-4, III-2

Genetic Testing and Gene Therapy, page SG-80

1. Gene therapy could potentially treat SCID but there are significant risks that need to be overcome.

2. The immune system of SCID babies cannot protect them from diseases so they are often placed in sterile disease-free plastic bubbles.

3. **a. Pros:** families have hope for curing a potentially lethal disorder; more effective than bone marrow transplants; patient's immune system function improves. **Cons:** may raise false hopes of a cure; unknown side effects such as triggering the gene for leukemia; always risks associated with new technologies

   b. Answers may vary. For example, the trials should stop until scientists know more about the genes they are manipulating so they do not cause diseases. Or, the trials should continue because it cures some children who are terminally ill so it's worth the risk.

Chapter 5 Practice Test, page SG-82

1. B	**2.** A	**3.** C	**4.** B
5. D	**6.** B	**7.** E	**8.** *BB* or *Bb*

9. The chromosome theory of inheritance.

10. **a.** tall

   b.

	T	t
T	TT	Tt
T	TT	Tt

   c. 100%   **d.** 2:2:0

11.

	BG	Bg	bG	bg
BG	BBGG	BBGg	BbGG	BbGg
Bg	BBGg	BBgg	BbGg	Bbgg
bG	BbGG	BbGg	bbGG	bbGg
bg	BbGg	Bbgg	bbGg	bbgg

12. Huntington disease is an autosomal dominant disorder, so offspring with one *H* with inherit the disorder. In the cross *Hh* × *HH*, all offspring will inherit at least one *H*, so they will all have the disorder.

Chapter 6 Self Assessment, page SG-84

1. D	**2.** E	**3.** B	**4.** A
5. C	**6.** A	**7.** D	**8.** B
9. A	**10.** D	**11.** B	**12.** B
13. C	**14.** E	**15.** E	

Incomplete Dominance and Codominance, page SG-86

1. $C^R C^R$; homozygous; red flowers. $C^R C^W$; heterozygous; pink flowers. $C^W C^W$; homozygous; white flowers

2. a. In incomplete dominance, neither allele is dominant. In codominance, two alleles are both fully expressed (dominant).

b. If the trait is co-dominant, the heterozygote individual will display both traits equally.

3. P phenotypes   normal   ×   normal
                 hemoglobin   hemoglobin
P genotypes $Hb^A Hb^S$ × $Hb^A Hb^S$
Pgametes Hb^A Hb^S × Hb^A Hb^S
Punnett square should indicate this predicted genotype of children:
$Hb^A Hb^A$, $Hb^A Hb^S$, $Hb^A Hb^S$, $Hb^S Hb^S$; 50%

4. C^B; C^W; predicted genotypes: $C^B C^W$, $C^B C^W$, $C^B C^W$; $C^B C^W$; roan

Polygenic Traits, page SG-88

1. a. Traits that are controlled by two or more pairs of alleles.

b. long ears, genotype $AABB$; short ears, genotype $aabb$

2. a. When a trait is controlled by multiple alleles, the gene exists in several allelic forms. There are three alleles that determine the blood type in humans I^A, I^B, and i.

b. $I^A i$ or $I^A I^A$

3. ii; type O; none. $I^A i$; type A; A. $I^A I^A$; type A; A. $I^B i$; type B; B. $I^B I^B$; type B; B. $I^A I^B$; type AB; A and B.

4. i; I^B i; I^A; i; genotopye of offspring: $I^B i$, $I^A I^B$; genotype ratio I^B, ii; phenotype ratio: A, AB, O

Linked Genes, page SG-90

1. Linked genes are genes found on the same chromosome. This illustration shows that the alleles for eye colour, body colour, and wing type are all found on the same chromosome in fruit flies.

2. Diagrams should show key features of Figure 4.19 on page 175 of the student textbook. Crossing over can take place when the non-sister chromatids in a tetrad exchange pieces of a chromosome. If the point at which a crossover occurs is between two genes, the previously linked alleles will end up on separate chromosomes and will therefore migrate into different gametes.

Sex-linked Traits, page SG-91

1. Males only have one X chromosome. A recessive allele on the X chromosome in males behaves as a dominant chromosome.

2.

Mother Phenotype	Father Phenotype	Mother Genotype	Father Genotype	Offspring Phenotype
normal vision	normal vision	$X^B X^b$	$X^B Y$	colour vision deficient son
normal vision	colour vision deficient	$X^B X^B$	$X^b Y$	normal vision son
normal vision	colour vision deficient	$X^B X^b$	$X^b Y$	colour vision deficient daughter
colour blind	normal vision	$X^b X^b$	$X^B Y$	all sons colour vision deficient

3. a. First Punnett Square: $X^B X^b$, $X^B Y$, $X^b X^b$; Second Punnett Square: $X^B X^b$, $X^B Y$, $X^b Y$ **b.** I-3: $X^B Y$, male normal; II-1: male normal, II-2: $X^B X^b$, female, carrier, normal; II-3: $X^b Y$, male, affected; II-4: $X^B X$, female, carrier, normal; III-1: $X^b X^b$ or $X^B X^b$, female, normal, possibly carrier; III-4: $X^B Y$, male, affected

Genetic Research, page SG-94

1. a. Is closely tied to genomics and proteomics. Allows studies of huge amounts of information to be completed reasonably quickly.

b. Studies the expression, function, identification, interaction, and structure of proteins. Genes code for the proteins in a cell.

c. Can be used to study which genes are active and which are inactive in different cell types. Helps scientists understand how these cells function normally and how they are affected when various genes do not perform properly.

d. Epigenetics is the study of changes in gene activity that do not involve alterations to the genetic code but still get passed down to at least one successive generation.

e. SNPs occur normally throughout a person's DNA. Researchers have found SNPs that may help predict an individual's response to certain drugs, susceptibility to environmental factors such as toxins, and risk of developing particular diseases such as heart disease, diabetes, and cancer.

2. Epigenetics is the study of changes in gene activity that do not involve alterations to the genetic code but still get passed down to at least one successive generation. It is through epigenetic marks that environmental factors like diet, stress, temperature, and prenatal nutrition can make an imprint on genes that is passed from one generation to the next.

3. Pros: The discovery of disease-causing genes. The design of new drugs. New understanding of developmental processes. Ability to determine the origin and evolution of the human race.

Cons: Many privacy issues if others know your genetic profile before you develop a disorder. This knowledge can also cause mental distress. Patented genes could delay research and development of new tools or treatments. Prenatal testing could be used to select for traits not related to health such as gender, height, or intelligence.

Chapter 6 Practice Test, page SG-96

1. B   **2.** E   **3.** B   **4.** A

5. D   **6.** A   **7.** B

8. Presence of multiple alleles.

9. A Barr body is an inactive X chromosome.

10. The study of genomes and how genes work together to control phenotype.

11. SNP single nucleotide polymorphism has occurred. Individual B had an A replace a G.

12. The son could not inherit the type B blood type since no antigen B (I^B) is found in either parent.

13. The genotype of the woman's uncle with hemophilia would be X^hY. Her mother may have one copy of the recessive gene X^h, which she may have passed on to her daughter. This would make her a carrier.

14. Answers will vary. Discussions should include advantages and potential disadvantages of the sharing of the genetic information including ethical issues.

Unit 2 Practice Test, page SG-99

1. B   **2.** D   **3.** B   **4.** A

5. C   **6.** D   **7.** D   **8.** C

9. B   **10.** A   **11.** B   **12.** E

13. D   **14.** E   **15.** B

16. The diploid cell ($2n$) would have sixty-six chromosomes.

17. Meiosis increases genetic diversity.

18. Semi-conservative refers to the conservation of half the original DNA.

19. A plasmid is a small circular piece of DNA.

20. karyotyping

21. Animal cells: An indentation forms and deepens to pinch the cell in two. Cytoplasm divides evenly between the two daughter cells. **Plant cells:** A cell plate forms between the two daughter nuclei. Cell walls then form on either side of the cell plate. **Prokaryotic cells:** In binary fission, the cell membrane grows and pulls the two nuclei apart. Two daughter cells are produced.

22. Vector DNA is the foreign genetic material being introduced into the cell. Recombinant DNA is DNA from two or more sources (the vector DNA and the cell's DNA).

23. SCID is an X-linked genetic trait. Fathers have only one X chromosome and pass it on to their daughters, so all daughters will have this trait.

24. Diagrams should show key features of Figure 4.7 on textbook page 165.

25. a.

	T	t
T	TT	Tt
t	Tt	tt

b. Embryos with homozygous recessive genotypes (*tt*) do not develop.

26. a. *Hh*

b. *Hh*

c. 75%

27. Mitosis: asexual, two diploid daughter cells have identical genetic information, one division occurs, centromeres split in anaphase. **Meiosis:** sexual, four haploid daughter cells do not share genetic information, two divisions occur, centromeres split in anaphase II.

28. Benefits could include increased nutritional value, new medical treatments, increased resistance to disease. Risks could include environmental threats, new diseases, social and economic issues.

29. Answers should include a position and facts related to genetic testing to support that position.

Chapter 7 Self Assessment, page SG-104

1. D	**2.** C	**3.** A	**4.** E
5. D	**6.** C	**7.** B	**8.** A
9. A	**10.** B	**11.** C	**13.** E

Adaptation and Variation, page SG-107

1. Predators will be think it is poisonous and be afraid of it. It is les likely to be eaten.

2. a. physiological

b. There is no need to maintain the digestive system during long non-feeding periods. The energy normally required to maintain their digestive system can be used for other life processes.

3. physiological

4. a. The thick bark would help protect the tree in a fire. Few branches could reduce the spread of the fire, and the deep roots might survive a fire.

b. structural adaptations

5. For example, a frog lives part of its life cycle in ponds and part on land. This helps the species to survive wet and dry seasons.

Variations, Mutations, and Selective Advantage, page SG-109

1. range in length, colouration, number of "saddles" along their back, number of dark blotches on their sides, colour of their belly, colour of the band running diagonally across their eye

2. mutation → variation → environmental change → some individuals have traits that provide a selective advantage

3. C

4. E

Natural Selection, page SG-111

1. variation; selective advantage; fit; reproduce; offspring; natural selection; selective advantage; Fewer

2. *Physical fitness* describes how effectively a person's muscles and cardiovascular system can help the person carry out a physical task. In terms of evolution, *fitness* describes the number of offspring produced.

3. Selective pressures are environmental forces such as scarcity of food or extreme temperatures that result in the survival of only certain organisms with characteristics that provide resistance.

4. Natural selection is a result of selective pressures in the environment. It is the process by which genetic mutations that enhance reproduction become, and remain, more common in successive generations of a population. It produces populations of individuals that are well adapted to their environment. Selective advantages are different in different environments. Selective advantages in one environment may be disadvantages in another. Natural selection can only take place when there is variation in the population.

5. Individuals with favourable phenotypes are more likely to survive and reproduce than those with less favourable phenotypes. Natural selection acts on individual traits to cause shifts in the phenotypes of whole populations and species. The genotypes associated with the favourable phenotypes will increase in frequency as natural selection proceeds.

Artificial Selection, page SG-113

1. Natural Selection: results because individuals with different sets of inherited characteristics have unequal chances of surviving and reproducing; the natural environment determines which individuals survive and reproduce; some poorly adapted individuals in each generation will be lucky enough to survive and reproduce, while other well-adapted members of the population will not; may take many, many generations. **Artificial Selection:** breeding of domesticated plants and animals; results from the deliberate human choice of which individuals to propagate; all unwanted phenotypes can be eliminated in just a few generations, bringing about about rapid change.

2. a. natural **b.** artificial **c.** artificial **d.** natural

3. Advantages: fruit is uniform in size and ripening date resulting in low cost for labour, harvesting, and shipping; every plant has the same desirable traits. **Disadvantages:** monoculture reduces variations in the population making it vulnerable to disease and pests, original genetic variability has been lost.

4. a. A gene bank stores seeds as a source for planting in case seed reserves elsewhere are destroyed. **b.** For example, to provide genetic resources in case disease threatens monoculture crops, or populations are wiped out by environmental events such as floods.

Chapter 7 Practice Test, page SG-116

1. C   **2.** A   **3.** B   **4.** A

5. D   **6.** C   **7.** E

8. Gradual, accumulative changes in the DNA of a group of organisms.

9. Examples could include predators, parasites, disease, and competition for resources.

10. environmental conditions

11. Thick fur and layers of fat for warmth, white fur to hide from prey, large paws for traction and swimming, and small ears and tail to minimize heat loss

12. Individual intestinal bacteria may have developed a new allele from a random genetic mutation that made them resistant to tetracycline. Bacteria can exchange generic material through conjunction and can reproduce very quickly which gives them a selective advantage. So, after 40 years, most of the bacteria may have the mutation.

13. Artificial selection: usually intentional, selective pressure imposed by humans, change is designed or controlled. **Natural selection:** situational, gradual change over generations, selective pressure by environmental conditions, occurs naturally, change not anticipated. **Both:** selective pressure, modification of genetic traits, genetic processes altered, gene pools affected, impact on survival of populations.

14. The breeders will produce animals that have a stronger expression of the trait they are selecting for but they will also introduce traits that are undesirable as a consequence. For example, bulldogs were bred to have flat faces but many have breathing problems.

Chapter 8 Self Assessment, page SG-118

1. D   **2.** B   **3.** D   **4.** E

5. C   **6.** E   **7.** A   **8.** A

9. C   **10.** A   **11.** D   **12.** E

13. E   **14.** D

Developing the Theory of Evolution by Natural Selection, page SG-121

1. It has been supported by significant amounts of evidence from several fields of science.

2. The individuals most fit for their environment will pass more genes on to offspring. Over time, this results in more fit individuals in the population. This is known as survival of the fittest, or natural selection. Over large amounts of time, it causes the characteristics of the population as a whole to change in significant ways—evolution.

3. 1707–1708: George-Louis LeClerc hypothesized that similarities between humans and apes might mean they had a common ancestor. early 1800s: Georges Cuvier proposed that some species disappeared, or became extinct, over time as new ones appeared
1830: Charles Lyell stated that geological processes operated at the same gradual rate in the past as they do today. Jean-Baptiste Lamarck hypothesized that organisms acquire characteristics through their lifetime, and pass those on to offspring.
1858: Darwin and Wallace develop theory of evolution by natural selection.

4. Diagrams and captions should illustrate the key steps of evolution, for example,

   1: In nature, organisms produce more offspring than can survive.

   2: In any population, there is variation between individuals.

   3: Individuals with certain useful adaptations, for example speed, survive and pass those adaptations on to their offspring.

   4: Over time, individuals with those useful variations make up most of the population. The population has evolved, or changed.

Evidence for Evolution: Fossils and Biogeography, page SG-124

1. The fossil record is not complete, but does contain many well-documented examples of the transition from one species into another, as well as the origin of new physical features. Although scientists do not have fossils for all of the changes that occurred, they can still understand the overall picture of how most groups evolved.

2. **a.** a vestigial organ **b.** Vestigial organs provide evidence of a common ancestor. In this case, the human appendix is a derivative of the caecum found in our mammal ancestors.

3. While all continents began as one landmass, they drifted apart and became separated by large bodies of water. Different plants and animals evolved in different biogeographic regions, and barriers such as mountain ranges and oceans prevented them from migrating into other regions. Zebras evolved in Africa after it had separated from South America.

More Evidence for Evolution: Anatomy, Embryology, and DNA, page SG-126

1. Homologous structures. Pharyngeal pouches are present in the embryos of animals as different as fish and mammals, but develop into different structures in the adult animal. This is evidence of common ancestry.

2. Analogous structures. Although the wings of both animals perform a similar function, they do not have a common structure or evolutionary origin.

3. Macaques. Macaques are more closely related to humans than frogs are, so they should share more proteins with humans than frogs do.

4. Concept map should show these ideas and how they relate to evolution. **Anatomy:** homologous structures such as vertebrate limbs, vestigial organs (human appendix). **Embryology:** overall similarity, homologous structures (dorsal rods and paired pouches). **DNA:** similarities in base sequences.

Chapter 8 Practice Test, page SG-128

1. C   **2.** B   **3.** B   **4.** E

5. E   **6.** D   **7.** D

8. Gondwana

9. Examples could include pelvic bone in whales, wings of flightless birds, and appendix in humans.

10. *The Origin of Species*

11. Organisms produce more offspring than can survive, therefore organisms competed for limited resources. Individuals in a population vary extensively and much of this variation is hereditary. Individuals that are better suited to local conditions survive to produce more offspring. Processes for change are slow and gradual.

12. Mendel found out that traits were inherited in a predictable manner. Darwin could not account for how traits were passed down from generation to generation.

13. Each species of finch filled a different niche on each island. They all started as similar populations, but evolved to become more fit for their particular environments.

14. Ray (1627–1705): classification system for plants and animals based on anatomy and physiology; Linnaeus (1707–1778): classification system; Leclerc (1707–1788): apes and humans common ancestor; Malthus (1766-1834) *Essay on the Principles of Population*; Anning (1799–1847): fossil collection; Cuvier (1769–1832): science of paleontology, catastrophism; Lyell (1797–1875): uniformitarianism; Lamarck (1744–1829): "line of descent", inheritance of acquired characteristics; Wallace (1823–1913): similar theories to Darwin's.

15. **Fossils:** Fossil layers are chronological so species in older rocks are ancestors to species in younger rocks. Not all organisms appear in fossil records at the same time showing some species evolved from others. Transitional fossils show the intermediary links between groups of organisms. **Biogeography:** Geographically closed environments tend to be populated by related species. Animals on islands often resemble animals found on the closest continent. Fossils of the same species can be found on the coastlines of neighbouring continents. Closely related species are very rarely found in the same habitat or location. **Evidence from anatomy:** Homologous structures are similar because they were inherited from a common ancestor. Vestigial structures are not used but show evidence of common ancestors. **Evidence from embryology:** Embryos of different organisms have similar stages of embryonic development suggesting they have a common ancestor. **Evidence from DNA:** Similar patterns in DNA bases indicate a common ancestor.

Chapter 9 Self Assessment, page SG-130

1. D	**2.** C	**3.** E	**4.** B
5. B	**6.** C	**7.** A	**8.** E
9. D	**10.** B	**11.** A	**12.** C
13. D			

How Do Populations Evolve?, page SG-134

1. **a.** the total of all genes in a population at a given time **b.** the percentage of any specific allele in a gene pool **c.** when the allele frequency for a specific gene remains the same over generations **d.** the occurrence of small-scale changes in allele frequencies in a population

2. **a.** Mutations provide new alleles and therefore produce variation, the raw material for evolutionary change. **b.** Most mutations have no effect, or affect only the individual, and are not passed on. Mutations that affect gametes can be passed on and produce variation in the population.

3. Diagram should show that in any population, not all of the individuals in each generation reproduce, and that environmental pressures can make individuals with certain traits more likely to reproduce and to survive.

4. The bottleneck effect occurs when a population size is reduced by a natural disaster or by human interference. The founder effect occurs when a small number of individuals colonize a new area. In both, certain alleles are overrepresented or underrepresented in the reduced population. Genetic drift follows and the genetic variation in the population is reduced.

5. **a.** non-random mating, or inbreeding **b.** Inbreeding results in a population with more homozygous individuals. Inbreeding can lead to a decrease in the genetic diversity in a population resulting in an increase in certain diseases and conditions.

Evolution by Natural Selection, page 135

1. **a.** disruptive **b.** stabilizing **c.** directional **d.** stabilizing **e.** directional

2. For example, male moose with large antlers have the advantage of being chosen as a mating partner, so the frequency of the alleles responsible for large antlers will increase in the population.

Speciation, page SG-138

1. Pre-zygotic barriers impede mating between species or prevent the fertilization of the egg. Examples include habitat isolation, temporal isolation, behavioural isolation, mechanical isolation, and gamete isolation. Post-zygotic barriers prevent hybrid zygotes from developing into normal, fertile individuals. Examples include hybrid inviability, hybrid sterility, and hybrid breakdown.

2. two populations interbreed → gene flow is interrupted by a geographical barrier → genetic drift causes gene pools of the populations to become different from one another → populations can non longer interbreed

3. a. Polyploid organisms have three or more sets of chromosomes in the nucleus of each cell. **b.** If chromosomes do not separate during meiosis (non-disjunction), the gametes produced will have two sets of chromosomes (diploid − 2n), instead of one set (haploid − n). Then, if two diploid gametes fuse, the offspring will have four of each chromome (tetraploid – 4n). **c.** Polyploidy in plants is possible because many species are able to self-fertilize and can reproduce vegetatively. **d.** Any offspring from this mating would be triploid (3n). Normal meiosis requires paired chromosomes to produce viable daughter cells. An even number of chromosomes is required to create pairs.

4. Graph should show a gradual, constant increase in speciation as time goes on. Possible caption: Evolution occurs at a slow, steady rate, with small, adaptive changes gradually accumulating over time. Species originate through these gradual adaptations.

5. The *punctuated equilibrium* hypothesis states that speciation occurs relatively quickly, in rapid bursts separated by long periods of genetic equilibrium. The diagram shows that most species undergo most of their physical changes when they first diverge from the parent species.

Adaptive Radiation, page SG-139

1. Divergent evolution is a pattern of evolution in which populations that were once similar adapt to different environmental conditions and diverge, or become increasingly distinct. Crossbills originated from an ancestral species, and become less and less alike as they adapted to feeding on different size coniferous cones, eventually resulting in new species of birds.

2. In convergent evolution, similar traits arise because each species has independently adapted to similar environmental conditions, not because they share a common ancestor. Birds and bats evolved independently and at different times, yet natural selection favoured variations suitable for the same environment—air. But since birds and bats do not have a common ancestor, they evolved very different wings.

Human Activities and Speciation, page SG-140

1. For example, major highway constructed through a valley → grizzly bear habitat fragmented by this highway → highway prevents the normal gene flow between split populations → bottleneck effect and genetic drift occur → resulting small populations may become extinct if there is insufficient genetic diversity to permit adaptation.
Wildlife corridors and overpasses could have been created as the highway was built to allow movement and interbreeding between populations.

2. Humans are causing vast physical changes on the planet. As the human population grows and our demand for natural resources increases, more and more habitats are devastated. Today, we may be losing thousands of species a year. This rate of species extinction is occurring at a much faster rate than at any time since the last great extinction 65 million years ago that wiped out most of the dinosaurs.

Chapter 9 Practice Test, page SG-142

1. B   **2.** C   **3.** B   **4.** D
5. E   **6.** C   **7.** A
8. natural selection
9. competition and predation

10. pre-zygotic and post-zygotic reproductive isolating mechanisms

11. a. directional, selects against one extreme
b. stabilizing, eliminates extreme individuals
c. disruptive, eliminates intermediate individuals

12. Diagrams should show similar steps to those described in the flowcharts on page SG-137.

13. Divergent evolution occurs when populations change as they adapt to different environmental conditions. The populations become less and less alike resulting in two different species. These species do share a common ancestor. Convergent evolution occurs when similar traits arise because each species has independently adapted to similar environmental conditions. These species do not share a common ancestor.

14. The isolated or reduced populations may undergo adaptive radiations. Severely fragmented populations may die out if genetic diversity is insufficient to permit adaptation to environmental changes.

Unit 3 Practice Test, page SG-145

1. D   **2.** C   **3.** C   **4.** D
5. E   **6.** C   **7.** B   **8.** A
9. D   **10.** B   **11.** E   **12.** A

13. C

14. an environmental agent that can cause mutations in DNA

15. uniformitarianism

16. the movement or flow of alleles between populations

17. a. stabilizing selection **b.** directional selection
c. disruptive selection.

18. Organisms produce more offspring than can survive. Therefore, organisms compete for limited resources. Individuals of a population vary extensively, and much of this variation is heritable. Individuals that are better suited to local conditions survive to produce more offspring. Processes for change are slow and gradual.

19. Biogeography shows that ecosystems that are similar but widely spaced do not usually include the same organisms. Ecosystems on an island often include organisms that also exist on the nearest mainland.

Darwin and Wallace hypothesized that species evolve in one location and then spread out to other regions. They cannot spread beyond geographic barriers such as mountains and oceans. Examples could include cacti found in deserts in North, Central and South America but not in Australia and Africa. Lizards found on Canary Islands are similar to lizards in west Africa. Reference may be made to fossils found on neighbouring continents.

20.

Scientist	Theory/area of study	Summary
Cuvier	Paleontology	Proposed catastrophism as explanation for fossil history.
Lyell	Uniformitarianism	Earth's geological features change at a slow, continuous rate.
Lamarck	Inheritance of acquired characteristics	Parents pass on learned adaptations to their offspring.
Darwin	Natural selection	Changing environments convey advantages to some traits and make individuals with these traits the fittest, or the most likely to pass on their genes.

21. The founder effect limits the gene pool due to the few individuals that start an isolated population. There is a lack of genetic diversity in the population.

22. In convergent evolution, similar traits arise because each species has independently adapted to similar environmental conditions. For example, birds and bats. In divergent evolution, populations change and become more unique as they adapt to different environmental conditions, for example: Darwin's finches.

23. Mechanisms represented in concept map should include pre-zygotic including behavioural isolation, habitat, temporal, mechanical, gamete isolation and post-zygotic including hybrid inviability, hybrid sterility, and hybrid breakdown.

Chapter 10 Self Assessment, page SG-151

1. D	**2.** B	**3.** D	**4.** A
5. C	**6.** E	**7.** A	**8.** E
9. B	**10.** B	**11.** D	**12.** E
13. C	**14.** E		

Macromolecules and Essential Nutrients, page SG-153

1. Answers may vary. For example: Carbohydrates provide the cells with quick energy; rice. Lipids insulate and cushion internal organs; butter. Protein helps muscles move; salmon.

2. water and enzymes

3. Calcium helps build bones, vitamin D helps the body absorb calcium, vitamin A helps maintain bones.

4. Answers may vary. For example: Iron and vitamin E work together to make healthy red blood cells.

5. a. Protein, lipids, calcium, magnesium, potassium, and vitamin B1 to promote muscle growth and coordination (nerves). b. Simple carbohydrates for quick energy, to balance body fluids and replace fluids lost by sweating.

6. Humans need carbohydrates, lipids, proteins, water, vitamins, and minerals for our bodies to function.

Obtaining and Processing Food, page SG-154

1. a. bulk feeder **b.** substrate feeder **c.** filter feeder **d.** fluid feeder

2. a. mouth, throat, esophagus **b.** gizzard, stomach, small intestine **c.** intestines

3. a. The digestive tracts would be similar since they are both mammals. The mouse's intestine and cecum would be comparatively longer than the cat's so it can digest the cellulose in its diet and store more undigestible waste.

Organs in the Human Digestive System, page SG-156

1. a. mouth **b.** esophasus **c.** liver **d.** stomach **e.** gall bladder **f.** pancreas **g.** large intestine **h.** small intestine **i.** rectum

2. For example, the tongue and teeth work together to chew the food.

3. a. villus **b.** capillary network **c.** and **d.** artery and vein

4. Their liver might produce fewer bile salts, so they would be less able to absorb fat.

5. a. small intestine, large intestine **b.** A greater surface area in the intestines means more nutrients and water can be absorbed through the intestine wall into the capillaries. c. Answers may vary. For example, a shaggy towel has a greater surface area than smooth fabric so it absorbs more water.

Chemical Digestion and Absorption, page SG-158

1. mouth, stomach, small intestine

2. a. sucrase **b.** pancreatic lipase **c.** pepsin **d.** pancreatic amylase

3. Macromolecules are too large to fit into the capillaries.

4. The stomach has a pH of 2 and pepsin, which breaks down protein, works best at a low pH.

5. Monosaccharides (other than glucose) are converted into glucose in the liver. Excess glucose is converted to glycogen and stored. In the liver, amino acids are converted into sugars, and used in energy releasing reactions; in cells, they are used to make proteins and enzymes. Glycerol and fatty acids are made into triglycerides, which are then broken down in the bloodstream and used as energy by cells.

6. They may not be able to digest their food because they will lack the pancreatic enzymes used to break down carbohydrates, lipids, and proteins.

7. Carbohydrates: mouth, small intestine; salivary amylase, carbohydrases (pancreatic amylase, sucrase, maltase, and lactase); monosaccharides; energy. **Proteins:** stomach, small intestine; pepsin, proteases (trypsin and chymotrypsin), peptidases; amino acids; energy, enzymes, protein. **Lipids:** small intestine; bile, lipases; glycol, fatty acids; energy, cushioning.

Digestive System Disorders, page SG-160

1. Answers may vary. For example: **a.** peptic ulcer **b.** ulcerative colitis **c.** hepatitis

2. Advantages could include: non-invasive; can see problems that are hard to observe using other methods; can view entire alimentary canal; can take samples, perform minor surgery, and record images.

3. There is no cure for hepatitis A or B, and hepatitis C can lead to cirrhosis.

4. **a.** It will leave the patient with less surface area in the colon for water absorption. **b.** They might be unable to absorb sufficient water to produce feces. Their waste might need another route out of the body.

Chapter 10 Practice Test, page SG-162

1. B   2. A   3. B   4. D

5. D   6. C   7. C

8. the pancreas

9. **a.** protease **b.** lipase **c.** maltase **d.** sucrase **e.** amylase

10. temperature, pH level

11. They are not part of the alimentary canal but fluids from these organs aid digestion.

12. Their bodies need more water to cope with increased temperature, sweating, body toxins, joint and muscle movement, and need for energy.

13. In the mouth, starch is chewed and chemically broken down by salivary amylase. In the small intestine, it is broken down further by enzymes such as pancreatic amylase to become maltose. Maltose is broken down by maltase to become glucose. Glucose enters the bloodstream.

14. Insulin can now be produced in large quantities using genetically engineered bacteria. This method costs less, is faster and easier, and can be better controlled so the product is safer.

Chapter 11 Self Assessment, page SG-164

1. D   2. B   3. E   4. A

5. D   6. A   7. B   8. D

9. D   10. A   11. B   12. C

13. E   14. E   15. B

Respiratory Systems of Animals in Aquatic or Moist Environments, page SG-166

1. To get oxygen into the body and carbon dioxide out of the body.

2. Diagram should show concentration of carbon dioxide increasing in the water and decreasing in the blood.

3. We do not live in a moist environment and our body is too large compared to its surface area to obtain enough oxygen this way.

Respiratory Systems of Land Animals, page SG-167

1. **Insect:** direct respiration near every body cell. **Mammal:** uses muscles to draw air in; once in the body oxygen must be transported to cells. **Both:** get oxygen into body and carbon dioxide out of body

2. **a.** It increases the amount of air that comes into contact with the respiratory surface. **b.** It allows for more gas exchange, and provides more oxygen to cells.

3. It might indicate a problem with the rib cage, muscles, or diaphragm; or damage to part of a lung.

The Human Respiratory System, page SG-169

1. **1.** nostrils **2.** nasal passages **3.** pharynx **4.** larynx **5.** trachea **6.** bronchus **7.** bronchioles

2. **a.** alveoli **b.** bronchioles **c.** capillaries **d.** To increase the area of the respiratory surface.

3. Heat from the blood in the capillaries warms air entering the body.

4. Answers may vary. For example: both air and food can enter through the mouth and pass through the pharynx.

5. alveoli → bronchioles → bronchi → trachea → larynx → glottis → pharynx → nasal passages → nostril

Gas Exchange and Transport in Humans, page SG-170

1. a. Arrows should show carbon dioxide diffuses out of cells into capillaries and oxygen diffuses out of capillaries into cells. **b.** It gets oxygen into the cells where they need it for metabolic processes and removes carbon dioxide produced during metabolic processes.

2. Less oxygen would diffuse into their blood and their body cells. They might breathe more frequently to increase the amount of air coming into contact with their respiratory surface.

3. Iron is necessary to manufacture hemoglobin, which carries oxygen through the blood.

Respiratory System Disorders, page SG-172

1. Laryngitis: loss of voice; caused by infection, allergy, or over use of voice; no treatment usually given. **Tonsillitis:** swollen tonsils and neck glands, sore throat, and fever; caused by viral infection; in serious cases, treated by removing the tonsils.

2. Answers may vary. For example: **a.** chest X-ray, allergy tests **b.** "sweat" test, genetic tests **c.** chest X-ray, CT scan

3. For example, **Cause:** genetic mutation. **Effects:** inflammation, bacterial infection, thick mucous in alveoli of lungs and in pancreas, difficulty breathing.

Chapter 11 Practice Test, page SG-174

1. E	**2.** A	**3.** B	**4.** C
5. B	**6.** D	**7.** A	

8. Moisture and a large surface area.

9. the diaphragm and the intercostals (rib muscles)

10. mostly as bicarbonate ions

11. The alveoli are one cell thick, they have a large surface area and are surrounded by capillaries, and they are moist.

12. They have moved their respiratory surface farther inside, where it can be kept moist. They have developed ways of using muscles to keep air flowing over the respiratory surface.

13. a. Oxygen diffuses from the air through the alveoli into capillaries, where it is transported to body cells. Carbon dioxide is transported from body cells to the capillaries around the alveoli. It diffuses through into air in the lungs.

b.

HCO₃⁻ Bicarbonate	+	H⁺ Hydrogen Ions	→	H₂CO₃ Carbonic acid	→	CO₂ Carbon Dioxide	+	H₂O Water

14. Answers could include breathing in tobacco smoke (first hand and second hand), air pollution, and exposure to radon or asbestos.

Chapter 12 Self Assessment, page SG-176

1. E	**2.** A	**3.** D	**4.** C
5. D	**6.** B	**7.** A	**8.** D
9. B	**10.** E	**11.** A	**12.** C
13. D	**14.** E		

The Circulatory System Supports other Systems, page SG-178

1. a. the alveoli in the lungs **b.** Oxygen diffuses from the alveoli to capillaries, to the pulmonary vein and te left atrium, to the left ventricle, to the aorta, through arteries to capillaries, then diffuses to body cells **c.** the alveoli

2. a. in the villi of the small intestine **b.** Nutrients diffuse from the villi to capillaries. Many travel to the liver, eventually to the heart and to capillaries around the body where they diffuse into body cells.

3. a. Capillaries have a large surface area, so warm blood in the capillaries warms the air in the nasal passages, which results in warmer air reaching the lungs. **b.** It protects delicate structures in the lower respiratory system from damage caused by cold air.

4. a. a clot forms **b.** Protection against blood loss and against disease entering the body.

The Human Heart, page SG-180

1. **a.** right atrium **b.** left atrium c. atrioventricular valve
   d. right ventricle **e.** left ventricle

2. **a.** atrioventricular valve **b.** To keep a constant supply
   of oxygen available to body cells.

3. **a.** aorta **b.** pulmonary artery **c.** *vena cavae*
   d. pulmonary vein

4. It emits an electric signal that is transmitted to
   cardiac muscle cells in the atria causing the muscles
   to contract. This signal is also transmitted to the AV
   node, which emits an electric signal causing the cardiac
   muscle in the ventricles to contract.

5. stethoscope, electrocardiogram

6. *vena cavae* → right atrium → atrioventricular valve →
   right ventricle → semilunar valve → pulmonary
   artery … pulmonary vein → left atrium →
   atrioventricular valve → left ventricle → semilunar
   valve → aorta

7. For example: Valves prevent blood (and oxygen and
   nutrients) from flowing backward. Separate right and
   left sides provide an efficient flow of oxygen and carbon
   dioxide to and from lungs and to and from body.
   Strong cardiac muscle pumps and maintains a steady
   flow of blood to the body.

The Blood Vessels, page SG-182

1. **a.** veins **b.** capillaries **c.** arteries

2. **a.** the pumping of the heart and muscles in the artery
   walls **b.** valves to prevent backward flow and skeletal
   muscles surrounding the veins

3. **a.** the pressure in an artery during a ventricular
   contraction **b.** the pressure in an artery between
   ventricular contractions

4. Body cells need more oxygen during exercise, so the
   heart pumps blood faster, causing increased pressure.

5. Higher. They will require more oxygen while running
   so the heart will pump blood more quickly.

6. **a.** 54 mL **b.** The athlete's cardiac muscle is strong and
   the heart can pump more blood with each beat—a
   higher stroke volume.

Blood and Its Components, page SG-184

1. **a.** platelets **b.** plasma **c.** plasma **d.** white blood cells

2. red blood cells and white blood cells

3. Some produce a substance that attracts other white
   blood cells, which engulf and destroy pathogens.

4. Oxygen is transported bound to hemoglobin, so
   the more hemoglobin there is, the more oxygen can
   be transported.

5. This allows more blood to flow to body cells so
   that they can obtain sufficient oxygen to maintain
   the activity.

6. **Cause:** blood vessels tear. **Effects:** chemicals are
   released by the vessel that attract platelets, platelets
   travel to the injury and release chemicals that result
   in formation of thromboplastin. Thromboplastin
   reacts with other chemicals to produce a fibrous mesh
   of fibrin to stop blood flow and eventually form a clot.
   Cause: bacteria enter the injured blood vessel. **Effects:**
   white blood cells (basophils) release a chemical that
   attracts phagocytes, phagocytes engulf and destroy
   the bacteria.

Circulatory System Disorders, page SG-186

1. **a.** heart valve disorders, arrhythmia, congenital
   heart defects **b.** stroke, aneurysm, arteriosclerosis
   c. hemophilia, leukemia

2. For example: cancer causes leukemia, a genetic sex-
   linked trait causes hemophilia.

3. The build up of plaque in atherosclerosis increases
   blood pressure, which can cause damage to arteries.
   The plaque can result in blood clots, potentially leading
   to strokes, aneurysms, or heart attacks.

4. Having time to practise and plan can lead to fewer
   surgical errors, greater precision, and shorter surgery
   times, which require less anesthetic and reduce
   blood loss.

5. **Xenotransplants:** living cells, tissues, or organs are transplanted from other species into humans. Still experimental. Advantages: Animal tissue and organs can be more readily available than human tissue and organs. Potential problems or issues include organ rejection, introduction of diseases, and the fact that animals must be killed to obtain the organs. **Artificial hearts:** transplanting a mechanical pump with batteries and a controller to function (temporarily) as a heart. Advantage: Can keep a person alive until a suitable human heart becomes available. Potential problems or issues: An external battery pack must be worn most of the time, risk of mechanical or battery failure. **Targeted drug delivery:** drugs are released only when they come into contact with specific enzymes or pH range (indicating cancerous or diseased tissue). Advantages: Chemicals used to kill pathogens or cancerous cells will not harm healthy body cells. Potential problems or issues: unknown.

Chapter 12 Practice Test, page SG-188

1. B   **2.** D   **3.** A   **4.** D
5. C   **6.** E   **7.** B

8. tricupsid valve, or atrioventricular valve

9. albumin, globulins (antibodies), and fibrinogen

10. calcium

11. Answers could include genetics, activity, stress, body temperature, diet and, medications.

12. a. elastic walls; allow artery to expand during contraction of ventricles **b.** thick middle layer; more force for movement of blood **c.** one cell thick; allows gases to pass through **d.** smooth cells; reduces friction **e.** valves; prevent backflow of blood **f.** smooth inner layer; reduces friction

13. a. SA node fires and atria contract. **b.** AV nodes fires, ventricles contract, and AV valves close. **c.** Ventricles relax and semilunar valves close.

14. Issues could include the ethics of using tissues from different species, increased risks of transmitting diseases, risk of recipient's immune system rejecting the tissues, long-term effects, and potentially unknown risks.

Unit 4 Practice Test, page SG-191

1. E   **2.** B   **3.** C   **4.** B
5. A   **6.** E   **7.** B   **8.** A
9. C   **10.** C   **11.** E

12. 6 to 8

13. inspiration and expiration

14. gills and the counter-current exchange mechanism

15. Blood links all the cells and organs in the body.

16. the SA node

17. continuous high blood pressure

18. a. Gastric juice includes hydrochloric acid (activates pepsin), mucus (protects the walls of the stomach) and salts, enzymes, and water (aid chemical digestion). **b.** Bile breaks lipids into smaller fat droplets, increasing the surface area for chemical digestion of fats. **c.** Pancreatic fluid contains enzymes (aid chemical digestion), bicarbonate ions (alter the pH of chyme), water (transport), and insulin (allows glucose to enter body cells).

19. Exhalation is a return to the normal state where the diaphragm and rib muscles are relaxed.

20. Sweating releases heat. Blood vessels widen to increase blood flow near the skin.

21. Cancer cells produce certain enzymes that can be used as biomarkers. Nanotechnology allows scientist to deliver drugs directly to cancer cells by locating these biomarkers.

22. Mouth: Polysaccharides breakdown into disaccharides: starch + water + salivary amylase → maltose; glycogen + water + salivary amylase → maltose. **Small intestine:** Polysaccharides breakdown into disaccharides: starch + water + pancreatic amylase → maltose; glycogen + water + pancreatic amylase → maltose. Disaccharides breakdown into monosaccharides: sucrose + water + sucrase → glucose + fructose; maltose + water + maltase → glucose; lactose + water + lactase → glucose + galactose

23. Both involve the exchange of oxygen and carbon dioxide using diffusion. **External respiration** occurs in the alveoli and capillaries; oxygen diffuses out of alveoli into blood; carbon dioxide diffuses out of blood into alveoli. **Internal respiration** occurs in the capillaries and body tissues; oxygen diffuses out of blood into tissues; carbon dioxide diffuses out of the tissues into the blood.

24. The digestive tract provides nutrients for the formation of blood cells and plasma proteins. The liver detoxifies the blood, makes plasma proteins, and destroys old red blood cells. The cardiovascular system transports nutrients from the digestive tract throughout the body, and also services the accessory organs of the digestive tract.

Chapter 13 Self Assessment, page SG-196

1. A	**2.** E	**3.** E	**4.** B
5. A	**6.** D	**7.** C	**8.** D
9. C	**10.** A	**11.** B	**12.** E
13. B	**14.** C	**15.** D	

Plants Are Valuable Bioresources, page SG-199

1. a. source of food **b.** source of fibres **c.** source of fibres **d.** source of biochemicals **e.** control erosion

2. Diagram should clearly show how plants played a role in several activities, for example, stepped into cotton (plant fibre) slippers, turned up furnace (biochemicals from plants).

3. For example, birds use trees for shelter, fungi use plants for food, beavers build homes and dams with tree branches.

4. For example, grass → mouse → snake → owl → bacteria

5. Both practices can upset the balance of the ecosystem by upsetting soil and water quality, and result in decreased sustainability. Due to increased resistance to pesticides, you may need to use increasing amounts each year, costing more and more money.

Types of Plant Cells, page SG-200

1. a. cell wall **b.** vacuole **c.** chloroplast **d.** nucleus

2. a. parenchyma; they are flexible and think-walled **b.** sclerenchyma, they have thick walls

3. a. for support. **b.** the skeletal system

Types of Plant Tissues, page SG-201

1. a. dermal **b.** vascular (phloem) **c.** meristematic **d.** ground

2. sclerenchyma. They have cell walls, but no cytoplasm.

3. Sketch and labels should resemble Figure 13.13 on textbook page 550.

4. a. guard cell **b.** to control the opening of the stoma

5. a. carbon dioxide **b.** oxygen

6. It refers to transporting nutrients and other substances from one part of the organism to another.

7. meristematic

Plant Organs and their Functions, page SG-204

1. a. taproot **b.** fibrous root **c.** taproot

2. They are protected by a root cap.

3. a. epidermis **b.** cuticle **c.** palisade mesophyll cell **d.** spongy mesophyll cells **e.** epidermis **f.** stoma **g.** guard cell

4. Oxygen is produced by chloroplasts and needs to move to a stoma to be released. Carbon dioxide enters the stoma and needs to find its way to a cell conducting photosynthesis.

5. a. Diagram should show parallel venation. **b.** Diagram should show palmate or pinnate venation.

6. For example, monocot root systems are typically fibrous and dicot root systems are typically taproot.

7. soil → root epidermis → root cortex → root vascular tissue → xylem in stem → veins in leaf → cells of leaf

Transport in Plants, page SG-206

1. a. For example: osmosis, concentration, transpirational pull, root pressure **b.** For example: source, sink, translocation, pressure-flow model

2. Osmosis is the movement of water from an area of low solute concentration to an area of high solute concentration.

3. A: Sucrose enters the phloem in the leaf. The concentration of sucrose in the leaf's phloem is now high. B: Water moves into the leaf's phloem by osmosis. This increases the pressure in the phloem. C: The sucrose solution flows from the source (with high pressure) to the sink (with low pressure). D: Sucrose is removed from the phloem at the sink. This causes the concentration of sucrose in the phloem to fall, and water also moves out, decreasing the pressure.

4. The diagram should show transpiration removing water from leaves and reducing pressure, a column of water moving up the xylem tissue due to cohesion and adhesion, and more water entering the xylem at the roots to replace the water that is moving up to the leaves.

5. A plant uses active transport to make the concentration of minerals in the roots higher than diffusion would make it. This causes water to move into the roots, which increases the pressure causing the column of water in the xylem to move up the stem to the leaves.

Chapter 13 Practice Test, page SG-208

1. C	**2.** B	**3.** C	**4.** D
5. B	**6.** A	**7.** D	

8. For example, plants carry out photosynthesis and contain the fibre cellulose.

9. corn, climbing beans, and squash

10. Vascular tissue tranports water, minerals and other substances and provides support.

11. transpiration

12. Diagram should resemble Figure 13.19 on page 556 of the student textbook.

13. flowers are in five parts, veins are palmate

14. Transpirational pull: the evaporation of water from the interior of leaves to the outside causes a negative pressure in the xylem that pulls water from the roots and soil. Root pressure: the osmotic pressure within the cells of a root system causes positive pressure in the roots and moves water upward in the xylem.

15. Ogans are made of different types of specialized tissue working together. Epidermal, ground and vascular tissues work together in the leaf, stem, and roots. These plant parts are organs.

16. Xylem allows plants to transport water against gravity, from roots to leaves, and allow plants to move nutrients and water from one part to another. Without them, plants cannot support themselves in air and cannot grow very big.

Chapter 14 Self Assessment, page SG-210

1. D	**2.** C	**3.** A	**4.** D
5. B	**6.** B	**7.** E	**8.** D
9. A	**10.** C	**11.** B	**12.** E
13. B	**14.** D		

Reproduction in Seedless Plants, page SG-212

1. **a.** n **b.** $2n$ **c.** n **d.** mosses **e.** a moist or wet environment **f.** meiosis

Flowers and Sexual Reproduction, page SG-213

1. Clockwise from top right: stigma, pistil, sepal, petal, stamen, anther

2. incomplete, imperfect

The Life Cycle of Flowering Plants, page SG-215

1. **a.** anther **b.** stigma **c.** ovary **d.** seed

2. **a.** an ovule and embryo sac grow in the ovary → four haploid megaspores are produced in the ovule → three megaspores disintegrate leaving one female gametophyte **b.** microspores are produced in the anther → each microspore forms a tube cell and a generative cell → a thick wall forms around this mature male gametophyte (or pollen grain)

3. The polar nuclei fuse with one sperm cell to produce a triploid ($3n$) cell that divides to form nutrient-rich endosperm in the seed.

4. Two sperm cells are involved—one fuses with the egg to form a zygote, and the other fuses with the polar nuclei to form endosperm.

5. pollination in which the egg and the sperm come from different flowers or different plants.

6. **Similarities:** new plant produced, haploid gametes and diploid sporophytes, sperm travels to egg. **Seed plants:** pollination is often by wind or animal transport, flowers are involved in most, the gametes are not free-living plants, male gametophytes develop into pollen grains. **Non-seed plants:** male gametes (sperm) have flagella, a moist or wet environment is required for sperm migration.

Asexual Reproduction in Flowering Plants, page SG-216

1. **a.** stem cutting; simple, inexpensive **b.** simple layering; rooting is assisted by water and nutrients from the parent plant

2. **a.** root cuttings; a small section of root is placed in a growth medium **b.** grafting; a bud or piece of stem is cut from one plant and joined to another so the vascular cambium of the two plants is in contact

3. **a.** air layering **b.** produces daughter plants faster than they can be grown from seed, suitable for use with woody trees such as lilac

4. **a.** grafting **b.** Can produce a tree with characteristics of two or more individuals

5. meristematic cells

Plant Growth and Development, page SG-218

1. phototropism

2. thigmotropism

3. ethylene

4. The apical meristem produces auxins, which cause the main shoot of the plant to grow tall. Cutting off the apical meristem decreases the amount of auxins present, so side branches grow instead.

5. Gravitropism causes roots to grow down, which enables them to access deep water and to anchor the plant securely in the soil, and leaves to grow up toward sunlight.

6. Photosynthesis: N, K, Mg, Fe, Mn. Growth, maintenance, and repair: N, Ca, Mg, P, S, Cl, Fe, B, Zn, Cu, Mo. Reproduction: B

7. For example, a cytokinin and indoleacetic acid work together to promote rapid growth.

8. **a.** auxins **b.** Auxins regulate the expansion of root cells so the plant can grow in response to gravity.

9. It might not be able to produce chlorophyll to carry out sufficient photosynthesis for its energy needs, so it might stop or slow growing.

Succession and Sustainability, page SG-220

1. **a.** 6 **b.** 2 **c.** 4 **d.** 10 **e.** 7 **f.** 8 **g.** 9 **h.** 1 **i.** 3—As these small plants die, soil is created. **j.** 5—Animals move into the ecosystem.

2. For example, a forest that has been cut down for roads or buildings, a field that has flooded, a lake that has been polluted, a forest fire.

3. **a.** For example, a park that was all lawn is being naturalized. **b.** A wider variety of species of plants are being introduced and protected in the park, plants are becoming taller, plants are spreading out of the protected area as animals and wind carry their seeds.

4. The more diverse the ecosystem, the more positive ways the ecosystem will have available to respond. Variation provides resilience when the environment changes. Diversity ensures more variation.

5. Small plants would be involved in primary succession, larger plants would move in as opportunities to anchor themselves became available, animals would move in as those plants provided shelter and food.

6. For example, diversity of life, specialization; genetic variation, survival of the fittest; plant specialization, photosynthesis.

Chapter 14 Practice Test, page SG-222

1. C   2. B   3. D   4. A
5. C   6. B   7. E

8. a male haploid gamete uniting with a female haploid gamete to produce a diploid zygote

9. the gametophyte

10. ethylene

11. negative trophism

12. pollen structure, pollen tubes, and seeds

13. Two sperm nuclei of a pollen grain unite with nuclei of the embryo sac of an angiosperm plant. One sperm nucleus unites with the egg to form the diploid zygote, from which the embryo develops. The other sperm unites with the two nuclei located in a single cell at the centre of the embryo sac. Together these form the triploid nucleus of the cell from which the endosperm develops

14. a. Primary succession. Lichens begin to grow. Soil forms. Plants such as mosses begin to grow. Insects, micro-organisms, and other organisms move in. Grasses, wildflowers, and shrubs begin to grow. More insects and micro-organisms move in. Tree seeds are transported by animals. Small, then larger trees grow. Plants that cannot tolerate shade die. **b.** Secondary succession. Exposed soil contains micro-organisms, worms, insects, and seeds (wildflowers, weeds, grasses, and trees). Other seeds may blow in or be carried in by animals. Small plants grow, and die as trees grow taller and provide shade. Mature community may only take decades to establish.

15. Rate of species increase is relatively rapid, then slower, then rapid again. **A.** There is no vegetation. **B.** Grasses and wildflowers cover the landscape. Small shrubs and trees are beginning to grow. **C.** A mature community is visible, including a variety of tall trees, and several types of animals. Few grasses and wildflowers are visible.

Unit 5 Practice Test, page SG-225

1. D	**2.** A	**3.** C	**4.** D
5. B	**6.** E	**7.** C	**8.** B
9. E	**10.** B	**11.** A	**12.** E
13. D			

14. the difference in concentration between two areas

15. root pressure and transpirational pull

16. active transport

17. the development of the flower

18. Corn, climbing beans and squash. Companion planting involves planting the three crops close together. Each of the crops benefits the others. The corn acts as a vertical structure for the beans to climb. When the bean plant dies, nitrogen is added to the soil for the corn and squash. The squash protects the corn and beans from dehydration, weeds, and other pests.

19. Two of the following: to take in water and dissolved minerals, to anchor the plant, and to store carbohydrates.

20. Diagrams should show: **Phototrophism:** a plant exposed to a light source. The stem curves in the direction of the light. **Negative gravitropism:** a stem of a plant growing upwards. **Thigmotropism:** a plant growing in response to a physical stimulus, for example, a vine twining around a post.

21. Dicot: two seed leaves, palmate or pinnate venation, flower parts in multiples of four or five, taproot. **Monocot:** one seed leaf, venation usually parallel, flower parts in multiples of three, fibrous roots.

22. Genetically identical plants will produce crops that are uniform and lacking in genetic diversity. The crops will be vulnerable to new crop-specific pests.

23. Dandelions have taproots that grow deep into the soil to tap into water sources far below ground level. Cacti generally have fibrous roots what spread wide and shallow to collect water near the surface. Aquatic plants have evolved aerenchyma—a spongy tissue that allows oxygen to move through spaces in their root systems.

24. In dicots, the cotyledon absorbs most of the endosperm tissue as the seed matures and provides much of the nourishment for the embryo.

25. Asexual reproduction offers a quick, means of reproducing plants with known characteristics; however, it does not lead to genetic variability.

26. They produce large quantities of light pollen grains and the stigma of the plant often extends beyond the petals.

27. For example: soil erosion, water cycle disruptions, loss of biodiversity, flooding and drought, leading to climate change and destruction of animal habitats.

Study Guide Index

For more detail about these topics, refer to the index in your textbook.

peristalsis, SG-155
petals, SG-213
pharynx, SG-168
phenotype, SG-70
phloem, SG-201
photosynthesis, SG-198
phototropism, SG-217
pioneer species, SG-219
pistils, SG-213
plants, SG-35–SG-37, SG-198–
  SG-205, SG-212–SG-217
pollination, SG-213
polygenic traits, SG-88
polypeptides, SG-152
polysaccharides, SG-152
prenatal testing, SG-62, SG-79
pressure-flow model, SG-205
primary succession, SG-219
prions, SG-20
prokaryotic cells, SG-10
protists, SG-27, SG-28
pulmonary arteries, SG-179
pulmonary circulation, SG-179
pulmonary veins, SG-179

radicle, SG-214
recessive, SG-70
reproductive technology, SG-63
respiration, SG-166
respiratory system, SG-166–
  SG-171
root cap, SG-203
root hairs, SG-201
root pressure, SG-205

saliva, SG-155
salivary glands, SG-155
secondary succession, SG-219
selective advantage, SG-108,
  SG-110
semilunar valves, SG-179
sepals, SG-213
sex-linked traits, SG-91
sinoatrial (SA) node, SG-179
somatic cell, SG-59
speciation, SG-136–SG-140
species, SG-6–SG-8, SG-11
spermatogenesis, SG-61
spirillium, SG-21
spirograph, SG-167
spongy mesophyll, SG-203
sporophyte, SG-36

stamens, SG-213
stroke volume, SG-181
sustainable agriculture, SG-199
sympatric speciation, SG-137
systemic circulation, SG-179
systolic pressure, SG-181

tap root, SG-203
taxonomy, SG-7
test cross, SG-72, SG-73
textiles, SG-198
thigmotropism, SG-217
timber, SG-198
trachea, SG-168
transgenic organisms, SG-64
translocation, SG-205
transpiration, SG-205
trisomy, SG-62
true breeding (plants), SG-70

uniformitarianism, SG-120

variation, SG-108
vascular plants, SG-36, SG-37
vascular tissue, SG-201
venation, SG-203
vertebrate, SG-41
vestigial structures, SG-123
villi, SG-155
viruses, SG-20

xylem, SG-201